BIBLICAL
imagination
SERIES

LUKE

The Gospel of Amazement

MICHAEL CARD

IVP Books

An imprint of InterVarsity Press
Downers Grove, Illinois

InterVarsity Press
P.O. Box 1400, Downers Grove, IL 60515-1426
World Wide Web: www.ivpress.com
Email: email@ivpress.com

InterVarsity Press® is the book-publishing division of InterVarsity Christian Fellowship/USA®, a movement of students and faculty active on campus at hundreds of universities, colleges and schools of nursing in the United States of America, and a member movement of the International Fellowship of Evangelical Students. For information about local and regional activities, write Public Relations Dept., InterVarsity Christian Fellowship/USA, 6400 Schroeder Rd., P.O. Box 7895, Madison, WI 53707-7895, or visit the IVCF website at <www.intervarsity.org>.

Scripture quotations, unless otherwise indicated, are taken from the Holman Christian Standard Bible, *copyright ©1999, 2000, 2002, 2003 by Holman Bible Publishers, Nashville, Tennessee. Used by permission HCSB Holman Bible Publishers. All rights reserved.*

Design: Cindy Kiple
Images: The Last Supper. From the MS "The Four Gospels", Folio 135r from Mount Athos Monastery, Iberon, Greece at National Library, Athens, Greece. Erich Lessing/Art Resource, NY

ISBN 978-0-8308-3835-6

Printed in the United States of America ∞

Library of Congress Cataloging-in-Publication Data

Card, Michael, 1957-
   Luke: the gospel of amazement / Michael Card.
      p. cm.—(The biblical imagination series)
   Includes bibliographical references.
   ISBN 978-0-8308-3835-6 (pbk.: alk. paper)
   1. Bible. N.T. Luke—Commentaries. I. Title.
   BS2595.53.C37   2010
   226.4'077—dc22

                                                                                          2010041412

P   20   19   18   17   16   15   14   13   12   11   10   9   8

Y   28   27   26   25   24   23   22   21   20   19   18

CONTENTS

THE BIBLICAL IMAGINATION

"Though seeing, they may not see;
though hearing, they may not understand."

LUKE 8:10 NIV, FROM ISAIAH 6:9

When we hear these words of Jesus, something inside us shudders. We wince at the thought of someone—anyone—who has the ability to see and hear and yet stubbornly refuses to perceive and understand. Our greatest fear is that inwardly *we* might be just that person.

He had just told the parable of the sower. And we will learn in Luke that a parable demands the use of the imagination. If we are to take our place alongside the disciples as ones to whom these "secrets of knowledge" have been entrusted, then we too must learn what it means to read, to perceive, to understand the Bible with our imaginations.

It is impossible, when a seed is planted in you, to know just what sort of fruit it will eventually produce. Almost thirty years ago, when Dr. William Lane smiled at me over his crooked glasses and said, "I am going to teach you how I read Scripture," how could I have known that I would spend the rest of my life in pursuit of his stated goal: reading the Scriptures with my imagination.

"We must learn to read the Bible at the level of the informed imagination": this was how he encapsulated his approach to studying God's Word. In the years that followed, he never once explained *how* we were supposed to do this. Instead, he simply *did it*. That is, Bill incarnated for his students a deep interaction with the biblical text by means of his remarkably informed imagination. A Ph.D. from Harvard, he spoke fourteen languages. You saw his imagination when he simply opened the Bible; it seemed to tremble in his hands. You heard it when he read with his booming voice, usually from the New Testament. You saw it in your mind's eye when he used primary source backgrounds to paint the image of Jesus the rabbi. Sometimes you even smelled it when Bill recounted a scene like the anointing of Jesus' feet. "'The smell of the perfume filled the house' [Jn 12:3]: now, why do you think John included that detail?" he would ask, his voice modulating for effect.

In our own way, those of us who studied with Bill in the religion department of Western Kentucky University adapted and adopted this luminous approach. We absorbed the primary sources for ourselves: Suetonius, Eusebius, Tacitus, Josephus and the rest. We learned to ask the same sort of questions he might ask of the text: "Why is this detail there?" "What does it mean?" "How would the first hearers of this document have understood this?" "Why did the writer leave that out?" In time, on our own, we would learn to ask even better questions . . . questions of our own.

Precisely because he neglected to present this method as a full-blown system, we were left to struggle on our own. His refusal to provide a systematic, didactic outline had a powerful purpose: we were left to engage with Scripture at the level of our imaginations, by ourselves.

And now, all these years later, I would like to show you how *I* read Scripture, to show you what I've come to understand about engaging with the Scriptures at the level of the informed imagination. I do not intend to present a system or an outline of my own, even if I could. In this new series of explorations of the Gospels, I would simply like to share some of the discoveries I've made along the way.

DISINTEGRATION/*RE*INTEGRATION
AND THE HOLY SPIRIT

We are a disintegrated people. The signs of it are all around us. Every bird that flees when you're taking a walk is a reminder that the integrated place we once had with creation has been violated. We experience this when we witness the disintegration of every human relationship while our souls tell us that wife belongs with husband, friend with friend, child with parent. Yet at every turn we find it almost impossible to fit the fragmented pieces of the puzzles of our lives together.

This disintegration affects the way we come to the Scriptures as well. Some of us embrace the Bible with our hearts, which is right to do, and yet we do not bring disciplined minds into the process. Sometimes the reverse is true: we apply first-rate minds to the Bible and yet fail to be sensitive to what the Word is whispering to our hearts. In the end, it is not a heart problem, nor is it a head problem. It is an *integration* problem. We must ask the Lord to help us bring our whole self to the task of listening to the Bible. How can we begin to reconnect what became disconnected at the Fall? How can the heart and mind become reintegrated?

The imagination is the vital bridge between the heart and the mind. It is the means by which the Spirit begins to reconnect what was disintegrated by the Fall. This explains why the majority of the Bible is seeking to recapture our imaginations, whether it is the poetry of the psalms, the imagery of the prophets or the luminous parables of Jesus.

It is appropriate, then, that we start this series with Luke's Gospel, because he is more preoccupied with the Holy Spirit than any other Gospel writer. After all, it is Luke who, in his second volume, tells us the story of the coming of the Spirit at Pentecost. From the very beginnings of the church, the Holy Spirit was recapturing the imaginations of the first followers of Jesus, reintegrating their hearts and minds. The Spirit enabled them to bring selves made whole once more to the task of understanding those "secrets of the kingdom" (Lk 8:10).

As we proceed in this process, we will discover a new appreciation for the work of biblical scholarship, for the men and women who have received the call to vocationally study the Word and share the fruits of their strenuous labor with you and me. Along the way we will discover a fresh appreciation of scholarship—not as an end in itself but as a beginning. Often we are tempted to believe that the commentary or the lecture is an end, the final word. Here are the facts: record, digest, and the work is done. To the contrary, I hope we will see that the thoughtful commentary is only where you and I begin. The lecture is only the seed, not the fruit. You and I are called to move forward on our own, interacting with heart and mind, continually asking what all the facts mean. This is our calling, just as academic scholarship is the calling of the commentator. Most of us are not scholars. Perhaps we should begin thinking of ourselves as "imaginators," or "biblical imaginators"—or, better yet, "christological biblical imaginators." We are being conformed to his image as we engage our hearts and minds, by means of the imagination, with the Word of God.

THE BIBLICAL IMAGINATION SERIES

This series intends to work its way through all four Gospels, illustrating all along what it means to take the imagination seriously in the understanding of the Bible. These are not, strictly speaking, a collection of academic books, although I intend to draw from the best scholarly sources. Instead, I hope to present a fresh way to approach the Gospels for the lay reader. If the scholarly book or article represents not the end but only the beginning, I intend to take what responsible scholars have faithfully and arduously fought for and demonstrate what it might look like to engage with their facts and with the Scripture on our own, to take their facts and ask what they mean in a larger sense.

Beginning with the Gospel of Luke, the Biblical Imagination Series is an invitation to work through the Gospels along with me. I will take seriously the individual life of each Gospel writer, as well as the life situations that called forth each individual book. Instead of dealing with the texts line by line, or even word by word, we will work with larger blocks of material, looking for major themes and trying to grasp the flow of the story of the life of Jesus. I will do my best to ask good questions and to always be aware of your presence on the journey with me. So consider this my personal invitation to join me as we make our way through the Gospels.

Introduction

WHO IS LUKE?

A COMPANION OF PAUL'S

*T*he middle of Acts 16 tells the mysterious, unprecedented and some-what cryptic story of a portion of Paul's roundabout journey through the Roman province of Asia. It serves as a wonderful example of the benefits of engaging the text with the informed imagination and asking what the facts might mean. If you simply read Acts 16:6-8, you are left with a list of long-forgotten regions and cities. (It took me some time to find a map that listed all of the sites mentioned in the passage.) But once your mind is armed with the information on the map, you can trace this frustrating leg of what is commonly referred to as the second missionary journey. Then your heart just might engage with the story in a fresh way. So let's get started.

Paul and his companions had been traveling within the regions of Phrygia and Galatia, telling the good news about Jesus of Nazareth. When they wanted to travel west, into the Roman province of Asia (not Asia as we define it), the Holy Spirit kept them from doing so (Acts 16:6). Next we are told they set out to the north, in the direction of Mysia, hoping to enter the town of Bithynia, but the "Spirit of Jesus" would not allow them to (Acts 16:7). If you look at the map, you'll see that the only way left for them to go was west, to the town of Troas. In other words, traveling west to Asia, the Spirit said, "No." Then north to Mysia, Jesus said, "No." In essence, they were being funneled to Troas. Once in Troas, Paul had a vision of a man from Macedonia (a region farther west, across the Aegean Sea, Acts 16:9). Acts 16:10 says that after the vision, "we" got ready to leave. This is the first of the "we" passages in Acts, and it indicates that the narrator of Acts had joined Paul's team. During that frustrating time of trying to go west and then north and then southwest to Troas, the Spirit was driving Paul, as it were, to the solitary man who would be his companion for the rest of his life. As they set out on this, their first missionary journey together, they never could have guessed just how deep their friendship would eventually become. The man's name was Luke.

In the letter to Philemon, Paul refers to Luke as simply one of his "fellow workers" (Philem 1:24 NIV). By the time he writes Colossians, Paul, in prison in Rome, mentions Luke again, next to Demas, but now he singles him out as "our dear friend" (Col 4:14 NIV). By the end of his life, Paul confesses in 2 Timothy 4:11 that "only Luke is with me." Although we do not know that much about Luke, something tells me that this is all we really need to know. Luke had become his most faithful friend. Who is to say that he did not stay by Paul's side until the very end, perhaps claiming and caring for the decapitated body? So fact one concerning Luke is this: *he was a companion of Paul.*

NOT AN EYEWITNESS

In the opening verses of his Gospel, Luke indicates that he was not an eyewitness to the stories he is recording but has in fact spoken to those "who from the first were eyewitnesses" (Lk 1:2 NIV). Fact two concerning Luke: *he was not an eyewitness.* This means he had to self-consciously pick and choose which eyewitness accounts he would utilize as he wove together the story of Jesus.

A DOCTOR

Could it be that Paul simply needed a doctor to travel with him to help treat whatever his "thorn in the flesh" might have been? Some believe the mysterious ailment might have been progressive blindness. (At one point Paul speaks of having to write in such "large letters" [Gal 6:11].) Others think he might have suffered from malaria contracted on an earlier mission trip. Or could it have been that their mutual respect and concern for the marginal men and women of their time brought Paul and Luke together in ministry? Or was it the fact that they both cared so deeply for the universality of the gospel that their hearts resonated together with compassion for the Gentiles? Perhaps it was for all these reasons and others we may never know. In Colossians 4:14, Paul refers to Luke as an *iatros*, or doctor. Fact three concerning Luke: *he was a doctor.*

PERHAPS A SLAVE

In Paul's day, many doctors were recruited from the slave community. So based on his profession, there is at least a chance that Luke might have been a slave. Whereas the Greeks forbade slaves to practice medicine, the Romans promoted the idea. In fact, even Augustus's personal physician was a freedman (former slave) named Antonius Musa. By the end of the first century, the emperor Domitian was forced to issue a decree that forbade any more slaves to study the medical arts, presumably because the profession was becoming overloaded with slave doctors.[1] Many of the most respected Roman doctors were in fact slaves.[2]

Another piece of evidence that points in the direction of Luke being a slave is his very name. "Luke" is technically known as a hypocorism, a fancy word for "nickname." In the first century, slaves were usually renamed each time they were purchased. Some slave names bespeak qualities, like the name Onesimus, which means "useful." Other slaves were given shortened forms of their masters' names, or nicknames. Hence, a slave purchased by someone named Demetrius might receive the name Demos. If I were to have owned a slave in the first century (God forbid), I might have named him Mike. Likewise, someone named Lucius would have renamed his new slave Luke. I find it most interesting that Paul has a relative named Lucius (Acts 13:1; Rom 16:21). I admit that this idea is quite a stretch, and my scholarly friends have told me this theory would never wash in the halls of academia, but I suggest to you that Luke *may* have been a slave who was perhaps freed and given to Paul to serve him as his personal physician by his relative Lucius. We will look for more evidence for this later, but for now let us put forth, not as a fact but as a distinct possibility: *Luke might have been a slave.*

A GENTILE

It is widely accepted that Luke was a Gentile. First, there is his Greek name. Then there is the fact that Paul first meets up with him in Asia. Also, a close look at the text of his Gospel indicates that he is writing to a Greek audience. In Colossians 4:10-17, Paul lists his "co-workers." In verses 10-11 he names Aristarchus, Mark and Justus, mentioning that they are the only fellow workers who are "of the circumcision," meaning they are the only Jews. In verses 12-17, Paul lists the other, presumably non-Jewish coworkers. In verse 14 he lists Luke, "the loved physician." So *Luke was a Gentile.*

Here is where we stretch out and try to apply our method of engaging with the imagination. We have listed some facts and possible truths about Luke. Facts rest well in the mind, but our imaginations need to do something with the facts. So let's try to ask some better questions based on what we have seen so far. Let's try to interact with the facts at the level of the informed imagination.

If it is true that Luke was a companion of Paul's, then what would we expect from a companion of Paul's? Here's where it gets interesting.

First, Paul is not shy about confessing the fact that he was once a Pharisee (Acts 23:6; 26:5; Phil 3:5). When we come to the Gospel of Luke, we find that Luke deals with the Pharisees differently than the other Gospel writers do. In fact, in Luke's Gospel we see Jesus sharing meal fellowship with the Pharisees on three separate occasions (Lk 7:36; 11:37; 14:1). Only in Luke do the Pharisees come to warn Jesus about Herod's plan to take his life (Lk 13:31). In the final chapters that record all that leads up to the crucifixion, we see that the Pharisees are not implicated in the plot. So what we might expect from the traveling companion of a Pharisee like Paul is exactly what we find. Luke has a broader perspective on the Pharisees.

Shortly after they first met (Acts 16), Paul and Luke set out on a journey. For the vast majority of the remainder of their time together they would be traveling. It is interesting then, when we turn to the Gospel of Luke, to see that 40 percent of the book, what is known as the great central section, records Jesus' final journey to Jerusalem. It is also known as the travel narrative (Lk 9:51–18:14). From the time he spent traveling with Paul, Luke seemed to understand the spiritual life as a journey. And so when he comes to tell the story of Jesus, he emphasizes Jesus' final journey to Jerusalem. In fact, someone has said that Luke is simply the story of a journey from Galilee to Jerusalem, while Acts is the story of a journey from Jerusalem to Rome. So what we would expect to find from the traveling companion of Paul is exactly what we find in the Gospel of Luke.

Paul was also not ashamed to acknowledge himself as an "apostle to the Gentiles" (Rom 11:13). So you might expect that a companion of Paul would be unusually sensitive to the Gentile world. And that is precisely what you find in the Gospel of Luke, as well as in the larger context of Luke and Acts. In Matthew, where the genealogy of Jesus is recorded, Matthew begins with Abraham, pointing to the Jewishness of Jesus. But in Luke 4, when Luke records the genealogy of Jesus, he goes all the way back to Adam, stressing that Jesus is the savior who has come for all humankind, including the Gentiles. In chapter 2 the angel speaks of the good news, which has come for "all the people." In the same chapter Simeon sings about "a light for revelation to the Gentiles" (Lk 2:32). This might also be seen as a confirmation that Luke was himself a Gentile. As we work our way through the Gospel of Luke, we will be on the lookout for more of these examples.

We have seen that Paul clearly states that Luke was a doctor. That, in and of itself, is an interesting fact. But let's go deeper and ask the question: what would you expect from a Gospel writer who was a doctor?

Once again, what we might expect is exactly what we find. There is a wealth of medical detail in the accounts of the healings of Jesus' ministry. In chapter 4, Luke records that Peter's mother had a "high" fever. Even as today we speak of high-grade and low-grade fevers, doctors in the ancient world differentiated between great and small ones. In chapter 3, John the Baptist baptizes for the remission of sin. Luke uses the same word for remission that we use when we speak of the remission of cancer. Only Luke speaks of the man with "dropsy" (Lk 14:2 NIV). In chapter 9, the man in the crowd asks Jesus to examine his son. Here Luke uses the same word that is used of a doctor examining a patient.

One of the best examples of the medical background in the Gospel of Luke is a detail that Luke leaves out. In Mark 5, the story is told of a woman who has had a hemorrhage for twelve years. Mark tells us that she has suffered much at the hands of many doctors and has spent all she has, and that instead of growing better, she has grown worse. Interestingly enough, when Luke tells the same story in Luke 8, he leaves out that detail! This is precisely the kind of omission we would expect from someone invested in a particular profession.

Earlier we posited the idea that because of his name and his profession, Luke might have been a slave. If this is so, then what might we expect from a writer who was a slave? Once again, what we might expect is precisely what we find. Luke is known as the Gospel of the poor and marginalized because he shows more concern for women, who were the most marginalized group in the first century, and for those who existed on the bottom rung of Jewish society. Luke alone tells us of the shepherds who are the first recipients of the good news of the birth of Jesus. Shepherds were regarded as outcasts in first-century Judaism, barred even from testifying in a court of law. Only Luke tells of the impoverished baby who sleeps in a cattle trough. Only Luke tells us the story of the widow of Nain, as well as the widow who offers both of her remaining coins to the temple treasury.

We might expect that a slave would have longed to see the world turned upside down, and this is also exactly what we find in Luke's Gospel. From Mary's song of the radical reversal that the coming of Messiah will bring, to the Beatitudes of Jesus, which announce that those who are laughing now will mourn while the mourners will soon find reason to laugh, Luke the slave celebrates the coming of Jesus. He longs for and wonders at the world being turned upside down by this arrival.

Luke loved songs. In the opening chapters everyone seems to be singing. Mary sings her Magnificat. The angels pronounce their Gloria in Excelsis. The father of John the Baptist, Zechariah, sings his Benedictus as he holds the infant prophet in his arms. And as Simeon embraces the infant Jesus, he sings his swan song, his Nunc Dimittis. While I would love to make a connection back to his companion, I do not see Paul as a very musical person. There are only a few fragments of hymns in his writings (Phil 2:6-11). All I can conclude is that Luke, in his own right, was a lover of songs. Perhaps in his experience as a slave he found that singing was an effective way to cope with his suffering. Whenever one of his eyewitnesses spoke or perhaps even sang a song to him, Luke was careful and, it seems to me, delighted to put it down.

Luke believed in prayer. More than any other Gospel writer, Luke shows us the prayer life of Jesus. Jesus went into the wilderness and prayed all night (Lk 5:16). He prayed before the Twelve were chosen (Lk 6:12). Only Luke tells us that "as He was praying" Jesus was transfigured (Lk 9:29). Jesus pronounces two parables on the subject of prayer (Lk 11:5-13; 18:1-8). And finally, the reason for the second temple expulsion in Luke was so that a place of prayer might be reestablished for the Gentiles (Lk 19:46). Interestingly, after a long wait, when we finally get to hear Jesus himself at prayer in Luke, it is the shortened Lord's Prayer—sometimes called the Lukan Lord's Prayer—which can be spoken with a single breath (Lk 11:2-4).

We have a long journey ahead as we make our way through Luke's Gospel. As we go, I hope we will learn to listen to the tone of his voice, for he is our principal guide, our companion on the journey. All along the way we will continue to ask questions of his life and particular interests in telling the story of Jesus. He has already been revealed to be a courageous, faithful, prayerful and sensitive person. I can think of no one better at this present moment to accompany us.

MAJOR THEMES

THE GOSPEL OF AMAZEMENT

They were, all of them, quite simply amazed. Zechariah's friends, the shepherds, all who heard the shepherds, Joseph and Mary, the people in his hometown of Nazareth, those in Capernaum, those who heard the boy Jesus in the temple, the disciples, the parents of the girl who had died, even the Pharisees: all were amazed, astonished, in awe and afraid. Three decades later, as Luke interviews the ever-decreasing group of eyewitnesses, he finds them still amazed, still struggling to put into words just what it was like to encounter the rabbi from Nazareth. And thirty years away from the event that was Jesus' life, Luke still finds himself amazed as well.

Luke exhausts the language of amazement. They were "amazed," "astonished," "in awe," "astounded," "spellbound." Surely Matthew, Mark and John were amazed as well: Matthew speaks twelve times of the people being amazed, and Mark does it fifteen times. John only uses the term six times. There are five Greek words that can be translated "amazed," and only Luke uses every one of them. Sometimes he uses two different words in the same sentence (see Lk 5:26)!

thaumazo: "amazed," "marvel," "wonder," "astonished" (Lk 1:63; 2:18; 4:22; 7:9; 9:43; 11:14; 20:26)

ekplēsso: "astonished," "astounded," "spellbound" (Lk 2:48; 4:32; 5:26; 9:43)

ekstasis: "amazement," "trance" (Lk 5:26)

thambos: "astonishment" (Lk 4:36; 5:9; this appears only in Luke)

existēmi: "amazed" (Lk 2:47; 8:56; 24:22)

I used to sum up this material by asking the convicting question, "Why am I not amazed?" But I have found a better question. If we truly engage with the text of Luke, I hope that we will rediscover a sense of wonder and amazement at this remarkable, mysterious, amazing person called Jesus. With Luke, we might just begin to ask the world, "Is he not amazing?" After all, Bonhoeffer was right: "Bewilderment is true comprehension."[3]

WHEN THOSE WHO SHOULD *DON'T*

Luke is a self-conscious writer; we will see this clearly in his introduction. He has set himself the task of interviewing eyewitnesses of Jesus' ministry some thirty years after the event. This means that, with the Holy Spirit's guidance, he must pick and choose his material. The man whom God has created Luke to be will shape the final form of the material. This is one facet of the backgrounds of all the Gospels that makes them endlessly complex and fascinating.

As Luke went about the task of collecting eyewitness accounts of the life of Jesus, he noticed a pattern emerging. Time and time again religious leaders—supposedly spiritual men, people who should have understood what Jesus' ministry was about—were simply unable to comprehend the rabbi from Nazareth. On the other hand, simple, run-of-the-mill people—most of them women—were able to almost immediately grasp the gift of grace that Jesus was offering them. Eventually the sheer weight of examples caused Luke to develop these stories into a literary theme which, for lack of a better term, I call "when those who should *don't*, and those who shouldn't *do*."

We will take a closer look at each example when we get into the chapter-by-chapter discussion of the text. So for now, I will simply provide an annotated list.

- Zechariah (the father of John the Baptist) and Mary (Lk 1:5-56, 67-79)

  Zechariah, a priest serving in the holy place in the temple, is given a promise directly from the mouth of the angel Gabriel and yet does not believe. Mary, on the other hand, a simple young girl from the backwater town of Nazareth, hears Gabriel and immediately responds by submitting herself as the "Lord's slave" (v. 38).

- Jews and the centurion (Lk 7:1-10)

  The Jewish friends of the pagan soldier come to Jesus, insisting that he "deserves" Jesus' attention (v. 4 NIV). The Roman centurion, however, sends word, "I am not worthy" (v. 6). Nevertheless, he still asks for Jesus' gift of healing for his slave. His faith amazes Jesus.

- Simon the Pharisee and the "sinful" woman (Lk 7:36-50)

  Simon, a Pharisee who has invited Jesus for meal fellowship, inwardly judges both Jesus and the sinful woman who has crashed the party. While the woman who is a "sinner" (v. 37) weeps over the feet of Jesus and dries them with her hair, Jesus responds to Simon, "Do you see this woman?" (v. 44) because Simon has only viewed her as one of his categories.

- Jesus' family and the listeners (Lk 8:19-21)

  Jesus' mother and brothers come to "see" Jesus. We know from Mark's account that they have decided that Jesus is out of his mind and needs to be taken away from the presence of the crowd. The crowds, however, who are apparently listening to the words of Jesus, are relabeled as his mothers and brothers. Jesus' own family, for the moment, doesn't understand, while the group of strangers does. They become the new, listening family of Jesus.

- The unpossessed Gerasenes and the possessed man (Lk 8:26-39)

  After having been delivered from the legion of demons, the man pleads to go with Jesus, while the townspeople plead for Jesus to leave.

- The priest and Levite and the good Samaritan (Lk 10:25-37)

  So pervasive is this literary theme that it even makes it into the parables of Jesus. Here the priest and Levite pass by the wounded traveler, while the Samaritan goes far out of his way to help.

- Those invited to the banquet and those on the streets (Lk 14:15-24)

Those who are initially invited to the extravagant banquet bow out at the last minute with a host of lame excuses, while the "street people" are invited and dragged into the feast.

- The older brother and the lost son (Lk 15:11-32)

  The younger son, who has wasted his father's inheritance, limps home and asks to become a servant. The older brother scorns the father's forgiveness and complains that he is really a slave.

- The rich man and Lazarus (Lk 16:19-31)

  Here the rich man, who would have been seen as blessed, ends up in hell. The "cursed" beggar, on the other hand, finds himself in Abraham's bosom. Even in hell the rich man still does not "get it."

- The nine lepers and the one who returned (Lk 17:11-19)

  Out of the ten lepers who are healed, only one comes back to give thanks, and he is a Samaritan.

- The Pharisee and the tax collector (Lk 18:9-14)

  The religious Pharisee is praying "about himself" (v. 11 NIV) before God and goes home unjustified. Unthinkably, the tax collector seems to understand the grace and forgiveness of God when he merely blurts out, "God, have mercy" (v. 13 NIV).

- The rich young ruler and Zacchaeus (Lk 18:18-30; 19:1-10)

  The young man cannot give up his possessions. Zacchaeus, the tax collector, repents and pays restoration.

- The rich people and the poor widow (Lk 21:1-4)

  The poor widow puts more into the treasury than the rich people.

- The religious leaders and the thief and soldier (Lk 23:35, 40-41, 47)

  The religious leaders mock Jesus on the cross, while the thief and the Roman soldier protest that he is innocent.

- The eleven disciples and the women (Lk 24:8-12)

  After the resurrection, the women come to the eleven disciples, believing Jesus has been raised from the dead. The disciples think they are merely speaking "nonsense" (v. 11).

PARABLES AT WORK

Of all the Gospel writers, Luke makes the most of Jesus' parables. Matthew and Mark record several, going so far as to say that Jesus said nothing to the people without a parable (Mt 13:34; Mk 4:34). But Luke tends to show us parables at work. Whereas Matthew and Mark say things like, "And then Jesus spoke to them this parable," Luke gives us places and names. He gives us context—for example, the stubborn widow (Lk 18:1-8) and the Pharisee and the tax collector (Lk 18:9-14). He tells us why Jesus is speaking a particular parable. And Luke, far more than the other writers, shows the parables taking effect—for example, Simon the Pharisee responding to the parable of the two debtors (Lk 7:36-50), and the lawyer responding to the story of the good Samaritan (Lk 10:25-37). In reference to the parable of the minas in Luke 19:11-27, Luke says Jesus told it *because* he was nearing Jerusalem for the last time and knew that the people had false expectations about the coming of the kingdom.

The parables of Christ are a mystery. They are not equations to be solved. You are never done with a single parable of Jesus—or perhaps it is better to say that his parables are never done with you. The simplest parable will continue speaking for the rest of your life—that is, if you choose to listen. No one understood this better than Luke.

Two aspects of Jesus' parables give them great persuasive power: identification and lack of closure. Identification seeks to engage our imaginations by drawing us into the story. Once there, we identify with one or more characters. I am the father whose son has run away with his inheritance, or the woman who has lost the precious coin. The character with whom you identify in any given parable can tell a lot about who you truly are.

Lack of closure is seen in Jesus' tendency to leave off the moral summing up at the end of the story. The stories have endings in and of themselves. The boy returns home, the judge finally listens to the widow, the pearl is found. But what is left silent is the moral, the conclusion. Within the freedom of the form of the parable, Jesus leaves the "aha!" to us. The moment of realization is ours to savor. Explaining the parables to death can rob them of this, their most important character-istic. So in one sense, the parable's greatest strength is also its greatest weakness. The transcendent moment of the opening of the eye of the heart is left to you alone with the Spirit. (See the appendix for a list of the parables of Jesus.)

AN UNIMAGINABLY PARADOXICAL PROTOTYPE

"We have seen *paradoxical* things today" (Lk 5:26, author's translation). Whenever we work closely with the text of Scripture, we will notice levels of structure. Sometimes the structure is intentional. For example, in Luke's nativity narratives, he contrasts the births of Jesus and John the Baptist. If you look closely, you will see that Luke intentionally pres-ents them in a parallel structure. I believe that the same is true of the travel narrative. Luke's opening statement of the travel narrative "He determined to journey to Jerusalem" is a literary device that intentionally opens the story of Jesus' final trip to Jerusalem and the cross (Lk 9:51).

Other times it is not so clear. Sometimes it's difficult to say whether what seems to be a literary structure to us was actually intended by the author. The theme of the paradoxical prototype (Lk 5:1–7:30) cannot be conclusively proven to be intentional. But does it need to be? It rep-resents a segment of the life of Jesus that was dominated by a central theme of unorthodoxy. Or perhaps it is a small window into a life that was continuously dominated by it. This literary block on the "unortho-doxy" opens with a statement that sounds, to my ear, like a literary device. See what you think: "Then everyone was astounded, and they were giving glory to God. And they were filled with awe and said, 'We have seen incredible things today!'" (Lk 5:26).

Two different terms in this statement speak of the amazement of the crowd: "astounded" *(ekstasis)* and filled with "awe" *(phobos)*. They give "glory" *(doxa)* to God and conclude that they have seen "incredible" *(paradoxos)* things. This is the only time the Greek word *paradoxos* ap-pears in the New Testament. It is translated elsewhere "remarkable" (NIV, NASB) or "strange" (KJV) or even "amazing" (NLT). But I would like to propose a somewhat unorthodox phrase to translate it. I wonder if it is only a coincidence that the word *doxa*, which means "glory" and represents half of the word *paradoxos*, appears in the same sentence. Could the two be linked somehow? Did the people give *doxa* to God and then respond, "We have seen things that might otherwise *(para)* bring glory *(doxa)* to God."

I propose this translation because what follows it is a long collection of stories that have to do with the unorthodoxy—even the "paradoxy"—of Jesus. In the very next incident Jesus chooses Levi, the tax collector, as one of his disciples. Given the fact that tax collectors were always listed next to murderers and adulterers in the rabbinic literature, the choice of Levi should be seen as nothing less than wildly unorthodox. In Luke 5:31-32, Jesus says he has come for sinners. In the next passage, it is pointed out that Jesus and his disciples do not fast and pray in an orthodox way. Jesus responds with the parable of the wineskins. The old orthodoxy—that is, the old wineskins—cannot contain the new orthodoxy that is the new wine of Jesus' message.

Next, Jesus and his disciples violate the Sabbath by harvesting grain. Then Jesus heals on the Sabbath, something the Pharisees thought he should not do. This is followed by the radically reversed blessings and woes we have come to know as the Beatitudes. This is followed by the impossible command to love our enemies. Jesus' rationale? God loves his enemies.

And on it goes. Next we meet the Gentile centurion who understands the grace of Jesus better than the Jewish elders. Later John the Baptist, the one who should have been least likely to ask this question, asks whether Jesus is the Messiah or whether they should look for someone else. Surely this remarkable question, coming from the one who had leaped in his mother's womb, signals the fact that Jesus' ministry is highly unorthodox, thoroughly paradoxical and contrary to what might otherwise bring glory to God.

This block seems to end, or at least to ebb, with another literary statement in Luke 7:29-30 that sounds like a bookend to me: "And when all the people, including the tax collectors, heard this, they acknowledged God's way of righteousness, because they had been baptized with John's baptism. But since the Pharisees and experts in the law had not been baptized by him, they rejected the plan of God for themselves."

HESED IN LUKE

I have had a lifelong love affair with words, especially untranslatable ones. Of all the biblical words I have encountered, no single one is more fascinating than the Hebrew word *hesed*. It is the word God uses to define himself again and again in the Old Testament (for example, Ex 20:6; 34:6-7; Num 14:18-19; Deut 5:10). The best translation I have found for this untranslatable word takes an entire sentence: "When the person from whom I have a right to expect nothing gives me everything." Without requiring an entire book, that phrase pretty well captures the meaning of *hesed* in the Old Testament. When the concept of *hesed* appears in the New Testament, it is usually translated "grace" or "mercy."

Despite Luke's non-Jewish background and the fact that he writes in Greek and not Hebrew, we find the notion of *hesed* reflected in the text over and over. We do not simply see mercy or grace portrayed in a one-dimensional way. Rather, the fully formed Hebrew notion of *hesed* is what we inevitably find.

Mary's Magnificat is full of *hesed*. In Luke 1:50, "His mercy is from generation to generation" is an echo of Exodus 20:6. In Luke 1:54 we are told again that he is "mindful of His mercy." Then, four verses later in Luke 1:58, we read that mercy has been shown to Elizabeth, the mother of John. It becomes the theme of Zechariah's song a few verses later (Lk 1:72, 78). When Jesus makes the impossible demand on his disciples to love their enemies, they are reminded that God loves his enemies, that "He is gracious to the ungrateful and evil" (Lk 6:35). Sound familiar? *When the person from whom I have a right to expect nothing gives me everything.* In Luke 10, the Samaritan shows compassion. Though the wounded man on the ground has no right to expect anything from a no-good Samaritan, behold, he receives over-the-top mercy: first aid, a donkey ride to the hotel, room and board, and the promise that the Samaritan will be back to check on him. And when Jesus forces the legal expert who called for the story in the first place to decide who his neighbor is after all, he is forced to mumble, "The one who showed *mercy*" (Lk 10:37).

Time and time again in Luke's Gospel, we will hear that perfect prayer coming from the poor and the leper, "Have *mercy!*" Once again the people who are asking know they do not deserve what they are asking for. Nonetheless, they ask because of the defining characteristic of Jesus: *hesed*, or undeserved mercy. Ultimately, upon the cross Jesus will forever define *hesed*.

THE LONG JOURNEY TO JERUSALEM

The largest literary block in the book of Luke has to do with Jesus' final journey to Jerusalem. It begins in Luke 9:51, when Jesus "determined to journey to Jerusalem." It ends in Luke 19:44 when Jesus arrives at last. This block comprises almost 40 percent of the Gospel. In Matthew, this period is covered in two chapters (Mt 19–20). Mark covers it in chapter 10. But Luke takes up ten chapters out of twenty-four to tell what he clearly understands as a major event in the story of Jesus. The final journey does not begin until the question "Who is Jesus?" is finally answered by the transfiguration and the confession of Peter.

Once the journey has begun, Luke's language continually reminds us that we are on the road with Jesus: "As they were traveling on the road" (Lk 9:57); "He sent them ahead of Him in pairs to every town and place where He Himself was about to go" (Lk 10:1); "While they were traveling" (Lk 10:38); "When He left there" (Lk 11:53); "He went through one town and village after another, teaching and making His way to Jerusalem" (Lk 13:22); "Yet I must travel today, tomorrow, and the next day, because it is not possible for a prophet to perish outside of Jerusalem" (Lk 13:33); "Now great crowds were traveling with Him" (Lk 14:25); "While traveling to Jerusalem" (Lk 17:11); "Listen! We are going up to Jerusalem" (Lk 18:31); "As He drew near Jericho" (Lk 18:35); "When He had said these things, He went on ahead, going up to Jerusalem" (Lk 19:28); "As He approached and saw the city" (Lk 19:41).

Luke is always moving us along with these phrases. We will see that the closer Jesus comes to Jerusalem, the more concentrated his teaching becomes. You sense urgency in his voice to complete his teaching ministry before time runs out. As we work through this section, we too must feel the sense of urgency; otherwise, we have failed to engage the text with our imaginations.

LUKE AS A BRIDGE

If indeed we regard the imagination as a bridge between the heart and mind, then Luke's Gospel is the best beginning place for a series on the biblical imagination. Luke itself is a bridge.

Luke is a literary bridge between the Gospels and the letters. In fact, some believe it was originally a cover document for a collection of Paul's letters to be used at his trial.

It is a generational bridge, spanning from the first generation of Christian believers, who were actual eyewitnesses, to the second generation, who had only heard about the things Jesus said and did.

It is a bridge between two worlds of Christian leadership: the world of having one perfect leader, namely, Jesus, and the world of having many decidedly imperfect leaders.

Finally, it is a bridge between the Old Testament world, in which having faith meant waiting like Simeon, and the world in which having faith meant following, like the twelve disciples.

So in more than one sense, reading the Gospel of Luke will be like crossing a bridge. On one side, those first witnesses are encouraging us to move forward. Those from the old world of waiting call out to us, "What are you waiting for?"

On the far side, the followers are bidding us to come. They welcome us to cross over to the new world of expressing our faith by following—really following—Jesus, with all that it costs and means.

Lord Jesus, as we begin our journey through Luke's great work, grant us perseverance, for the way can sometimes seem long. Give us focus so we might shut out the noise and busyness of the world that would distract us from you. Grant us peace when we are confronted by the disturbing nature of your kingdom and the impossible demands of your call.

Most of all, Lord, grant us empowered imaginations, that we may see and feel and hear your Word, your voice, your call, your great love.

We ask this in the name of Jesus, the Amazing One!

LUKE 1

A SELF-CONSCIOUS WRITER

1:1-4 Formal prologue.

PARALLEL PRE-BIRTH STORIES

*1:5-25 Details of the birth of John the Baptist.
Focus on Zechariah's disbelief and request for a sign.*

*1:26-38 Details of the foretelling of the birth of Jesus.
Focus on Mary's willingness to believe.*

MARY SINGS

1:39-45 Mary visits Elizabeth.

*1:46-56 Mary responds with a song
(compare to the song of Hannah in 1 Sam 2).*

ZECHARIAH SINGS

1:57-66 Birth of John.

*1:67-79 Zechariah's tongue loosed.
He responds with a song.*

*1:80 Single-verse summary of the growing up of John
(compare to Lk 2:40).*

A SELF-CONSCIOUS WRITER

¹Many have undertaken to compile a narrative about the events that have been fulfilled among us, ²just as the original eyewitnesses and servants of the word handed them down to us. ³It also seemed good to me, since I have carefully investigated everything from the very first, to write to you in orderly sequence, most honorable Theophilus, ⁴so that you may know the certainty of the things about which you have been instructed.

Luke sits down with his pen and parchment and writes his opening statement in perfect Greek. It is an educated man who writes. Over seven hundred words appear in Luke's writing that can be found nowhere else in the New Testament. This opening paragraph is one single perfectly balanced and constructed sentence!

He acknowledges that many others have already accomplished what he is only beginning to do. Other accounts of the life of Jesus have already been written and apparently circulated. If Luke has the sort of mind we believe him to have, we can be sure he has read them all and fully digested their content. Moreover, Luke has collected eyewitness accounts; one of the most interesting exercises as you read his Gospel is to try to determine who his source might have been.

When we read the nativity accounts, we see that Luke knows what Mary was thinking and feeling. He knows about the secret things she treasured and pondered in her heart. He has eyewitness detail about the twelve-year-old Jesus in the temple—especially the exasperation of his parents who, after having been entrusted with the raising of the Messiah, have lost him for three days. Who would have been able to tell Luke all of that information?

Then Luke mentions an "orderly" account. But certainly this means more than the fact that he has simply gotten his chronological details straight. Indeed, he has "ordered" the story of Jesus. He has collected stories and grouped them together in meaningful ways. And so Theophilus is entrusted with one of the greatest pieces of literature on the planet, all for the purpose of being sure of his original catechism.

Don't believe anyone who claims that they know the true identity of Luke's patron. I will outline the choices, and, armed with these facts, you can make as valid a choice for yourself as anyone. Just don't be dogmatic about what the Bible is not dogmatic about!

First, Theophilus could be nobody—a made-up person who represents all those who are "lovers of God." That is what his name means.

Lately there has been an attempt to identify him with a high priest by the same name who served between A.D. 37-41. Josephus mentions him in his *Antiquities of the Jews.* This would place the writing of Luke within four to eight years of Jesus' death. And Luke does tell us that many of the priests had come to believe in Jesus (Acts 6:7). The problem is this seems too early a date for the writing of the book. And if Luke was written for a Jewish high priest, how do we explain the emphasis on Gentiles? How do we explain the fact that he never even uses the word *rabbi?*

One final theory—and one, it seems to me, that is fairly believable— is that Theophilus was a Roman official who was involved in Paul's trial. This accounts for his official title "most honorable," which was used to designate those who belonged to the upper-middle or equestrian class in Rome. It also explains the focus on the innocence of Jesus in the closing chapters.

So, finally, we can never be sure of the identity of the mysterious Theophilus. But that is not, strictly speaking, true either. He is you. He is me. For we have received some initial instruction on Jesus' life and ministry. We need to know with more certainty the truth of what we have heard. And you would not be holding Luke's book in your hands if you weren't in some sense a "lover of God," or at least someone who longed to become one.

PARALLEL PRE-BIRTH STORIES

[5]In the days of King Herod of Judea, there was a priest of Abijah's division named Zechariah. His wife was from the daughters of Aaron, and her name was Elizabeth. [6]Both were righteous in God's sight, living without blame according to all the commandments and requirements of the Lord. [7]But they had no children because Elizabeth could not conceive, and both of them were well along in years.

⁸*When his division was on duty and he was serving as priest before God,* ⁹*it happened that he was chosen by lot, according to the custom of the priesthood, to enter the sanctuary of the Lord and burn incense.* ¹⁰*At the hour of incense the whole assembly of the people was praying outside.* ¹¹*An angel of the Lord appeared to him, standing to the right of the altar of incense.* ¹²*When Zechariah saw him, he was startled and overcome with fear.* ¹³*But the angel said to him:*

> *Do not be afraid, Zechariah,*
> *because your prayer has been heard.*
> *Your wife Elizabeth will bear you a son,*
> *and you will name him John.*
> ¹⁴*There will be joy and delight for you,*
> *and many will rejoice at his birth.*
> ¹⁵*For he will be great in the sight of the Lord*
> *and will never drink wine or beer.*
> *He will be filled with the Holy Spirit*
> *while still in his mother's womb.*
> ¹⁶*He will turn many of the sons of Israel*
> *to the Lord their God.*
> ¹⁷*And he will go before Him*
> *in the spirit and power of Elijah,*
> *to turn the hearts of fathers*
> *to their children,*
> *and the disobedient*
> *to the understanding of the righteous,*
> *to make ready for the Lord a prepared people.*

¹⁸*"How can I know this?" Zechariah asked the angel. "For I am an old man, and my wife is well along in years."*

¹⁹*The angel answered him, "I am Gabriel, who stands in the presence of God, and I was sent to speak to you and tell you this good news.* ²⁰*Now listen! You will become silent and unable to speak until the day these things take place, because you did not believe my words, which will be fulfilled in their proper time."*

²¹*Meanwhile, the people were waiting for Zechariah, amazed that he stayed so long in the sanctuary.* ²²*When he did come out, he could not speak to*

them. Then they realized that he had seen a vision in the sanctuary. He kept making signs to them and remained speechless. ²³When the days of his ministry were completed, he went back home.

²⁴After these days his wife Elizabeth conceived and kept herself in seclusion for five months. She said, ²⁵"The Lord has done this for me. He has looked with favor in these days to take away my disgrace among the people."

²⁶In the sixth month, the angel Gabriel was sent by God to a town in Galilee called Nazareth, ²⁷to a virgin engaged to a man named Joseph, of the house of David. The virgin's name was Mary. ²⁸And [the angel] came to her and said, "Rejoice, favored woman! The Lord is with you." ²⁹But she was deeply troubled by this statement, wondering what kind of greeting this could be. ³⁰Then the angel told her:

> *Do not be afraid, Mary,*
> *for you have found favor with God.*
> *³¹Now listen:*
> *You will conceive and give birth to a son,*
> *and you will call His name JESUS.*
> *³²He will be great*
> *and will be called the Son of the Most High,*
> *and the Lord God will give Him*
> *the throne of His father David.*
> *³³He will reign over the house of Jacob forever,*
> *and His kingdom will have no end.*

³⁴Mary asked the angel, "How can this be, since I have not been intimate with a man?"

³⁵The angel replied to her:

> *The Holy Spirit will come upon you,*
> *and the power of the Most High will overshadow you.*
> *Therefore the holy One to be born*
> *will be called the Son of God.*

³⁶And consider your relative Elizabeth—even she has conceived a son in her old age, and this is the sixth month for her who was called barren.

³⁷For nothing will be impossible with God."

³⁸"I am the Lord's slave," said Mary. "May it be done to me according to your word." Then the angel left her.

*W*hen Luke opens this passage with a historical reference to Herod, he is not merely setting the date of 4 B.C. for us. Whenever a historical figure—especially someone like Herod—is mentioned, the writer intends that an emotion come along with it. When we read that it was "in the days of King Herod," a chill should run down our spines. Quite simply, Herod was a monster. He came to power amid a bloodbath with the help of two Roman legions in 37 B.C. He murdered both of his brothers-in-law and his beloved wife Miriamne, as well as her mother. Just before his own death he ordered that prominent citizens in Israel be gathered together into the hippodrome. The decree was that upon his death they would be executed, so that there would be mourning in Israel. With this kind of rap sheet, it's not hard to understand why the slaughter of the innocents recorded for us in Matthew 2 did not even make it into the history books.

Zechariah was a member of one of the twenty-four priestly divisions. His division was Abijah's. His wife, Elizabeth, was also of priestly descent. And Luke believes that it is important for us to know one additional fact: that they were righteous and without blame. In spite of this, there is a disconnect; you see, Elizabeth was barren. Given the fact that they were keepers of the law, it does not follow that the couple should have been stricken by infertility. In Judaism and, sadly enough, in some strains of modern-day Christianity, to be childless is seen as the result of sin.

On the day in question, Zechariah draws the third lot. This means that he will have the once-in-a-lifetime opportunity to enter the sanctuary and burn incense. As he is inside the holy place, serving God before the table of incense, the people are outside praying. That is, what Zechariah is doing symbolically, the people are doing in reality.

Inside, the holy place is dark and full of smoke. As Zechariah stands before the altar of incense, it must dawn on him that this is indeed the greatest day of his life. All at once, he becomes aware of another presence in the room standing on the right side of the altar of incense (this kind of detail indicates an eyewitness). Zechariah could make out the figure of a man. Perhaps something inside him thinks, *This is no man.*

Do not be afraid: these are almost always the first words that come from the lips of angels. Presumably the sight of an angel is a fearful thing. The prophetic pronouncement of the angel is poetic in form. You would expect an angel to speak in poetry. It is all good news. Their prayers have been heard. Elizabeth will bear a son. He will be a joy and delight. He will be great. The Lord will use him to turn the hearts of the fathers back to their children.

The greatest day of his life, the best good news he has ever heard, spoken by the lips of an angel, within the confines of the holy place in the temple—and yet Zechariah asks in Luke 1:18, "How can I know this?" Of all the people gathered around the temple, of everyone in Israel, Zechariah should have heard and accepted this word.

You can almost hear the tone of Gabriel's voice as he responds, "*I* am *Gabriel, I* stand before *God*, I came to tell you this good news, and now you won't say a word until my words all come true." This is the same Gabriel who spoke to Daniel, saying, "As soon as you began to pray, an answer was given" (Dan 9:23 NIV). Daniel said he looked like a man.

When Zechariah finally limps out of the temple, those who are waiting outside immediately know that something is wrong. He cannot speak; they guess that he must have seen a vision. All that is left for the old man is to go home.

It is important to note that Elizabeth does not become pregnant until after Zechariah comes home. Luke tells us the story of two miraculous births, but the nature of the miracles is completely different. Zechariah and Elizabeth, in their old age and despite their barrenness, conceive a child in a natural way. Jesus will be born of a virgin.

This opening scene of the story closes with a focus on Elizabeth. We are told that she secludes herself for five months, apparently to wait until she is showing. She is a grateful old woman, rejoicing that the Lord has taken away her disgrace.

In verse 26, in the sixth month of Elizabeth's pregnancy, we learn

that the same Gabriel is sent to an obscure town in Galilee called Nazareth. He comes to a young woman who is twice described as a virgin.
Her name is Miriam. We have come to know her as Mary. She finds
the angel's greeting troublesome. What is she to make of his statement
that "the Lord is with you"? And then come those familiar angelic
words, "Do not be afraid, Mary."

Once again in poetry, Gabriel pronounces the name the world has
waited an eternity to hear: "You will call His name Yeshua." We have
come to know him as Jesus. In a parallel pronouncement we are told
that, like John, Jesus will be great. But quite unlike John, he will be the
Son of God. His reign and his kingdom will never end.

Mary responds with a legitimate question, not a faithless one. Not
"How can I be sure?" but "How can this be?" She is a virgin. It is a rea-
sonable question. And Gabriel is glad to give her a gentle and reasonable
answer. Using the most discreet language, he describes how the Holy
Spirit will "come upon" her and the Most High will "overshadow" her.
He uses the same word used in the Greek Old Testament to describe the
Spirit of God hovering over the face of the waters upon creation.

There is an ongoing debate as to whether Mary was perfect or
not. One thing seems certain to me: she was the perfect mother for
Jesus. Her final response to the angel is conclusive proof. Essentially she responds, "Look, the slave of the Master." Of all that she
does not know, one thing seems perfectly clear to her. It is a perspective that will help her navigate the deep waters into which the
small vessel of her life is about to go. It will be the source of her
disturbingly clear obedience. She perfectly articulates this fundamental reality with her first response to the angel's troubling news:
"I am the Lord's slave."

Different translations soften the language. Some render the word
(*doulē*, the feminine form of *doulos* for "slave") "servant"; others use the
even softer "handmaiden." But Mary is affirming that she is the slave
of the Lord. She is surrendering her rights, her hopes and dreams and
her own body absolutely to him. Mary seems to know that she is owned
by Another. The message that has come to her through the angel is
absolute and life-changing.

The call on Mary's life is an impossible demand. The call of God always is. To impotent Abram and sterile Sarah he says, "Make a son." To the young virgin slave, kneeling at the feet of the angel, he says, "You will have a Son." To become obedient to his call always means becoming a slave to the impossible.

MARY SINGS

³⁹In those days Mary set out and hurried to a town in the hill country of Judah ⁴⁰where she entered Zechariah's house and greeted Elizabeth. ⁴¹When Elizabeth heard Mary's greeting, the baby leaped inside her, and Elizabeth was filled with the Holy Spirit. ⁴²Then she exclaimed with a loud cry:

> *You are the most blessed of women,*
> *and your child will be blessed!*

⁴³How could this happen to me, that the mother of my Lord should come to me? ⁴⁴For you see, when the sound of your greeting reached my ears, the baby leaped for joy inside me! ⁴⁵She who has believed is blessed because what was spoken to her by the Lord will be fulfilled!"

⁴⁶And Mary said:

> *My soul proclaims the greatness of the Lord,*
> *⁴⁷and my spirit has rejoiced in God my Savior,*
> *⁴⁸because He has looked with favor*
> *on the humble condition of His slave.*
> *Surely, from now on all generations*
> *will call me blessed,*
> *⁴⁹because the Mighty One*
> *has done great things for me,*
> *and His name is holy.*
> *⁵⁰His mercy is from generation to generation*
> *on those who fear Him.*
> *⁵¹He has done a mighty deed with His arm;*
> *He has scattered the proud*
> *because of the thoughts of their hearts;*
> *⁵²He has toppled the mighty from their thrones*

and exalted the lowly.
⁵³He has satisfied the hungry with good things
and sent the rich away empty.
⁵⁴He has helped His servant Israel,
mindful of His mercy,
⁵⁵just as He spoke to our ancestors,
to Abraham and his descendants forever.

⁵⁶And Mary stayed with her about three months; then she returned to her home.

So right around the sixth month of her cousin Elizabeth's pregnancy, Mary hurries to her home. As soon as her greeting reaches Elizabeth's ear, the fetal John jumps. Upon this, Elizabeth is filled with the Holy Spirit and pronounces an Old Testament *berakah*, or benediction. Mary, she says, is the most blessed of women. And now this blessed woman has come to visit her and she can hardly believe it. She is blessed because, unlike Zechariah, she believes.

Upon hearing this, Mary bursts into song. It seems to come from the overflow of her heart. With wisdom far beyond her years, she sings with gratitude that the Lord has looked with favor upon her, his slave. She sings of the *hesed*, or mercy, that he shows from generation to generation.

As she comes to the end of her song, there is an almost imperceptible shift. At one moment she is singing of the Mighty One who has scattered the proud, and then in the next moment she sings that he has exalted the lowly. Mary has begun to sing of the radical reversal that will so captivate the heart of her son Jesus. She celebrates that the hungry have good things but the rich are sent away empty. This is all just as God had promised it would be to the ancestors and to Abraham.

Breathless, Mary comes to the end of her song. She has sung more than she knows. Elizabeth, the elderly mother-to-be, smiles at the pregnant virgin. Together their miracle children will change the world: they will gain it all and they will lose it all. When Elizabeth reaches her ninth month, Mary slips away, back to Nazareth to wait for the impossible to come true.

ZECHARIAH SINGS

⁵⁷Now the time had come for Elizabeth to give birth, and she had a son. ⁵⁸Then her neighbors and relatives heard that the Lord had shown her His great mercy, and they rejoiced with her.

⁵⁹When they came to circumcise the child on the eighth day, they were going to name him Zechariah, after his father. ⁶⁰But his mother responded, "No! He will be called John."

⁶¹Then they said to her, "None of your relatives has that name." ⁶²So they motioned to his father to find out what he wanted him to be called. ⁶³He asked for a writing tablet and wrote:

HIS NAME IS JOHN

And they were all amazed. ⁶⁴Immediately his mouth was opened and his tongue [set free], and he began to speak, praising God. ⁶⁵Fear came on all those who lived around them, and all these things were being talked about throughout the hill country of Judea. ⁶⁶All who heard about [him] took [it] to heart, saying, "What then will this child become?" For, indeed, the Lord's hand was with him.

⁶⁷Then his father Zechariah was filled with the Holy Spirit and prophesied:

> *⁶⁸Praise the Lord, the God of Israel,*
> *because He has visited*
> *and provided redemption for His people.*
> *⁶⁹He has raised up a horn of salvation for us*
> *in the house of His servant David,*
> *⁷⁰just as He spoke by the mouth*
> *of His holy prophets in ancient times;*
> *⁷¹salvation from our enemies*
> *and from the clutches of those who hate us.*
> *⁷²He has dealt mercifully with our fathers*
> *and remembered His holy covenant—*
> *⁷³the oath that He swore to our father Abraham.*
> *He has given us the privilege,*
> *⁷⁴since we have been rescued*
> *from our enemies' clutches,*

to serve Him without fear
75 in holiness and righteousness
in His presence all our days.
76 And child, you will be called
a prophet of the Most High,
for you will go before the Lord
to prepare His ways,
77 to give His people knowledge of salvation
through the forgiveness of their sins.
78 Because of our God's merciful compassion,
the Dawn from on high will visit us
79 to shine on those who live in darkness
and the shadow of death,
to guide our feet into the way of peace.

80 The child grew up and became spiritually strong, and he was in the wilderness until the day of his public appearance to Israel.

With verse 57, it all starts coming true. There have been promises and prophecies. Now we have an actual, living baby! And Luke is careful to tell us that this is a sign of God's *hesed*, of his great mercy. On the eighth day, when a Jewish male infant was named and circumcised, everyone assumed that the custom of naming the son after the father would be followed and the boy would be called Zechariah. But Elizabeth has not forgotten Gabriel's words: the boy is to be called John. Amid the confusion, Zechariah asks for a writing tablet. (Actually, Luke uses the medical term for a prescription tablet.) The old man has spent at least nine months cut off from society, unable to speak. Grasping the wooden tablet he furiously scrawls, "His name is John." Upon writing these words, the spell is broken and Zechariah can speak once more. And Luke wants us to know that the people are all amazed and in awe.

Like his wife Elizabeth before, now Zechariah is filled with the Holy Spirit. And the first words that come from those lips that have been silent for so long are, "Praise the Lord." Holding the infant in his arms, Zechariah bursts into song. His is a song of remembrance. He sings of David and the holy prophets and the ancient times. Like Mary he sings of *hesed*, of the mercy shown to the fathers, of the knowledge of salvation through the forgiveness of sins, which is also a gift of God's "merciful compassion," almost certainly again *hesed*.

In the midst of Zechariah's song comes an interesting word from a priest. He sings that God has given the privilege "to serve Him without fear." Nine months earlier Zechariah had gone into the holy place with the knowledge that if he was not ritually clean, he might very well die in the temple. In the old world the emotion that predominated in the service of God was fear. In the old world you were not allowed to touch the bottom of a mountain that God was on the top of or else you would die. But Zechariah is singing a song about a new world where the condition in which one will serve God is love and faithfulness and joy. It is a new world after all, but we must never forget that it is a world framed in the light of Old Testament *hesed*. The grace that has always been the defining characteristic of God has nonetheless granted an old man with little faith the privilege of singing a new song.

LUKE 2

THE KING IN A CATTLE TROUGH

2:1-3 Historical marker for the birth of Jesus.

2:4-7 Details of Joseph and Mary.
Simple statement of the birth.

2:8-20 Story of the shepherds.
Attention given to the outcasts.

THE LINE BETWEEN OLD AND NEW

2:21-24 Jesus presented at the temple.
Focus on the law.

2:25-35 Simeon's song and prophecy.

2:36-38 Reference to Anna.

2:39-40 The return to Galilee.

THE BOY WHO WOULD BE MESSIAH

2:41-52 Jesus in the temple.
Introduction of the question, "Who is Jesus?"

THE KING IN A CATTLE TROUGH

¹In those days a decree went out from Caesar Augustus that the whole empire should be registered. ²This first registration took place while Quirinius was governing Syria. ³So everyone went to be registered, each to his own town.

⁴And Joseph also went up from the town of Nazareth in Galilee, to Judea, to the city of David, which is called Bethlehem, because he was of the house and family line of David, ⁵to be registered along with Mary, who was engaged to him and was pregnant. ⁶While they were there, the time came for her to give birth. ⁷Then she gave birth to her firstborn Son, and she wrapped Him snugly in cloth and laid Him in a feeding trough—because there was no room for them at the inn.

⁸In the same region, shepherds were staying out in the fields and keeping watch at night over their flock. ⁹Then an angel of the Lord stood before them, and the glory of the Lord shone around them, and they were terrified. ¹⁰But the angel said to them, "Don't be afraid, for look, I proclaim to you good news of great joy that will be for all the people: ¹¹today a Savior, who is Messiah the Lord, was born for you in the city of David. ¹²This will be the sign for you: you will find a baby wrapped snugly in cloth and lying in a manger."

¹³Suddenly there was a multitude of the heavenly host with the angel, praising God and saying:

> *¹⁴Glory to God in the highest heaven,*
> *and peace on earth to people He favors!*

¹⁵When the angels had left them and returned to heaven, the shepherds said to one another, "Let's go straight to Bethlehem and see what has happened, which the Lord has made known to us."

¹⁶They hurried off and found both Mary and Joseph, and the baby who was lying in the feeding trough. ¹⁷After seeing [them], they reported the message they were told about this child, ¹⁸and all who heard it were amazed at what the shepherds said to them. ¹⁹But Mary was treasuring up all these things in her heart and meditating on them. ²⁰The shepherds returned, glorifying and praising God for all they had seen and heard, just as they had been told.

Caesar Augustus was born Gaius Octavius in 63 B.C. He became *princeps* in 31 B.C., a term he appropriated to himself as the inaugurator of the restored republic, or *principate*. He is often referred to as the first emperor of Rome, but some scholars believe it is not that simple, since he ostensibly postured himself as a believer in the republic, giving lip service to the senate during his reign, which lasted until he died in A.D. 14. (Increasingly scholars are saying that Tiberius was the first true emperor.)

Octavius's (or Octavian's as he was otherwise known) mother was the niece of the dictator Julius Caesar, who adopted him as his son and heir, leaving his financial and political fortune to the eighteen-year-old Octavius. When Julius Caesar was declared a god of the Roman state, Octavius became a "son of god" and the eventual founder of the "Roman Peace," or *Pax Romana,* clearing the sea lanes of pirates and establishing law and order throughout the empire.

He was five feet, seven inches tall and handsome, though Suetonius states that his teeth were "small and few." He kept a piece of sealskin in his pocket to protect himself from lightning, of which he seems to have been inordinately afraid. When a house he was in the process of building was struck by lightning, he ceased construction and began a new one. Despite the aura classical scholarship sometimes casts around him, Augustus was a bloodthirsty tyrant, close to someone like Hitler or Mussolini.

All of this background is important because Luke mentions his name not just to fix the period of time between 31 B.C. and A.D. 14. There is a distinct emotionality involved in simply saying "Caesar Augustus." It connotes upheaval, since the republic, which was initially attacked by Julius Caesar, was becoming an empire. The very fact that a census was called for confirms this. Rome was dominating the world, even the backwater town of Bethlehem. The notion of rulers being divine was taking hold in Rome. Some scholars say it began with Julius Caesar's illicit affair with Cleopatra, since she was worshiped as a god in Egypt. Even the term *Pax Romana* is a misnomer. Perhaps to some degree it was a safer time. But it was a false sense of peace, provided by a false god.

The mention of Quirinius in Luke 1:2 presents a problem for some scholars. We know, from Josephus, who he was. We know that he was appointed a legate who ruled Syria with military force. The problem comes from the fact that the closest census we have record of under Quirinius occurred in A.D. 6. Josephus tells us he ruled from A.D. 6-9. This does not match the date of 4 B.C. that we derive from the earlier reference to Herod (Lk 1:5). One solution, and I believe it is the best one, comes from evidence from an inscription that says Quirinius may have been legate twice, first from 10-7 B.C. and then again from A.D. 6-9.[4]

Into this corrupt, confusing time, in an obscure corner of the empire, a nondescript couple comes to Bethlehem in obedience to a decree issued a world away. The entire earth-shattering event is captured in four verses. The couple comes to their ancestral home place. The engaged yet pregnant woman senses it is her time, and the baby is born, wrapped snugly and placed in a feeding trough because there is no room for them at the inn.

No room at the inn: how many songs and sermons have tried to describe the monumental disconnect of the King of the Universe sleeping in a trough in a stable? Modern Christians sometimes lose patience with unbelievers. "How can they not believe?" they sometimes blurt out. But if we stand outside the stable and look in at the scene of the impoverished baby, wrapped in rags, I believe the correct response is, "They're never going to believe this!"

As poor and outcast as Joseph, Mary and the newborn seem to be, there is a group in the country more outcast still. That would be the shepherds. The rabbis had placed a ban on them, barring them from testifying in court. They are the first marginalized group we meet in Luke's Gospel. It seems appropriate that the first recipients of the promised Lamb of God would be shepherds. They are probably spending all night in the fields because it is lambing season—the spring, not the December 25 we have inherited from the early church. What seems even more unbelievable is the host that is sent to announce to them the good news. Mary met only a single angelic messenger. Joseph only dreamed of an angel. But the shepherds experience (literally in Greek) a "myriad" of the heavenly host. The "glory of the Lord" shines all around them. In Greek, they literally "feared a great fear."

Once again the typical angelic greeting comes, "Don't be afraid." We are not told if this is Gabriel again, only that it is "an angel of the Lord." His proclamation of good news is for "all the people"; again we see Luke's concern to record the fact that the gospel is universal.

The angel seems to understand that the shepherds need a sign, a way to find their way to this miraculous baby. He gives them two. He will be wrapped in cloths and lying in a trough. Luke uses a medical term for *swathing*, wrapping someone up in strips of cloth. The commentaries all agree this was a custom performed on newborns to help their limbs grow straight. I have wondered if this term might not refer to the fact that the baby was wrapped in strips of cloth or rags as a token of his poverty. This, it seems to me, is more of a sign, something out of the ordinary. Clearly the second reference that the baby would be lying in a trough is out of the ordinary.

Then it is as if heaven can no longer contain itself, and the sky erupts. The theme of the angels' brief song? Glory in heaven and peace on earth.

When the shepherds look for and find the wrapped-up baby in the trough, they tell everyone who will listen to them. Luke reminds us that they are all "amazed." How else is one supposed to respond to such a message?

Amid the hubbub, as the sky crackles with angelic energy and excited shepherds run around telling the good news, Luke leaves us with Mary. She is meditating on "these things." She has locked them away to treasure them in her heart. She must have been Luke's eyewitness for the nativity. How else would he have known this if not from her?

THE LINE BETWEEN OLD AND NEW

²¹*When the eight days were completed for His circumcision, He was named JESUS—the name given by the angel before He was conceived.* ²²*And when the days of their purification according to the law of Moses were finished, they brought Him up to Jerusalem to present Him to the Lord* ²³*(just as it is writ-*

ten in the law of the Lord: Every firstborn male will be dedicated to the Lord) [24] and to offer a sacrifice (according to what is stated in the law of the Lord: a pair of turtledoves or two young pigeons).

[25] There was a man in Jerusalem whose name was Simeon. This man was righteous and devout, looking forward to Israel's consolation, and the Holy Spirit was on him. [26] It had been revealed to him by the Holy Spirit that he would not see death before he saw the Lord's Messiah. [27] Guided by the Spirit, he entered the temple complex. When the parents brought in the child Jesus to perform for Him what was customary under the law, [28] Simeon took Him up in his arms, praised God, and said:

> [29] Now, Master,
> You can dismiss Your slave in peace,
> according to Your word.
> [30] For my eyes have seen Your salvation.
> [31] You have prepared [it]
> in the presence of all peoples—
> [32] a light for revelation to the Gentiles
> and glory to Your people Israel.

[33] His father and mother were amazed at what was being said about Him. [34] Then Simeon blessed them and told His mother Mary: "Indeed, this child is destined to cause the fall and rise of many in Israel and to be a sign that will be opposed—[35] and a sword will pierce your own soul—that the thoughts of many hearts may be revealed."

[36] There was also a prophetess, Anna, a daughter of Phanuel, of the tribe of Asher. She was well along in years, having lived with her husband seven years after her marriage, [37] and was a widow for 84 years. She did not leave the temple complex, serving God night and day with fastings and prayers. [38] At that very moment, she came up and began to thank God and to speak about Him to all who were looking forward to the redemption of Jerusalem.

[39] When they had completed everything according to the law of the Lord, they returned to Galilee, to their own town of Nazareth. [40] The boy grew up and became strong, filled with wisdom, and God's grace was on Him.

*V*erses 21-24 might seem confusing if you don't take the time to untangle them. We are looking at two separate occasions and three rituals. Jesus' circumcision happens first, eight days after his birth. At this time he would also be named. This is a parallel to the story of the naming of John in chapter 1. Both babies had been named before they were born.

The second observance begins in verse 22. Here we are looking at two separate rituals. First comes the purification of Mary, which took place forty days after the birth of a son and would have taken place eighty days after the birth of a daughter. The offering of the two pigeons was reserved for the poor (Lev 12:1-8). The second ritual is the dedication of the firstborn (Ex 13:2-14). Within the scope of six verses, the observance of the "law" is mentioned four times. This is a picture of Mary and Joseph's exacting observance of the law. Of the nine times the word *law* occurs in Luke's writing, five of them are contained in this passage. It is a picture of the world that would, very soon, begin to pass away.

In this context Simeon steps forward. It is a miracle in itself that they have met at this precise moment within the crowded, massive thirty-five-acre temple complex. He too is a representative of the old world, the Old Testament world in which faith was expressed primarily by waiting for God to make good on his promises. Simeon represents an important line in the world of faith. Before Simeon, faith meant waiting. After him, faith will mean following. At this moment, the old world is meeting and embracing the new.

Luke describes Simeon in old-world terms. He is "righteous and devout," waiting for "Israel's consolation." But the Holy Spirit is also there, as he has been with the unborn John, Elizabeth, Zechariah and Mary. The elderly man has received a promise: that he will not die until he has seen the Messiah. Now, under the guidance of that same Spirit, he makes his way into the temple court at precisely the same moment that the child's parents arrive.

Taking the baby in his arms, Simeon sings a song. It is the last song he will sing. It is the last song we will hear in Luke's Gospel. It is a song that welcomes his death as a release and a dismissal. But it is also a song that welcomes in the Light of revelation to the Gentiles, for whom Luke and Paul also cared so much. What is rapidly becoming the norm in Luke happens next: Mary and Joseph are amazed!

Simeon pronounces a *berakah*, or blessing, on the three of them. Next he utters a prophecy, most of which he would have rather bitten his tongue than spoken. The baby will cause many to rise and fall. He will face opposition. And then: Mary's heart will be pierced by a sword. This is an ominous prophecy of the pain she will endure watching her Son die on the cross—all this, Simeon whispers, so that the thoughts of many hearts would be revealed.

At that moment Anna, of the tribe of Asher, a clan renowned for its beautiful daughters, comes forward to thank God for the baby as well. Luke, who cares so deeply for widows, tells us far more about her than he does about Simeon. Yet he neglects to tell us what she says.

After the shekels are offered and the pigeons sacrificed, Mary and Joseph are ready to go back to the obscurity of Nazareth. Then they disappear from us for twelve years, during which time we are told Jesus grows up strong and wise and full of God's grace.

THE BOY WHO WOULD BE MESSIAH

⁴¹Every year His parents traveled to Jerusalem for the Passover Festival. ⁴²When He was 12 years old, they went up according to the custom of the festival. ⁴³After those days were over, as they were returning, the boy Jesus stayed behind in Jerusalem, but His parents did not know it. ⁴⁴Assuming He was in the traveling party, they went a day's journey. Then they began looking for Him among their relatives and friends. ⁴⁵When they did not find Him, they returned to Jerusalem to search for Him. ⁴⁶After three days, they found Him in the temple complex sitting among the teachers, listening to them and asking them questions. ⁴⁷And all those who heard Him were astounded at His understanding and His answers. ⁴⁸When His parents saw Him, they were astonished, and His mother said to Him, "Son, why have You treated us like this? Your father and I have been anxiously searching for You."

⁴⁹"Why were you searching for Me?" He asked them. "Didn't you know

*that I had to be in my Father's house?" ⁵⁰But they did not understand what
He said to them.*

*⁵¹Then He went down with them and came to Nazareth and was obedi-
ent to them. His mother kept all these things in her heart. ⁵²And Jesus in-
creased in wisdom and stature, and in favor with God and with people.*

*T*he *shalosh regalim* are the three great feasts of Judaism: *Pesach* (Passover), *Shavuot* (Pentecost) and *Sukkot* (Tabernacles). By law everyone
living within a prescribed distance had to come to Jerusalem to celebrate them. Perhaps that's why we read that Jesus' parents came to the
city every year. Only this year Jesus is twelve, just coming to the age at
which he will be held responsible for observing the law. Luke completely neglects to tell us what happens, because apparently he doesn't
think we need to know. All he tells us is that after the feast, Jesus is
"misplaced." Imagine being entrusted with the raising of the Messiah
and losing him . . . for three days! Apparently the group from Nazareth
has traveled together for safety, and Joseph and Mary assume Jesus is
safe with the group of relatives and friends. But when they cannot find
him, they return to Jerusalem. The three-day time period is up for
grabs. You can decide as well as any scholar: do they simply spend
seventy-two hours frantically looking for him? Or do they leave on one
day, miss him on the second and return a day's journey, spending the
third day looking "everywhere"? You can decide.

Apparently it was the custom of the Sanhedrin to hold public discussions of the law during the three big festivals. Jesus seems to have become absorbed in this open debate . . . for three days! Sometimes Ren-
aissance paintings of the scene lead you to believe he, the precocious boy
from Nazareth, was doing all the teaching. But Luke says he is listening
and asking questions. True to Lukan form, the people are "astounded"
by the boy's understanding, while his parents are "astonished."

Once again, Mary has to be the source for this story. Her first anxious question is so profoundly maternal: "Why have You treated us like
this?" After all, they have been looking everywhere.

Here is where we must engage with our imaginations and try to hear the tone in the twelve-year-old's voice as he responds to his astonished parents. The only thing that he who understands so much *doesn't* understand is why they didn't come to the temple in the first place. Why in the world would you look everywhere when you must have known I would be here in my Father's house? Has he realized fully that the One for whom the temple stands is uniquely his Father? Is Joseph confused and perhaps wounded by this response? All we are told is that they do not understand what Jesus says. They don't understand that they should not have been looking everywhere but only here, in his Father's house.

Luke 2:51 means to clear up any confusion. Lest we be tempted to think this extraordinary young man is a "handful," that this sort of behavior is the norm: no. He is obedient and, in an echo of Luke 2:40, he grows in wisdom and he grows in height. All the people and God himself are favorable toward him.

LUKE 3

THE DOLEFUL DAYS OF TIBERIUS

3:1 Tiberius, Pilate, Herod, Philip, Lysanias.

3:2a Annas, Caiaphas.

THE VOICE OF A SLAVE IN THE WILDERNESS

3:2b–3 Introduction to the ministry of John.

3:4–6 Isaiah as background.

3:7–14 John as representative of the old world.

3:15–18 John's self-understanding as a slave.

3:19–20 Herod imprisons John.

THE BAPTISM OF JESUS

3:21–22 The Father's answer to the question, "Who is Jesus?"

THE GENETICS OF JESUS

3:23–38 Jesus' genealogy back to Adam.

THE DOLEFUL DAYS OF TIBERIUS

[1]In the fifteenth year of the reign of Tiberius Caesar, while Pontius Pilate was governor of Judea, Herod was tetrarch of Galilee, his brother Philip tetrarch of the region of Iturea and Trachonitis, and Lysanias tetrarch of Abilene, [2]during the high priesthood of Annas and Caiaphas, . . .

$\mathcal{R}$oughly eighteen years have passed since the closing of chapter 2. When we last saw Jesus, he was twelve. Now he is about thirty. Luke begins his historiographical introduction by telling us it is the fifteenth year of Tiberius. Since he began to reign around A.D. 14, this sets the date at A.D. 29.

When Augustus died in A.D. 14, his dour stepson Tiberius became emperor. Pliny the Elder called him "the gloomiest of mankind." If Augustus's reign speaks of upheaval, Tiberius's connotes a time of dread and darkness. Augustus had intended one of his two sons to rule, but they had both died. Tiberius was clearly his second choice, a cloud that followed him throughout his reign. His mother was the infamous Livia, the suspect of numerous poisonings. During the latter part of his reign, a shadowy figure named Lucius Aelius Sejanus slowly manipulated his way to the top, becoming Tiberius's intimate associate, the partner of his labors. As Tiberius distanced himself from his responsibilities as emperor, Sejanus seized more and more power. In A.D. 31 Sejanus became consul, virtually co-emperor. Eventually his plots were exposed and he was executed the same year. We will see that he is an important though unnamed player in the trial of Jesus, owing to the fact that he had obtained the office for Pilate. The end of Tiberius's reign was a time of instability and terror. He died in A.D. 37.

Luke makes his list in descending order of power. After Tiberius comes Pontius Pilate. He played a major part in the trial of Jesus, insisting again and again that he believed Jesus to be innocent. He was prefect of Judea from A.D. 26-36. Prefecture was a nonmilitary position mostly concerned with overseeing the collection of taxes, though he also had peacekeeping responsibilities. His administration was a turbulent one, marked by bribes and robberies. At one point he stole money from the temple treasury in order to finance a Roman-style aqueduct for Jerusalem. He printed coins that portrayed objects of divination and emperor-worship that outraged the Jews. He was eventually called back to Rome to answer charges of hostilities against the Jews. Tiberius died during the trip and Pilate disappeared. It is believed that he killed himself.

Next in order of power are three of the sons of Herod the Great who, before his death in 4 B.C., divided up his empire into four parts or tetrarchies. Of the three who are mentioned, only Herod Antipas figures into the story of Jesus. He is mentioned in Luke 9:7-9 as wondering about the true identity of Jesus, and in Luke 13:31-32 Jesus refers to him as "that fox." He is responsible for the imprisonment and execution of John (Lk 3:20; Mt 14:3-12). Like his father, he was hated by the Jewish population. He stole his brother Philip's wife, Herodias (Lk 3:19), and so earned the denunciation of John the Baptist. The emperor Caligula deposed him in A.D. 39.

At the end of the list Luke provides the religious authorities, Annas and Caiaphas. Without a doubt they were the two most powerful Jewish men in Jerusalem. Strictly speaking, there was only one high priest at a time. Annas was in office between A.D. 6 and A.D. 15. He was succeeded by five of his sons. (Between the years 37 B.C. and A.D. 26, there were no less than twenty-eight high priests!) In A.D. 18, his son-in-law Caiaphas took office. Though technically Caiaphas remained the reigning high priest, Annas was still very much in power. This is seen in the fact that when Jesus was initially arrested, he was taken first to Annas's house for questioning (Jn 18:13).

Although this collection of powerful men is meant to point to a date of A.D. 29, nonetheless each major person in Luke's list represents corruption, greed and the irresponsible wielding of power. The tone they set for the opening of Jesus' ministry is dark and foreboding. Into a world dominated by fear, injustice and corrupt power steps the Prince of Peace and the Light of the World.

THE VOICE OF A SLAVE IN THE WILDERNESS

. . . God's word came to John the son of Zechariah in the wilderness. ³He went into all the vicinity of the Jordan, preaching a baptism of repentance for

the forgiveness of sins, ⁴as it is written in the book of the words of the prophet Isaiah:

> *A voice of one crying out in the wilderness:*
> *"Prepare the way for the Lord;*
> *make His paths straight!*
> *⁵Every valley will be filled,*
> *and every mountain and hill will be made low;*
> *the crooked will become straight,*
> *the rough ways smooth,*
> *⁶and everyone will see the salvation of God."*

⁷*He then said to the crowds who came out to be baptized by him, "Brood of vipers! Who warned you to flee from the coming wrath? ⁸Therefore produce fruit consistent with repentance. And don't start saying to yourselves, 'We have Abraham as our father,' for I tell you that God is able to raise up children for Abraham from these stones! ⁹Even now the ax is ready to strike the root of the trees! Therefore every tree that doesn't produce good fruit will be cut down and thrown into the fire."*

¹⁰*"What then should we do?" the crowds were asking him.*

¹¹*He replied to them, "The one who has two shirts must share with someone who has none, and the one who has food must do the same."*

¹²*Tax collectors also came to be baptized, and they asked him, "Teacher, what should we do?"*

¹³*He told them, "Don't collect any more than what you have been authorized."*

¹⁴*Some soldiers also questioned him: "What should we do?"*

He said to them, "Don't take money from anyone by force or false accusation; be satisfied with your wages."

¹⁵*Now the people were waiting expectantly, and all of them were debating in their minds whether John might be the Messiah. ¹⁶John answered them all, "I baptize you with water, but One is coming who is more powerful than I. I am not worthy to untie the strap of His sandals. He will baptize you with the Holy Spirit and fire. ¹⁷His winnowing shovel is in His hand to clear His threshing floor and gather the wheat into His barn, but the chaff He will burn up with a fire that never goes out." ¹⁸Then, along with many other*

exhortations, he proclaimed good news to the people. [19]*But Herod the tetrarch, being rebuked by him about Herodias, his brother's wife, and about all the evil things Herod had done,* [20]*added this to everything else—he locked John up in prison.*

*W*hen we last saw him, John was eight days old and in the arms of his father, Zechariah, who was singing a prophecy over him. Even now, all these years later, he is called Zechariah's son. He comes from the wilderness, the place of Elijah, with Elijah's message on his parched lips. It is not Jesus' "good news." In fact, for most people, it is terrible news.

John comes preaching a baptism of repentance for the forgiveness of sins, an unfamiliar baptism in Judaism. Besides the daily ritual oblations, the only baptism they know is for those Gentiles who want to become full proselytes to Judaism. In John's Gospel an argument about "ritual cleansing" breaks out, as the Jews try to cope with this unfamiliar form (Jn 3:25).

It is hard to explain the wild popularity of the ministry of John, especially when we hear him screaming at the crowd that they are a "brood of vipers." Being Abraham's children won't save you, he shouts— only repentance and baptism will. Isaiah foresaw John's ministry. He saw the way being prepared, the mountains being brought low, the crooked ways being made straight. He saw that a new world was coming, only not quite yet. John is making ready for the upheaval, for the world to be turned upside down. But he is not the One who will overturn it. So for now, when the people ask him what they should do in response to his message, he gives them old-world answers. Do good, try harder, be generous, stop cheating: all are difficult but doable. The One who is the new world will make impossible demands on his followers, like loving their enemies and forgiving the way God forgives.

John understands all this. While others are debating whether he is the Messiah, he is clear about it: "I baptize you with water, but One is coming who is more powerful than I. I am not worthy to untie the strap of His sandals."

Untying sandals was the task of the lowliest slave. The rabbis had decreed that the overzealous followers of well-known teachers could perform any sort of humiliating task for their masters except one: they could not untie the sandal thong.[5] That was seen as too degrading for anyone—anyone, that is, except John. After all, he is only a voice, crying in the wilderness.

From his mother's womb, leaping for joy, to his father's arms, being sung to sleep, to the desert wilderness and the inviting wetness of the Jordan, we finally see John in the last place we would have ever expected to see him: in prison. He is not there for doing something wrong but for doing something right. He has spoken out against Herod's adulterous relationship with Herodias, his brother Philip's beautiful wife. Herod's tetrarchy is a place where innocent people are jailed while the guilty go free, where (as we will learn eventually) innocent people are beheaded and even crucified.

THE BAPTISM OF JESUS

[21]*When all the people were baptized, Jesus also was baptized. As He was praying, heaven opened,* [22]*and the Holy Spirit descended on Him in a physical appearance like a dove. And a voice came from heaven:*

> *You are My beloved Son.*
> *I take delight in You!*

*L*uke devotes sixteen verses to John the Baptist and his followers beside the Jordan, yet only two for the unexplainable baptism of Jesus. It is unexplainable because One who has never and would never sin submits to a baptism that is a sign of repentance. He is not repenting; he is *identifying.* It is the first step toward an eventual death on the cross. Here, with John, he submits to a baptism of repentance for sins he never committed. On Golgotha he will die for sins he never committed so that he can forgive each and every sin.

Only Luke, with his emphasis on prayer, tells us that "as He was praying" heaven opens and Jesus hears those words he most needs to hear at this, the beginning of his difficult ministry. They are the words that every son longs to hear from his father, but only a few ever do. "I am delighted in you; you are the one I love!"

Those words will help prepare Jesus for the wilderness he is about to endure. For the next three years of struggle, rejection and opposition, they will echo in his ears when he is most tempted to give up.

THE GENETICS OF JESUS

23As He began [His ministry], Jesus was about 30 years old and was thought to be the son of Joseph, [son] of Heli,

24[son] of Matthat, [son] of Levi, [son] of Melchi, [son] of Jannai, [son] of Joseph, 25[son] of Mattathias, [son] of Amos, [son] of Nahum, [son] of Esli, [son] of Naggai, 26[son] of Maath, [son] of Mattathias, [son] of Semein, [son] of Josech, [son] of Joda, 27[son] of Joanan, [son] of Rhesa, [son] of Zerubbabel, [son] of Shealtiel, [son] of Neri, 28[son] of Melchi, [son] of Addi, [son] of Cosam, [son] of Elmadam, [son] of Er, 29[son] of Joshua, [son] of Eliezer, [son] of Jorim, [son] of Matthat, [son] of Levi, 30[son] of Simeon, [son] of Judah, [son] of Joseph, [son] of Jonam, [son] of Eliakim, 31[son] of Melea, [son] of Menna, [son] of Mattatha, [son] of Nathan, [son] of David, 32[son] of Jesse, [son] of Obed, [son] of Boaz, [son] of Salmon, [son] of Nahshon, 33[son] of Amminadab, [son] of Ram, [son] of Hezron, [son] of Perez, [son] of Judah, 34[son] of Jacob, [son] of Isaac, [son] of Abraham, [son] of Terah, [son] of Nahor, 35[son] of Serug, [son] of Reu, [son] of Peleg, [son] of Eber, [son] of Shelah, 36[son] of Cainan, [son] of Arphaxad, [son] of Shem, [son] of Noah, [son] of Lamech, 37[son] of Methuselah, [son] of Enoch, [son] of Jared, [son] of Mahalaleel, [son] of Cainan, 38[son] of Enos, [son] of Seth, [son] of Adam, [son] of God.

*M*atthew opens his Gospel with a genealogy of Jesus. It is shorter than Luke's because it only goes back to Abraham. The two lists sometimes agree and run together for a few generations but they also part and go off in their own directions. Detractors from the accuracy of the Scriptures gleefully point out these apparent inconsistencies, failing to realize that they are different genealogies. Matthew represents Joseph's line, while Luke's almost certainly comes from Mary, who was surely one of Luke's principal witnesses.

The list in Luke 3 contains some of the most famous men in Jewish history as well as some of the most obscure. From verses 24-31, the thirty-nine names are unknown until we reach Nathan, David's third son, whose name we know from 2 Samuel 5:14 and 1 Chronicles 3:5. With him we are back on the known map, so to speak. Then there he is: David, the son of Jesse, the king of Israel and the one through whom Jesus bears the right to the Davidic throne. After David's father comes Obed, for whom Naomi cared (Ruth 4:16-22). Then comes Boaz, who married Ruth in the book by the same name. The next six names, except Salmon, can be found listed in the Old Testament. Perez, the last of the six, was Judah's son by Tamar. If you read the story leading up to his birth in Genesis 38, you may shudder that this kind of sordid affair is a part of the background of Jesus. After Judah, the patriarch of the great tribe, comes Jacob, another less-than-illustrious ancestor, yet still someone whom God claimed he loved. Next is Isaac, the one they named "laughter" when Abraham and Sarah guffawed at the thought of two senior citizens setting up their own nursery.

At this point Luke moves beyond Matthew's genealogy. Terah, the father of Abraham, and Nahor, whose granddaughter would eventually become the wife of Isaac, we know from Genesis 11. We know Noah as well, who gets us back to Genesis 6. The next six names, including the long-lived Methuselah, are found in the fifth chapter of Genesis. Seth brings us to Genesis 4, and finally, with Adam, we arrive at the very beginning, the first chapter of Genesis.

This is the genealogy of Jesus, the son of Joseph and Mary. But is it not also a record of what made up the human part of his genetics? The genetic pool of Jesus: where his dark eyes or curly or straight hair came from. Where his proclivity to creative expression came from, or the problem he might have had with numbers. The more we learn about the vast amount of information we all carry in our genes, the more I wonder if Jesus' courage might go all the way back to David. Had he not given up his life on the cross, could Methuselah's genetic longevity have made a difference? His skin color and fingerprints, the shape of his ears and the color of his eyes, his cholesterol level, his blood type: it would have all been there.

The mystery will always remain as to how he could have inherited all this and yet not the sin nature: not Jacob's lying or David's uncontrollable libido. Perhaps the proclivity was still there on each strand of DNA, to be wrestled with, to be overcome.

LUKE 4

THE SON IN THE DESERT

4:1-13 Jesus establishes his sonship in the wilderness, fulfilling what Israel was unable to do.

GOOD NEWS FOR THE POOR

4:14-15 (to 9:50) Ministry in the Galilee.

4:16–21 Focus on the poor.

4:22 Initial acceptance in Nazareth.

4:23–30 Jesus eventually rejected when he speaks of the universality of the gospel.

"BE MUZZLED"

4:31–37 Jesus demonstrates his power to cast out evil spirits.

THE RELUCTANT HEALER

4:38-44 Jesus demonstrates his power to heal the sick mother-in-law of Peter.

THE SON IN THE DESERT

¹Then Jesus returned from the Jordan, full of the Holy Spirit, and was led by the Spirit in the wilderness ²for 40 days to be tempted by the Devil. He ate nothing during those days, and when they were over, He was hungry. ³The Devil said to Him, "If You are the Son of God, tell this stone to become bread."

⁴But Jesus answered him, "It is written: Man must not live on bread alone."

⁵So he took Him up and showed Him all the kingdoms of the world in a moment of time. ⁶The Devil said to Him, "I will give You their splendor and all this authority, because it has been given over to me, and I can give it to anyone I want. ⁷If You, then, will worship me, all will be Yours."

⁸And Jesus answered him, "It is written:

> *Worship the Lord your God,*
> *and serve Him only."*

⁹So he took Him to Jerusalem, had Him stand on the pinnacle of the temple, and said to Him, "If You are the Son of God, throw Yourself down from here. ¹⁰For it is written:

> *He will give His angels orders concerning you,*
> *to protect you, ¹¹and*
> *they will support you with their hands,*
> *so that you will not strike*
> *your foot against a stone."*

¹²And Jesus answered him, "It is said: Do not test the Lord your God."

¹³After the Devil had finished every temptation, he departed from Him for a time.

One final step is required before Jesus begins his ministry proper. He must go into the wilderness to establish his true sonship. William Lane used to say, "True sonship is always established in the wilderness." Israel would wander in the wilderness for two periods of forty years and yet ultimately fail the test. Jesus now enters for a period of forty days. Having heard the voice of God declare his sonship (Lk 3:22), Jesus is led by the Spirit into the desert to demonstrate that he is indeed God's true Son.

The canvas is painted thickly with the Holy Spirit. In one breath Luke tells us Jesus is both "full of the Holy Spirit" and is being "led by the Spirit." The specific purpose is made clear from the outset: he is going to be tempted by the devil.

The word used by Luke to denote Satan is *diabolos*. It is a name that paints a picture for our imaginations. *Dia* means "across," while *ballō* is a verb that means "to throw." The devil is the one who "throws across" accusations, as in the throne-room scene in the early chapters of Job when Satan (which means "accuser") is hurling accusations at Job. Now, in the waterless waste of the desert, he is hurling the best he has at Jesus. After Jesus has fasted for forty days, the devil attacks him where he is weakest. "If You are the Son of God," he hisses, "tell this stone to become bread." Certainly, Jesus has the power to perform such a miracle. In chapter 9 he feeds thousands. The temptation is not simply to perform a miracle but to renounce trust in God. Israel failed this test in the wilderness. When they were hungry they began to grumble, saying God had only brought them out of Egypt to let them starve in the wilderness (Ex 16:3). But to truly be a son or daughter of God is to completely depend on him. And this is precisely what Jesus is prepared to do. He combats the temptation of the devil with the same weapon any believer can use: Scripture.

Though Jesus quotes only a segment of the verse here, its entirety is implied: "He humbled you by letting you go hungry; then He gave you manna to eat, which you and your fathers had not known, so that you might learn that man does not live on bread alone but on every word that comes from the mouth of the LORD" (Deut 8:3).

In Luke 23, the crowd torments Jesus on the cross by shouting, "He saved others; let Him save Himself" (Lk 23:35). Indeed, Jesus will save others precisely by refusing to save himself. Likewise, he will feed others but he will not feed himself. He will completely trust his Father to care for all his needs.

The imagination reels at the next temptation. Luke simply says "he took Him up," and yet what that means can hardly be imagined. From wherever Jesus has been taken, he is able to see all the kingdoms of the world at one time. Everything that can be offered is offered to Jesus. It will all be given to him if only he will worship the devil. This is another test that Israel failed in the wilderness. In Exodus 32, after Moses received the law, he returned to find the Israelites worshiping the golden calf. Although the land flowing with milk and honey was promised to them, they deliberately chose to worship the golden calf instead.

Once again, Jesus responds to the accuser by simply quoting the Bible, something any newborn Christian can do. "Worship the Lord your God, and serve Him only." Again Jesus quotes from Deuteronomy, a book that, for many of us, is becoming more and more obscure. Yet when Jesus is faced with temptation, it is the book to which he flees. He refuses a momentary temptation, although we must realize that in his weakened condition, it must have been a powerful one. No, Jesus is the true Son of God, and he will demonstrate his sonship in the wilderness by refusing to worship anyone but God alone.

Finally, Jesus is taken to the pinnacle of the temple. From this dizzying height he is tempted to throw himself off, trusting the angels to protect him. Having been twice thwarted by Jesus, who has used the Scriptures to defend himself, the devil now resorts to quoting or misquoting Scripture. He uses Psalm 91, which speaks of the angels' protection and of trusting God through any calamity. And yet once more Jesus will not yield. You can almost see Jesus shaking his head, remembering Psalm 91 in its true context. It is almost as if Satan has quoted the psalm that will strengthen Jesus in this, his calamity in the wilderness. Once more Jesus will go to the Scriptures. It is Deuteronomy again, this time Deuteronomy 6:16, which speaks of the failure of the Israelites in the wilderness. In Exodus 17, they came to a place called Rephidim. Because there was no water there, the people began once more to complain against Moses. He renamed the place Massah, which means "test." Now, as Jesus comes to his final test in the wilderness, he will triumph because of his complete dependence on the Father. Now that his sonship has been fully established through testing in the wilderness, he is ready to begin his ministry.

GOOD NEWS FOR THE POOR

14Then Jesus returned to Galilee in the power of the Spirit, and news about Him spread throughout the entire vicinity. 15He was teaching in their synagogues, being acclaimed by everyone.

16He came to Nazareth, where He had been brought up. As usual, He entered the synagogue on the Sabbath day and stood up to read. 17The scroll of the prophet Isaiah was given to Him, and unrolling the scroll, He found the place where it was written:

> *18The Spirit of the Lord is on Me,*
> *because He has anointed Me*
> *to preach good news to the poor.*
> *He has sent Me*
> *to proclaim freedom to the captives*
> *and recovery of sight to the blind,*
> *to set free the oppressed,*
> *19to proclaim the year of the Lord's favor.*

20He then rolled up the scroll, gave it back to the attendant, and sat down. And the eyes of everyone in the synagogue were fixed on Him. 21He began by saying to them, "Today as you listen, this Scripture has been fulfilled."

22They were all speaking well of Him and were amazed by the gracious words that came from His mouth, yet they said, "Isn't this Joseph's son?"

23Then He said to them, "No doubt you will quote this proverb to Me: 'Doctor, heal yourself.' 'All we've heard that took place in Capernaum, do here in Your hometown also.'"

24He also said, "I assure you: No prophet is accepted in his hometown. 25But I say to you, there were certainly many widows in Israel in Elijah's days, when the sky was shut up for three years and six months while a great famine came over all the land. 26Yet Elijah was not sent to any of them—but to a widow at Zarephath in Sidon. 27And in the prophet Elisha's time, there were many in Israel who had serious skin diseases, yet not one of them was healed—only Naaman the Syrian."

28When they heard this, everyone in the synagogue was enraged. 29They got up, drove Him out of town, and brought Him to the edge of the hill their town was built on, intending to hurl Him over the cliff. ³⁰*But He passed right through the crowd and went on His way.*

*J*esus returns from the fasting and temptation in the wilderness not exhausted as we might expect but rather, Luke says, "in the power of the Spirit." Although initially his ministry is acclaimed, this period of acceptance is brief and will come to an end in the synagogue in his hometown of Nazareth. In fact, this will be our only chance to hear his synagogue preaching.

On the Sabbath Jesus enters the synagogue. At the closing of the service comes what is referred to as the haphtarah, a portion of the Prophets that is read before dismissal. Any young man from the community could do the reading and make a comment on the passage if he wished. The attendant hands Jesus the scroll of Isaiah. He unrolls it and begins to read. As Isaiah's words had defined the ministry of John the Baptist (Lk 3:4-6), now they will perfectly describe what Jesus has come to do.

They are the very first words he speaks upon beginning his ministry. They are perfect words, therefore, simply because he speaks them, but they are not simply spoken. They are costly words. In the end they will cost him everything. If only he would have the good sense to identify with the rich and the powerful instead of the poor, if only he would act in accordance with their values, if only he would dance to their tune. . . . But Jesus does not, would not, dance (Lk 7:32).

In a religious world that has concluded that the poor are poor because they are sinners and cursed by God as a result, Jesus comes and pronounces on them God's blessing. "Blessed are you who are poor," he says, because this world is not the only world that exists (Lk 6:20). A kingdom is coming where rich and poor will change places, where those who weep will laugh and where the laughing ones will burst into tears. That world is here; it is coming. It is Luke's favorite world to describe.

Although Jesus does have a few wealthy friends, Joseph of Arimathea being the most noteworthy, by and large he gravitates toward the poor. They are drawn, gravitationally, to him. They follow him in droves not necessarily because they grasp fully what his life means or what the gospel is, but because they recognize in him a compassionate heart that will feed them if he can, even when he is forced to borrow bread and fish from a hungry little boy to do it.

Even those who, because of their lack of education, are unaware of another one of Isaiah's prophecies—that he would be a man of sorrows acquainted with our deepest grief—even these recognize in him someone whose tears are their tears as well. He not only weeps for them; he weeps with them, becoming acquainted with the darkest depths, with their poverty and pain. He does not explain away the pain, nor does he say that he has come with the answer or that he will fix everything. Instead he bows his head and allows the tears to flow. It is not about providing answers or fixing a problem; it is about entering fully and redemptively into their suffering, because Jesus knows that God uses suffering to save the world. He has not come to *fix* death and sorrow but to ultimately bring about their demise. He has not come to give answers; he has come to give himself. His presence, his tears are the solution, the answer, the truth. And in the midst of that moment when we don't get what we want, we get what we need.

Jesus closes his reading with a reference to the Jubilee, the year of the Lord's favor. This was a gift offered the Israelites in Leviticus 25. Every fifty years all debts would be canceled. Everyone who was a slave would be set free, to be followed by a yearlong celebration. Sadly, there is no indication that the Israelites ever celebrated Jubilee or accepted this extravagant gift the Lord had offered. Now, in the ministry of Jesus, an extravagant gift would once more be refused.

Amid the early adulation, in Luke 4:25, Jesus reminds his hearers that the Gentiles had frequently been the beneficiaries of God's favor. The widow of Zarephath in Sidon had been miraculously fed while the Israelites hungered (1 Kings 17:8-24). Naaman the Syrian, the commander of the army of Aram, had been healed while the sores of the Israelites festered (2 Kings 5:1-14). The faint praise of the synagogue crowd evaporates in an instant. The enraged Nazarenes drive Jesus out of town, intending to throw him over a cliff. Yet, says Luke, he simply passes right through them and goes on his way. Having been cast out of his hometown, we never see Jesus returning to Nazareth.

"BE MUZZLED"

³¹Then He went down to Capernaum, a town in Galilee, and was teaching them on the Sabbath. ³²They were astonished at His teaching because His message had authority. ³³In the synagogue there was a man with an unclean demonic spirit who cried out with a loud voice, ³⁴"Leave us alone! What do You have to do with us, Jesus—Nazarene? Have You come to destroy us? I know who You are—the Holy One of God!"

³⁵But Jesus rebuked him and said, "Be quiet and come out of him!"

And throwing him down before them, the demon came out of him without hurting him at all. ³⁶They were all struck with amazement and kept saying to one another, "What is this message? For He commands the unclean spirits with authority and power, and they come out!" ³⁷And news about Him began to go out to every place in the vicinity.

*A*fter the expulsion from Nazareth, Jesus relocates to Capernaum, the hometown of Peter. Matthew, in fact, refers to it as "His own town" (Mt 9:1). During the rest of the Galilean ministry, it appears to be the base of operations for Jesus and his disciples. They come and go and come and go from Peter's house until chapter 9, when Jesus will leave, never to return.

Once they are there, the people are "astonished" by the authority of his message. One reason may be that when rabbis taught, they tended to quote other rabbis. This is where they derived their authority—from the number of rabbinic sources they could quote on any given topic. Jesus, on the other hand, never quotes anyone. The people have never heard this kind of authority before. They are about to learn another dimension of his authority. Jesus does not simply speak authoritative sermons; he actually has the authority to command demonic spirits to leave the possessed.

While Jesus is in the synagogue, a demonic spirit who possesses a man begins to shout, "Leave *us* alone! What do You have to do with *us*, Jesus—Nazarene? . . . I know who You are—the Holy One of God!"

"I know who you are" was, in fact, a magical formula used to gain power over someone who was more powerful. It was used in ancient magic spells to subdue spiritual powers. It was believed that knowing the name of a spiritual opponent would give you power over them.

But the demon's spell has no power over Jesus. What's more, he does not want this confession to be heard from the mouths of demons. He commands the demon literally to "be muzzled" and to come out, which it has absolutely no choice but to do. In the process of leaving, it throws the man to the ground in an attempt to do some final harm to him, but Luke notes that it does not hurt him at all. Once more the response of amazement is recorded for us by Luke in his Gospel of amazement.

THE RELUCTANT HEALER

[38]*After He left the synagogue, He entered Simon's house. Simon's mother-in-law was suffering from a high fever, and they asked Him about her.* [39]*So He stood over her and rebuked the fever, and it left her. She got up immediately and began to serve them.*

[40]*When the sun was setting, all those who had anyone sick with various diseases brought them to Him. As He laid His hands on each one of them, He would heal them.* [41]*Also, demons were coming out of many, shouting and saying, "You are the Son of God!" But He rebuked them and would not allow them to speak, because they knew He was the Messiah.*

[42]*When it was day, He went out and made His way to a deserted place. But the crowds were searching for Him. They came to Him and tried to keep Him from leaving them.* [43]*But He said to them, "I must proclaim the good news about the kingdom of God to the other towns also, because I was sent for this purpose."* [44]*And He was preaching in the synagogues of Galilee.*

We move from the tumult of the synagogue to the quiet of Peter's house, just eighty-three feet down the narrow street from the synagogue and to the right. Jesus and his friends enter the house, no doubt exhausted from the demonic confrontation, to find Peter's mother-in-law in bed with what Luke the doctor notes as a "high" fever. A high-grade fever in the first century was nothing to take lightly. Around Capernaum a disease known as "lake fever" was common due to impurities in the water.

Even as he spoke to the demon, now Jesus "speaks" to the fever, which has no choice but to leave. This does not mean that Peter's mother-in-law was possessed, but rather that Jesus also has authority over sickness. His word has the power to heal.

Without hearing a word from her mouth, we come to know everything we need to know by Peter's mother-in-law's immediate response. She gets out of her sick bed, wipes the sweat from her now cool brow and serves Jesus and his men. I've often wondered whether Peter has her and her daughter (his wife) in mind when, decades later, he writes of the true beauty of the faithful woman (1 Pet 3:1-6). After sundown—that is, after Sabbath was over—the people crowd around the house, having heard of Jesus' ability to heal. Luke tells us of his graciousness, the way he lays his hands on the sick and casts out demons from those who are possessed.

If you read between the lines—that is to say, if you interact with the text through your imagination—you begin to think that Jesus does not want to become known simply as another faith healer. Several faith healers were traveling around at that time. In the morning Jesus goes out into the wilderness, which we will discover in Luke 5:16 is his habit. The crowds find him anyway, and he is confronted once more with their bottomless need. From this point on in the ministry, they will be following him everywhere. He will go into the wilderness for a break and turn around only to find five thousand of them, wanting more bread. They will press in to the point of crushing him so that he will not even know who is touching him (Lk 8:42, 45). In Luke 4:43 you can almost detect the tired tone in his voice. Jesus says he needs to leave and go preach in the surrounding towns "because I was sent for *this* purpose" (emphasis added).

He has just read those words from Isaiah that define his ministry: to preach good news to the poor. But now the emphasis has shifted to healing and casting out demons. The crowds are clamoring for provision, like the children in the wilderness who wanted bread and water. But Jesus has come to do so much more. He will continue to graciously heal and feed them by the thousands as an expression of his power and gracious lovingkindness. From even this point so early in the ministry, however, you can sense a growing sense of loneliness as the crowds beg for miracles and refuse to listen to what he has come to say.

LUKE 5

THE FIRST MIRACULOUS CATCH

5:1-11 The beginning of the community of disciples.

A PRACTICAL SECRET

5:12-16 Jesus touches an untouchable.

THE HEALING FAITH OF FRIENDS

5:17-25 Confrontation with the Pharisees over the healing of a paralytic.

PARADOXICAL UNORTHODOXY

5:26 An introduction to Jesus' preoccupation with the unorthodox.

5:27-28 The calling of Matthew.

5:29-32 The response of Matthew.

WEDDING GUESTS AND NEW WINE

5:33-39 A parable to explain the new and unorthodox nature of the ministry.

THE FIRST MIRACULOUS CATCH

¹As the crowd was pressing in on Jesus to hear God's word, He was stand-ing by Lake Gennesaret. ²He saw two boats at the edge of the lake; the fisher-men had left them and were washing their nets. ³He got into one of the boats, which belonged to Simon, and asked him to put out a little from the land. Then He sat down and was teaching the crowds from the boat.

⁴When He had finished speaking, He said to Simon, "Put out into deep water and let down your nets for a catch."

⁵"Master," Simon replied, "we've worked hard all night long and caught nothing! But at Your word, I'll let down the nets."

⁶When they did this, they caught a great number of fish, and their nets began to tear. ⁷So they signaled to their partners in the other boat to come and help them; they came and filled both boats so full that they began to sink.

⁸When Simon Peter saw this, he fell at Jesus' knees and said, "Go away from me, because I'm a sinful man, Lord!" ⁹For he and all those with him were amazed at the catch of fish they took, ¹⁰and so were James and John, Zebedee's sons, who were Simon's partners.

"Don't be afraid," Jesus told Simon. "From now on you will be catching peo-ple!" ¹¹Then they brought the boats to land, left everything, and followed Him.

Chapter 5 opens with the ever-present crowd crowding Jesus into the lake! Only Luke, who has sailed both the Mediterranean and the Adri-atic Seas with Paul, refers to it as "Lake" Gennesaret. For the other Gospel writers, it is always the "Sea" of Galilee. The boats have been left, apparently moored close to the shoreline, while the fishermen, tired from a long night of work, are washing their nets. Since fishermen are bound to catch more than fish, the nets need to be cleaned every morning.

Jesus helps himself to Simon's boat. We have not really met Simon Peter yet, though we did see his mother-in-law healed in the previous chapter. Jesus asks Simon to "put out"—a suspiciously nautical way of asking. Some scholars believe these examples of nautical speech in Luke and Acts hint that Luke might have been a ship's doctor before he left to be on the road with Paul. When you consider that Jesus is actively seeking these fishermen to be his disciples, you see that it is a brilliant transition to be using a boat for a pulpit.

When the sermon is over (and by the way, did you notice that Luke does not even bother to record for us the sermon?), Jesus asks Simon once more to "put out" into deep water. Notice he does not say, "to see if we can find a catch." Rather, he says simply, "let down your nets *for a catch*."

Simon, a slave to the obvious, reminds Jesus of what he already knows. Yet he adds a remarkable statement, saying more than he knows: "But at Your word, I'll let down the nets." He has witnessed an incident of Jesus' power. Perhaps he has even recognized some of his authority. In any case, the nets are lowered. The boat lurches to starboard, almost capsizing. The other boat is called for and races to the scene. Both are filled to the gunnels, water lapping occasionally over the sides.

Peter, the product of John's ministry, recognizes as fully as the moment allows just who Jesus might be. Thanks to the preaching of the Baptist, his response is a repentant one. "Go away," he blathers into Jesus' knees; "I am a sinful man!" Peter is asking for what, in his heart, he really does not want.

If you want to amaze a fisherman, a tremendous catch is the proper way to do it. And they are all amazed: Peter and James and John and Andrew. Jesus' response is the angelic "Do not be afraid." So often when he reveals himself in new ways, he will have to tell them not to be afraid: when he is about to raise the dead girl (Lk 8:50), when he walks on the water (Mt 14:27; Jn 6:20), at the transfiguration (Mt 17:7), when he was raised from the dead (Mt 28:10). Again and again they hear him say, "Do not be afraid."

And then he adds, "From now on you'll be catching people!" I used to picture that statement with Jesus smiling. The play on words seemed somehow delightful—that is, until Jeremiah 16:16 came to my attention: "'I am about to send for many fishermen'—the LORD's declaration—'and they will fish for them. Then I will send for many hunters, and they will hunt them down on every mountain and hill and out of the clefts of the rocks.'"

Jeremiah's words are not so delightful. He is, in fact, speaking of judgment. To become a fisher of men is serious business after all. And the disciples seem to understand just how serious it is. Luke tells us that they leave everything and follow him.

This passage reflects a first miraculous catch on two levels. First, there is the simple fact that there are two miraculous catches of fish in the Gospels and this is the first. The second miraculous catch is found in the last chapter of the book of John. But in a deeper sense, this first miraculous catch belongs to Jesus, for it is he who is the fisherman here. He casts his net and—behold!—catches four men who will become key leaders among the Twelve.

A PRACTICAL SECRET

[12]While He was in one of the towns, a man was there who had a serious skin disease all over him. He saw Jesus, fell facedown, and begged Him: "Lord, if You are willing, You can make me clean."

[13]Reaching out His hand, He touched him, saying, "I am willing; be made clean," and immediately the disease left him. [14]Then He ordered him to tell no one: "But go and show yourself to the priest, and offer what Moses prescribed for your cleansing as a testimony to them."

[15]But the news about Him spread even more, and large crowds would come together to hear Him and to be healed of their sicknesses. [16]Yet He often withdrew to deserted places and prayed.

$\mathcal{F}$or the second time in the span of five verses, we have another person falling before Jesus. This time it is a man with a serious skin disease. For centuries, biblical interpreters have lumped them all together under the title "leprosy." But increasingly scholars have begun to see that the term covers a wide range of diseases of the skin.

We are not told just how this man came to recognize Jesus' authority to heal, but clearly he understands that all Jesus has to do is *will* that he be healed and it will happen. And then Jesus does something no observant Jew would ever think of doing: he reaches out and touches the diseased skin. By doing so, he has of course rendered himself "unclean." If you use your imagination, you can picture the uncleanness creeping up Jesus' arm. And yet such is not the case. It is as if the flow has been reversed. "Cleanness" seems to flow out of Jesus. He touches the unclean and they become clean. He touches the dead and they become alive. It is just one indication that a new world is at hand and death and uncleanness have met their match.

If you look at the miracle straight on, you have to recognize that Jesus performs it in a very unmiraculous way. There's no waving of arms in the air, no incantations, no hocus-pocus. He says simply, "Be made clean." The vast majority of his miracles are performed in such unmiraculous ways. "Let down your nets" is a simple command that any one of the fishermen had said a thousand times before, only when Jesus says it, the boats almost sink with the weight of the catch. The point is that the miracle is rarely the point. There is always something more miraculous hiding behind the miracle. In this particular story, the true miracle is the faith of the diseased man. In the first miraculous catch, they left everything to follow Jesus. Is that not, in one sense, a greater miracle than a net full of fish?

In verse 14 of Luke 5 Jesus commands the man who was healed not to tell anyone what has happened, a further indication that the miracle is not the real point of the story. Jesus will make this request of others he will heal. But no one ever keeps quiet. How are you supposed to not tell about something so wonderful that has occurred in your life? Some schools of thought have attributed this request for secrecy to a desire on Jesus' part to keep his identity as Messiah a secret. The real reason is far more practical and is made clear in the very next verse. Because the news leaks out, the crowds, which were already large enough to push Jesus into the lake, continue to grow. We are told that, as a result, Jesus withdraws to desert places to pray.

THE HEALING FAITH OF FRIENDS

[17]On one of those days while He was teaching, Pharisees and teachers of the law were sitting there who had come from every village of Galilee and Judea, and also from Jerusalem. And the Lord's power to heal was in Him. [18]Just then some men came, carrying on a stretcher a man who was paralyzed. They tried to bring him in and set him down before Him. [19]Since they could not find a way to bring him in because of the crowd, they went up on the roof and lowered him

on the stretcher through the roof tiles into the middle of the crowd before Jesus.

²⁰*Seeing their faith He said, "Friend, your sins are forgiven you."*

²¹*Then the scribes and the Pharisees began to reason: "Who is this man who speaks blasphemies? Who can forgive sins but God alone?"*

²²*But perceiving their thoughts, Jesus replied to them, "Why are you reasoning this in your hearts?* ²³*Which is easier: to say, 'Your sins are forgiven you,' or to say, 'Get up and walk'?* ²⁴*But so you may know that the Son of Man has authority on earth to forgive sins"—He told the paralyzed man, "I tell you: get up, pick up your stretcher, and go home."*

²⁵*Immediately he got up before them, picked up what he had been lying on, and went home glorifying God.*

*B*y all indications they are back in Capernaum. Matthew tells us they have returned to "His own town" (Mt 9:1). If they are in a house, it is almost certainly Peter's. Jesus is there, doing what he has said he is primarily called to do—teaching—when the lesson is interrupted by a scraping sound from above. Because the miracle-seeking crowd is so large, the doorway has been completely blocked. Enterprising friends of a paralyzed man have climbed onto the roof and are taking apart the tiles in order to lower the man, stretcher and all, in front of Jesus. Notice the text: "Seeing their faith . . ." It is not the faith of the paralytic but the healing faith of his friends that causes Jesus to respond.

Jesus heals his body by pronouncing the forgiveness of his sins. The Bible is clear that a connection exists between sickness and sin, only it is not the connection most people make it out to be. The Pharisees begin reasoning that something here does not add up. Only God can forgive sin, not an itinerant rabbi from Nazareth. (You will notice that, in Luke, people who "think to themselves" are usually the "bad guys.")

It is a simple matter to clear up the confusion. Jesus asks, "Which is easier: to say, 'Your sins are forgiven you,' or to say, 'Get up and walk'?" The answer, of course, is that both are impossible. You don't simply tell paralyzed people to get out of bed, nor can you pronounce the forgiveness of sin. Having already said the first thing, Jesus now commands the second: "Get up."

PARADOXICAL UNORTHODOXY

²⁶Then everyone was astounded, and they were giving glory to God. And they were filled with awe and said, "We have seen incredible things today!"

²⁷After this, Jesus went out and saw a tax collector named Levi sitting at the tax office, and He said to him, "Follow Me!" ²⁸So, leaving everything behind, he got up and began to follow Him.

²⁹Then Levi hosted a grand banquet for Him at his house. Now there was a large crowd of tax collectors and others who were guests with them. ³⁰But the Pharisees and their scribes were complaining to His disciples, "Why do you eat and drink with tax collectors and sinners?"

³¹Jesus replied to them, "The healthy don't need a doctor, but the sick do. ³²I have not come to call the righteous, but sinners to repentance."

We looked at the opening verse of this section in the introduction (p. 27), so we will move on. Following the comment of the crowd concerning the "incredible" things of Jesus, he does something in the very next verse of Luke 5 that would have been mind-boggling to any observant Jew. Jesus calls Levi, the tax collector, as one of his first followers. The other Gospels also refer to him as "Matthew" in the listings of the Twelve (Mt 10:3; Mk 3:18; Lk 6:15). This is the first of a string of stories in Luke that will demonstrate the "unorthodoxy" of Jesus.

Of the two types of tax collectors, Levi was the most hated. He was known as a "tax farmer." His position allowed him to be more dishonest and more arbitrary than the income or poll-tax gatherers. In the Talmud he would have been included with robbers and murderers. He might have been in Capernaum collecting the fish tax, which would have led him into daily conflict with someone like Simon Peter. Both Luke and Mark tell us that, in response to Jesus' offer, Levi gives a party at his own house. When Levi tells the story in chapter 9 of his Gospel, he leaves out the detail that the party was in his house.

When the ever-present crowd of Pharisees objects, Jesus responds with a saying from one of their own books, a commentary on Exodus

(15:26) called the *Mekilta*. The healthy do not need a doctor, but the sick do. I find it fascinating that Jesus does not reject their distinction between the "righteous" and the "sinner." It is only that, when given the choice, Jesus chooses the sinners!

Levi and his many friends who are attending the feast apparently do not miss this openness in Jesus. Perhaps they have recognized a refreshing difference in this rabbi who seems so open to them.

Often, when I celebrate the Lord's Supper, I remember the question of the Pharisees at Levi's house: "Why do you eat and drink with tax collectors and sinners?" At those moments I hope I'm recovering just a bit of the experience of Levi and his friends. For Jesus has invited me, a sinner, to share the table with him. It makes me deeply glad that Jesus is the unorthodox One who came looking not for the righteous ones but for someone like you and me to share his extraordinary table.

WEDDING GUESTS AND NEW WINE

³³Then they said to Him, "John's disciples fast often and say prayers, and those of the Pharisees do the same, but Yours eat and drink."

³⁴Jesus said to them, "You can't make the wedding guests fast while the groom is with them, can you? ³⁵But the days will come when the groom will be taken away from them—then they will fast in those days."

³⁶He also told them a parable: "No one tears a patch from a new garment and puts it on an old garment. Otherwise, not only will he tear the new, but also the piece from the new garment will not match the old. ³⁷And no one puts new wine into old wineskins. Otherwise, the new wine will burst the skins, it will spill, and the skins will be ruined. ³⁸But new wine should be put into fresh wineskins. ³⁹And no one, after drinking old wine, wants new, because he says, 'The old is better.'"

*T*he final scene in chapter 5 is yet another story of the unorthodoxy of Jesus. It is not clear just who the "they" of verse 33 is, but whoever they are, they have noticed yet another discrepancy in the orthodoxy of Jesus' disciples. John's disciples and the Pharisees fast and pray often, while the disciples of Jesus "eat and drink."

Put yourself in the place of the Pharisees for a moment and try to see it from their point of view. What if a new religious group came to your town and rarely seemed to practice prayer, not to mention fasting? Honestly, even I, with my miniscule prayer life, would have a problem with that. Ask yourself: what is the fundamental purpose of prayer and fasting? Is it not to better experience the presence of God?

The answer seems so simple to Jesus. At a wedding, do you fast when the groom is there? Answer: no, you feast. And then he ominously mentions that a time is coming when the groom will be taken away. Then, he says, they will fast.

If the purpose of prayer and fasting is to better experience the presence of God, then in one sense they become irrelevant when Jesus, the Son of God, is there. But when he is taken away, they will become purposeful once more. A new world has come and is coming.

The presence of the new world is what the final parable is about. The new world, with its new orthodoxy, is like a new garment; you cannot take a piece of the new and stitch it to the old. And again, the new world and its orthodoxy are like new wine: if you pour it into old wineskins, they will not be able to take the expansion that inevitably comes. The old skins will burst because they cannot contain the new orthodoxy. New wine deserves new wineskins, just as the new world calls for a new orthodoxy.

Verse 39 of Luke 5 is Jesus' closing volley, and I confess that it has always bothered me. It has even been cut out of some ancient manuscripts. It seems to contradict what he has said before. Then I discovered that Jesus is quoting an ancient proverb that said, "The old is better." The statement should be seen, then, as ironic. Those who become attached to the old wine do not want to even try the new. All they can do is repeat the worn-out proverb "The old is better."

LUKE 6

LORD OVER ORTHODOXY

6:1–5 Unorthodox behavior in the grain field.

6:6–11 Unorthodox behavior on the Sabbath.

THE CHOICE OF THE TWELVE

6:12–16 Prayer followed by the calling of the Twelve.

THE SHAPE OF
THE NEW COMMUNITY

*6:17–26 Sermon on the "level place"
(vv. 20–26: the blessings and woes).*

THE IMPOSSIBLE COMMAND

6:27–36 Unorthodox advice on loving enemies.

HOW TO BUILD YOUR HOUSE
IN THE KINGDOM

6:37–45 Parable on the overflow of the heart.

6:46–49 Parable of the wise and foolish builder.

LORD OVER ORTHODOXY

¹On a Sabbath, He passed through the grainfields. His disciples were picking heads of grain, rubbing them in their hands, and eating them. ²But some of the Pharisees said, "Why are you doing what is not lawful on the Sabbath?"

³Jesus answered them, "Haven't you read what David and those who were with him did when he was hungry— ⁴how he entered the house of God, and took and ate the sacred bread, which is not lawful for any but the priests to eat? He even gave some to those who were with him." ⁵Then He told them, "The Son of Man is Lord of the Sabbath."

⁶On another Sabbath He entered the synagogue and was teaching. A man was there whose right hand was paralyzed. ⁷The scribes and Pharisees were watching Him closely, to see if He would heal on the Sabbath, so that they could find a charge against Him. ⁸But He knew their thoughts and told the man with the paralyzed hand, "Get up and stand here." So he got up and stood there. ⁹Then Jesus said to them, "I ask you: is it lawful on the Sabbath to do good or to do evil, to save life or to destroy it?" ¹⁰After looking around at them all, He told him, "Stretch out your hand." He did so, and his hand was restored. ¹¹They, however, were filled with rage and started discussing with one another what they might do to Jesus.

*T*he collection of Sabbath violations continues with the story of Jesus' disciples harvesting grain. Note in this story that it is not Jesus who is breaking their law but his disciples. The law provided that grain could be collected from a stranger's field as long as a sickle wasn't used. The disciples' violation does not have to do with the taking of the grain but with the fact that they rubbed their hands together—which, within the narrow definitions of the Pharisees, was considered work.

Jesus uses a passage from 1 Samuel 21 as his defense. He does not defend the disciples against the charge of violating the Sabbath per se, but rather makes the point that human need supersedes ritual observance. In the story, David and his companions are fleeing from Saul. When David comes to Ahimelech the priest, he asks for bread. Ahimelech responds that he can only give the consecrated bread to the men if they have "kept themselves from women" (1 Sam 21:4). When David assures him that "women are being kept from us" (1 Sam 21:5), the priest relents and provides the bread that was reserved for the priests. Conclusion: when David was in need, the ritual law was ignored on the basis of human need. The disciples are similarly hungry and so should be allowed to rub their hands together in order to "harvest" grain to satisfy their need.

Jesus' final statement comes like a bolt out of the blue. He uses his favorite self-designation from Daniel 7:13: "The Son of Man is Lord of the Sabbath." In essence, Jesus is claiming that even this most sacred observance of Sabbath rest comes underneath his lordship. What we think is right in terms of orthodox observance still comes under his lordship. He is Lord even over orthodoxy!

Verse 6 opens with a loose chronological connector: "On another Sabbath." It seems that Luke is collecting Sabbath-violation stories for his readers. This story specifically belongs here because it also deals with human need versus ritual observance.

A man who is attending the synagogue service has a hand that has atrophied or shriveled from an undisclosed cause. Luke the doctor, with his relentless eye for detail, wants us to know that it was the *right* hand. Jesus perceives that a trap lies before him and calls the man to the front.

The rabbinic litmus test in regard to Sabbath observance was the simple formula "choose the way that preserves life."[6] Jesus formulates his question based on their maxim but places it in the context of extremes: "Is it lawful to do good or to do evil, to save life or destroy it?" The form of Jesus' question elevates it out of the realm of theological debate. Are they supposed to answer, "No, it is lawful to do evil and destroy life"? As is his custom, Jesus leaves them speechless.

It is another unmiraculous miracle. There is no incantation, no hocus-pocus, but simply the command to stretch out the withered hand that is immediately and completely restored. The Pharisees are once more speechless. The Greek tells us they are literally filled with "senseless rage" and begin to discuss "what they might do to Jesus." Is it not ironic that on the Sabbath the Pharisees begin the plot to take Jesus' life? A few moments before they were outraged that he was giving life on that same Sabbath!

THE CHOICE OF THE TWELVE

¹²During those days He went out to the mountain to pray and spent all night in prayer to God. ¹³When daylight came, He summoned His disciples, and He chose 12 of them; He also named them apostles:

> *¹⁴Simon, whom He also named Peter,*
> *and Andrew his brother;*
> *James and John;*
> *Philip and Bartholomew;*
> *¹⁵Matthew and Thomas;*
> *James the son of Alphaeus,*
> *and Simon called the Zealot;*
> *¹⁶Judas the son of James,*
> *and Judas Iscariot, who became a traitor.*

*T*his is the first time in Luke that we are told of Jesus spending the entire night in prayer, although twice we have seen him moving out to solitary places for extended times of prayer (Lk 4:42; 5:16). You get the impression that he wanted to prepare his heart for the selection of the Twelve, as well as for the Sermon on the Plain that would immediately follow.

In the morning he calls all of the disciples together; there is no indication just how many there were at this point. Later, in chapter 10, he appoints seventy to help him make the final push to Jerusalem. I can imagine that a few hundred gathered around Jesus at this point, waiting to hear his choice.

He chooses twelve, clearly a meaningful number in Judaism because it speaks of the twelve tribes. To the chosen dozen he gives a specific title: apostle, or "sent one." Behind Luke's Greek *apostolos* lies the Hebrew word *shaliakh*.[7] The *shaliakh* was an authoritative representative —someone chosen to represent another as an appointed delegate. If I wanted to purchase a piece of land but was unable to go and look at it myself, I could appoint a *shaliakh* to evaluate it for me. I would give him my authority to the degree that any agreement he entered into would be binding on my behalf. His word would essentially be my word.

Later, when Jesus sends out the Seventy, his language reflects this same office of the *shaliakh:* "Whoever listens to you listens to Me. Whoever rejects you rejects Me" (Lk 10:16). William Lane, who was captivated by this idea of the *shaliakh,* summed up its significance: "We bear a concealed dignity as Jesus' apostles."

Simon Peter is always the first in every list of the Twelve. In him the others would come to find a corporate identity. He is part of the inner circle—the Three—along with James and John. He is clearly Jesus' closest friend and associate.

Andrew, Peter's brother, is one of the first followers of Jesus. Formerly he was a disciple of John the Baptist.

James and John are the "Sons of Thunder," or *Boanerges* (Mk 3:17). They earn the nickname when they ask Jesus if they can call down fire on a Samaritan village (Lk 9:54). John is probably the youngest of the Twelve. We deduce this from the fact that he lived into the reign of Trajan (A.D. 98-117), giving leadership in the great church at Ephesus, where he would also write his Gospel and care for Jesus' mother, Mary, until her death.

Philip is from Bethsaida, the original hometown of Peter and Andrew. In John 1:43 Jesus "finds" Philip and extends the call, "Follow Me." He was also first a disciple of John the Baptist.

Bartholomew we know absolutely nothing about! In fact, we don't even know his name. His father's name was Tolmai; *bar* simply means "son of." My mentor, William Lane, used to say that he was comforted by this fact: "Though people may not even know my name, still I am a servant of the Lord."

Matthew is the unorthodox choice Jesus made earlier in chapter 5. He is a tax collector, which means he would have been universally regarded as a traitor to his own people. He will go on to write the first Gospel.

Unfortunately, Thomas has been stuck with the label "doubting," because in John 20:25 he insists that he will not believe until he sees the marks of the nails and puts his hand into the wound in Jesus' side. In the next verse, when Jesus appears, he does not strictly condemn Thomas for his doubt. He simply encourages him to believe. He receives the nickname *Didymus*, or "twin" (Jn 11:16). There is one tradition that says this was because he looked so much like Jesus. James, the son of Alphaeus, was with the other disciples in the upper room, waiting for the "Father's promise" of the Holy Spirit (Acts 1:13).

Simon called the Zealot was a member of a burgeoning terrorist political party, also sometimes called the *Sicarii*. They opposed Roman rule with fanatical aggression. The fact that Jesus brings together someone like Simon with Matthew, the tax collector, is truly remarkable.

Judas the son of James is thought to be the same person as Thaddaeus (Mt 10:3). In John 14:22 he asks Jesus why he is revealing himself to the disciples and not to the whole world.

Judas Iscariot always appears last in the lists of the disciples. Often, as here, his name is followed by a circumlocution: "who became a traitor." The meaning of his second name is debated. Some say it simply means the man (*ish*) from the village of Kerioth. Others believe it means "man of the knife" or *ishsicarii*, which might mean that he too was a member of the Zealots. As treasurer, he is entrusted with the moneybag. Although John tells us he used to help himself to the money, Luke will tell us later that Satan enters Judas and that this leads to the betrayal of Jesus (Lk 22:3). Matthew says he went to the high priest earlier asking, "What are you willing to give me if I hand Him over to you?" (Mt 26:15). Later Judas, "full of remorse," tries to give back the money and kills himself (Mt 27:3-5).

THE SHAPE OF THE NEW COMMUNITY

[17]After coming down with them, He stood on a level place with a large crowd of His disciples and a great multitude of people from all Judea and Jerusalem and from the seacoast of Tyre and Sidon. [18]They came to hear Him and to be healed of their diseases; and those tormented by unclean spirits were made well. [19]The whole crowd was trying to touch Him, because power was coming out from Him and healing them all.

[20]Then looking up at His disciples, He said:

> *Blessed are you who are poor,*
> *because the kingdom of God is yours.*

21Blessed are you who are hungry now,
because you will be filled.
Blessed are you who weep now,
because you will laugh.
22Blessed are you when people hate you,
when they exclude you, insult you,
and slander your name as evil,
because of the Son of Man.

23"Rejoice in that day and leap for joy! Take note—your reward is great in heaven, because this is the way their ancestors used to treat the prophets.

24But woe to you who are rich,
because you have received your comfort.
25Woe to you who are full now,
because you will be hungry.
Woe to you who are laughing now,
because you will mourn and weep.
26Woe to you
when all people speak well of you,
because this is the way their ancestors
used to treat the false prophets.

*A*s Jesus comes down from the mountain, having appointed the twelve apostles, he finds a multitude that has gathered from hundreds of miles around. Some of them have even come to "hear Him." The picture is of the ever-present crowd, pressing in, straining to touch him. Alongside the seething crowd are the newly appointed Twelve with the rest of his disciples. If we are to engage this scene with our imaginations, we must not overlook the vital detail in the opening of verse 20. Before this mixed multitude, Jesus, "looking up at His disciples, . . . said . . .": in other words, the sermon that follows, although available to all the crowd, is directed at the disciples. It is the manifesto of the new kingdom—the radically reversed, upside-down world that Jesus has come to reveal to them. It is a sermon of a man who has stayed up all night praying.

The pronouncement of blessings *(birkot)* was a very rabbinic thing to do. But Jesus pronounces a disturbing list of blessings no one has ever heard before. Who would have ever thought of blessing the poor? Their poverty was thought to be a curse from God. The same could be said for the other unlikely recipients of Jesus' radical *birkot*. In the middle of this remarkable list, Jesus' blessing falls on those who weep, for often those who weep feel cut off or even cursed by God, as if they were on the other side of an uncrossable stream. In Jesus' kingdom such will not be the case: that stream will be crossed by a bridge of lament called into being by Jesus' blessing. It is a bridge made of his tears. Those who weep will be called to cross over from despair to hope. Those who weep are blessed because they recognize the depth of their sin and allow their hearts to be broken by it. Their tears are a testimony to the painful honesty that confession demands, just as they are tangible proof of the overflowing joy of knowing his forgiveness. Jesus' blessing is an encouragement to offer God what he wants the most from us: our broken spirits and contrite hearts (Ps 51).

In true covenant structure, the blessings are followed by curses. (Compare this to Deut 27–28; Is 65:13-16.) The woes represent the negative side of the blessings. Although the poor will receive the kingdom, the rich have already gotten all they will ever get. Likewise those who are full will swap places with those who are hungry. Jesus' words represent all the comfort the comfortless could ever hope to hear. His woes contain trouble and despair beyond the worst nightmares of the comfortable.

THE IMPOSSIBLE COMMAND

[27]*"But I say to you who listen: Love your enemies, do good to those who hate you, [28]bless those who curse you, pray for those who mistreat you. [29]If anyone hits you on the cheek, offer the other also. And if anyone takes away your coat, don't hold back your shirt either. [30]Give to everyone who asks from you, and from one who takes away your things, don't ask for them back. [31]Just as you want others to do for you, do the same for them. [32]If you love those who love you, what credit is that to you? Even sinners love those who love them. [33]If you do [what is] good to those who are good to you, what credit is that to*

you? Even sinners do that. ³⁴And if you lend to those from whom you expect to receive, what credit is that to you? Even sinners lend to sinners to be repaid in full. ³⁵But love your enemies, do [what is] good, and lend, expecting nothing in return. Then your reward will be great, and you will be sons of the Most High. For He is gracious to the ungrateful and evil. ³⁶Be merciful, just as your Father also is merciful.

*J*ust as the disciples are regaining their equilibrium after the first volley of blessings and woes, and just as the crowd begins to recover from the puzzling list of *birkot*, Jesus unveils the cornerstone of his master plan. It is the centerpiece of his radical value system. It is what turns the kingdom upside down. It is the one, single, unavoidable command he makes on all those who would be his followers. And it is impossible!

"Love your enemies." Those words are followed by seven statements of what loving your enemies might look like. Doing good to those who hate you. Praying for those who mistreat you. Offering someone who strikes you on one cheek the other. Giving your shirt to the person who steals your coat. Giving to everyone who asks. Do to others, especially your enemies, what you would want done to you.

It is interesting that Jesus even resorts to their language: "even *sinners* love those who love them"; "Even *sinners* do that." "But love your enemies," he says for the second time in verse 35. Love of enemies is the defining condition of sons and daughters of the Most High. If we want to act like, be like God, Jesus says, we must love our enemies. Why? Because God loves his enemies!

They are nine of the most wonderful, disturbing, shocking, comforting words Jesus ever spoke: "For He is gracious to the ungrateful and evil." That statement explains the life and motivation of Jesus. It explains grace. It describes *hesed:* that ancient Hebrew word that appears 250 times in the Old Testament and is translated by King James 14 different ways. This fact points to the notion that it may very well be an untranslatable word, like "love." The translators of the King James had to invent a new word—"lovingkindness"—to try to render *hesed*. It is linked linguistically to the Hebrew word for "stork," because the stork was regarded as the best mother in the animal kingdom. (In case you were wondering, the ostrich is the worst mother—Job 39:13-18; Lam 4:3.) It is a word by which God defines himself (Ex 20:6; 34:6-7; Num 14:18-19; Deut 5:10). It is the key concept in the worship of the psalms (Ps 23:6; 25:6-10; 51:1; 89; 107; 136). It is central to God's revelation in the prophets (Is 54:8; 63:7; Jer 32:18; Lam 3:21-22; Hos 6:6; Mic 6:8). When the Old Testament was translated into Greek, the word that was used most often to render *hesed* was *eleos*, or "mercy" (Rom 11:28-32). Less frequently, *charis*, or "grace," was used.

I believe *hesed* may very well have been the word Jesus originally spoke in Luke 6:36: "Do *hesed*, just as your Father also does *hesed*."

Compare Jesus' revolutionary words to those flat grey suggestions of John the Baptist in Luke 3:10-14. From this new point of view, from the borders of the new world, John's words are barely meaningful: "Be good." "Do better." "Stop cheating." That is the essence of what he said. It is the old world speaking—the world of the barely doable. But Jesus calls us, by means of his impossible command, to enter his unimaginable new kingdom, where men and women whose lives are being transformed are called upon to love each other the way God loves; to graciously give everything to those who, by all rights, should expect nothing from them. It is the way of the new kingdom that Jesus proclaims has arrived. It is the way of the King of that kingdom.

HOW TO BUILD YOUR HOUSE IN THE KINGDOM

37 "Do not judge, and you will not be judged. Do not condemn, and you will not be condemned. Forgive, and you will be forgiven. 38 Give, and it will be given to you; a good measure—pressed down, shaken together, and running over—will be poured into your lap. For with the measure you use, it will be measured back to you."

39 He also told them a parable: "Can the blind guide the blind? Won't they both fall into a pit? 40 A disciple is not above his teacher, but everyone who is fully trained will be like his teacher.

41 "Why do you look at the speck in your brother's eye, but don't notice the log in your own eye? 42 Or how can you say to your brother, 'Brother, let me

*take out the speck that is in your eye,' when you yourself don't see the log in
your eye? Hypocrite! First take the log out of your eye, and then you will see
clearly to take out the speck in your brother's eye.*

*43"A good tree doesn't produce bad fruit; on the other hand, a bad tree
doesn't produce good fruit. 44For each tree is known by its own fruit. Figs
aren't gathered from thornbushes, or grapes picked from a bramble bush. 45A
good man produces good out of the good storeroom of his heart. An evil man
produces evil out of the evil storeroom, for his mouth speaks from the overflow
of the heart.*

*46"Why do you call Me 'Lord, Lord,' and don't do the things I say? 47I will
show you what someone is like who comes to Me, hears My words, and acts
on them: 48He is like a man building a house, who dug deep and laid the
foundation on the rock. When the flood came, the river crashed against that
house and couldn't shake it, because it was well built. 49But the one who hears
and does not act is like a man who built a house on the ground without a
foundation. The river crashed against it, and immediately it collapsed. And
the destruction of that house was great!"*

*L*et's work our way backward through this last passage. The final
image has to do with the building of a house. One man digs a deep
footing for the foundation so his house will survive the storm. He just
happens to be the one who has listened to Jesus' words and responded
to them. In one sense, at least, Jesus is telling us how to build our house
in his kingdom. The other man, who though he may have heard did not
act on Jesus' words, ends up foolishly building a house right on the
ground which, of course, is destroyed by the flood. What then are the
words of Jesus that become the blueprints for our kingdom house? Let's
start back at verse 37.

Do not judge and your house will not be destroyed when the judgment turns on you. Do not condemn so that the final storm of condemnation will not sweep your house away. Forgive and the waves will be
forgiving. Give and you will receive back a good measure, shaken together and poured into your lap. You cannot possibly measure and saw

and hammer your house when there is a log in your eye. So does it make sense to be distracted by the sawdust in your brother's or sister's eye? Before you can get on with your work—much less help your brother or sister with his or her speck—take the log out of your own eye.

You have a storeroom. It's called your heart. If your heart is good, only good things will come out of the storeroom. If it is evil, then all you'll have stored up is evil. Out of the overflow of the storeroom of your heart your mouth speaks.

Whether it's the image of the house or the storeroom or the good tree or the thorn bush, Jesus is painting images to recapture our imaginations. I don't want my life to count for nothing, just as I wouldn't want my house to be washed away by a storm. I don't want to fall blindly into a deep pit, just as I don't want my discipleship to be shallow and meaningless. If it is an unimaginable kingdom into which you and I are being called, then only the parables and the Spirit can enable us to imagine our way in. If it is an impossible command that Jesus demands that we follow, then only by his *hesed* will we be able to obey.

LUKE 7

HOW TO AMAZE JESUS

7:1-10 Jesus amazed at the faith of the centurion.

A MEETING OF THE CROWDS

7:11-17 Jesus' compassion for the widow.

A MOST REMARKABLE QUESTION

7:18-30 Lengthy discussion of John the Baptist.

7:31-35 "Don't dance to the world's tune."

MOVING FROM THE HEAD
TO THE HEART

7:36-50 The anointing by the "sinful" woman.

HOW TO AMAZE JESUS

¹When He had concluded all His sayings in the hearing of the people, He entered Capernaum. ²A centurion's slave, who was highly valued by him, was sick and about to die. ³When the centurion heard about Jesus, he sent some Jewish elders to Him, requesting Him to come and save the life of his slave. ⁴When they reached Jesus, they pleaded with Him earnestly, saying, "He is worthy for You to grant this, ⁵because he loves our nation and has built us a synagogue." ⁶Jesus went with them, and when He was not far from the house, the centurion sent friends to tell Him, "Lord, don't trouble Yourself, since I am not worthy to have You come under my roof. ⁷That is why I didn't even consider myself worthy to come to You. But say the word, and my servant will be cured. ⁸For I too am a man placed under authority, having soldiers under my command. I say to this one, 'Go!' and he goes; and to another, 'Come!' and he comes; and to my slave, 'Do this!' and he does it."

⁹Jesus heard this and was amazed at him, and turning to the crowd following Him, He said, "I tell you, I have not found so great a faith even in Israel!" ¹⁰When those who had been sent returned to the house, they found the slave in good health.

*T*he nameless soldier has heard of the healings Jesus did earlier in his hometown. Now one of the centurion's slaves is gravely ill, and he cares enough to send for Jesus. Romans were notorious as the cruelest slave owners in history. Though laws concerning slaves became gradually more and more protective, the life of a slave in the first century could be unimaginable. Slaves were branded, mutilated, sexually abused and, worst of all, crucified. They had no rights to speak of and were at the mercy of their owners. (One Roman matron had her female slave killed because she did not like the way she had fixed her hair!)

None of this seems to be true of this centurion, for one single reason: he has come under the influence of the God of the Jews who, though they still owned slaves, were the kindest slave owners in history. Perhaps it is not correct to say that they themselves were kind, but rather it was their God whose grace extended even to the lowliest slave. We see it again and again in the laws protecting slaves in Deuteronomy and Leviticus.

The centurion is a "God-fearer": that is, a Gentile who worshiped the God of Israel but would not submit to ritual circumcision. He kept the regular times of prayer and worshiped through his gifts to the poor. According to the Jews who have come on his behalf, this man loves them and has even donated a synagogue. The basis of their appeal is found in the idea that the centurion *deserves* it. This is where the vast difference between the soldier and these Jewish men lies.

Jesus does not hesitate for a moment but follows the Jewish leaders in the direction of the soldier's home. But the centurion, sensitive to the fact that no Jewish person can enter the home of an "unclean" Gentile, sends a message to Jesus. He acknowledges that he is not worthy of a visit from the rabbi from Nazareth. He is a soldier acquainted with the horrors of ancient warfare. As a Roman soldier, he would have been prepared to fall upon his own sword at the command of his superior officer. He understands authority, and he recognizes that Jesus possesses a vast authority.

Jesus utters not a single word of healing. He only marvels at the faith of the Gentile God-fearer. Without even being present in the home that is "not worthy" for him to enter, and without a single word, Jesus heals the servant.

Behind the unmiraculous miracle of the silent, long-distance healing, there lies another miracle, miraculous enough to amaze even Jesus himself. Hidden within the story is the miracle of the faith of the centurion.

Luke is the Gospel of amazement. Thus far Zechariah's neighbors, those who heard the shepherds, Joseph and Mary, those who heard the boy Jesus in the temple, those who heard the adult Jesus in the synagogues at both Nazareth and Capernaum, Peter and his partners, and finally those who witnessed the healing of the paralytic have all been described as being "amazed." Eventually you begin to ask yourself, *When is Jesus going to be amazed?* This is that moment at last.

So what is it that amazes Jesus in this passage? Is it the fact that the Gentile, who isn't one of his followers, has already begun to live out Jesus' unorthodox command to love his enemies, the Jews? Is it that this powerful man attributes to Jesus a greater power and authority? Or is Jesus amazed that the soldier possesses a faith that still did not exist anywhere in Israel? He asks for what he knows he doesn't *deserve* and faithfully expects to get it anyway! He asks for *hesed*. He seems to intuitively understand that although he has a right to expect nothing from Jesus, still Jesus is willing to give him everything.

A MEETING OF THE CROWDS

¹¹Soon afterwards He was on His way to a town called Nain. His disciples and a large crowd were traveling with Him. ¹²Just as He neared the gate of the town, a dead man was being carried out. He was his mother's only son, and she was a widow. A large crowd from the city was also with her. ¹³When the Lord saw her, He had compassion on her and said, "Don't cry." ¹⁴Then He came up and touched the open coffin, and the pallbearers stopped. And He said, "Young man, I tell you, get up!"

¹⁵The dead man sat up and began to speak, and Jesus gave him to his mother. ¹⁶Then fear came over everyone, and they glorified God, saying, "A great prophet has risen among us," and "God has visited His people." ¹⁷This report about Him went throughout Judea and all the vicinity.

*L*uke is the only Gospel to tell the story of the widow of Nain. This fits into the theme of his concern for the outcast and marginalized. No group was more marginalized in the first century than women, and among women, widows were more desperate still. Only Luke tells us about Anna, the widow who prophesied over the infant Jesus (Lk 2:37). He tells us of the widow who gave both of her remaining coins (Lk 21:1-4). In Luke 20:47, the Jewish leaders particularly stir up Jesus' anger because they "devour widows' houses."

The ever-present throng is there as well as the disciples. They are all traveling into Nain as they see another crowd just leaving town. Luke even lets us know it is a "large" crowd. In my mind's eye, I see the two groups in silhouette against an afternoon sky.

According to Jewish custom in the first century, the widow would have been at the head of the funeral procession. The rabbis decreed that "woman, who brought death into the world, ought to lead the way in the funeral procession." So in addition to the grief of having lost an only son, guilty humiliation accompanies the widow as she walks ahead of the crowd. I also imagine Jesus at the head of his crowd of followers.

As the crowds approach, the woman looks up through her despair to see Jesus. Luke tells us that when Jesus sees her, he has compassion for her. After all, his own mother will be in a similar situation in a year or two. "Don't cry," he whispers.

When Jesus touches the coffin, he renders himself unclean from the corruption of the dead boy. But remember, in Jesus the flow has been reversed. His touch does not absorb uncleanness; rather, life flows the other direction, and the boy wakes from his death slumber. We are told that he begins to talk. I would love to have heard exactly what he said! And Jesus "gave him to his mother."

Technically, it is the boy who is given life. In reality, it is also the mother, the widow, who has her life given back to her on the road from Nain. This is the first time Jesus raises someone from the dead in Luke's Gospel. And as we are coming to expect, the people are amazed!

A MOST REMARKABLE QUESTION

18 Then John's disciples told him about all these things. So John summoned two of his disciples 19 and sent them to the Lord, asking, "Are You the One who is to come, or should we look for someone else?"

20 When the men reached Him, they said, "John the Baptist sent us to ask You, 'Are You the One who is to come, or should we look for someone else?'"

21 At that time Jesus healed many people of diseases, plagues, and evil spirits, and He granted sight to many blind people. 22 He replied to them, "Go and report to John the things you have seen and heard: The blind receive their sight, the lame walk, those with skin diseases are healed, the deaf hear, the dead are raised, and the poor have the good news preached to them. 23 And anyone who is not offended because of Me is blessed." 24 After John's messengers left, He began to speak to the crowds about John: "What did you go out into the wilderness to see? A reed swaying in the wind? 25 What then did you go out to see? A man dressed in soft robes? Look, those who are splendidly dressed and live in luxury are in royal palaces. 26 What then did you go out to see? A prophet? Yes, I tell you, and far more than a prophet. 27 This is the one it is written about:

> *Look, I am sending My messenger*
> *ahead of You;*
> *he will prepare Your way before You.*

28 I tell you, among those born of women no one is greater than John, but the least in the kingdom of God is greater than he."

29 (And when all the people, including the tax collectors, heard this, they acknowledged God's way of righteousness, because they had been baptized with John's baptism. 30 But since the Pharisees and experts in the law had not been baptized by him, they rejected the plan of God for themselves.)

31 "To what then should I compare the people of this generation, and what are they like? 32 They are like children sitting in the marketplace and calling to each other:

> *We played the flute for you,*
> *but you didn't dance;*
> *we sang a lament,*
> *but you didn't weep!*

33 For John the Baptist did not come eating bread or drinking wine, and you say, 'He has a demon!' 34 The Son of Man has come eating and drinking, and you say, 'Look, a glutton and a drunkard, a friend of tax collectors and sinners!' 35 Yet wisdom is vindicated by all her children."

We have been traveling through the part of Luke's narrative that highlights the unorthodoxy of Jesus' ministry. The story of the doubting John reinforces the truth that Jesus failed to meet everyone's expectations, even those of the man who knew him from the womb.

So unorthodox is this kingdom that John himself almost misses it! He has landed in prison, hardly where he expected to be as herald of the Messiah. While he sits in Herod's prison, he hears of all the wonderful things Jesus is doing. In verses 18-23 of Luke 7, John sends two of his disciples with an amazing question, considering its source. John, who has heard the voice of God, who first proclaimed Jesus as the Lamb of God (Jn 1:29-35), asks, "Are you the Messiah, or should we look for someone else?" It is the most remarkable question in the Gospels.

From his cell, John is unable to see the precious glimpses of the radical, unorthodox kingdom that is entering history with the presence of Jesus. In his mind this kingdom is about the Messiah overcoming the Romans, and fighting fire with fire. Never could he have dreamed of a kingdom in which the King dies for the enemies he loves. Not in his wildest dreams could John, the dreamer, have imagined a kingdom where the fire of hate would be conquered by the living water of love.

Jesus, who has been in some sense slighted by his cousin John, does not respond in kind. He sounds very straightforward. He tells John's messengers to go back and report to John that every prophetic sign connected to the coming of the Messiah is finding fulfillment. The blind see and the deaf hear. The lame are leaping like deer (Is 35:5-6).

When I imagine it, the messengers have already turned to report back to John when Jesus calls out to them, essentially, "Tell John, blessed is he who is not offended by me." How remarkable that Jesus responds with a *berakah* to John's doubt. But is that not what we are coming to expect from the One who commanded us to love our enemies?

After John's people leave, Jesus displays more of his graciousness. He tells the crowd what a remarkable person John is. In the words of Malachi, Jesus affirms that he is indeed God's unique messenger. In fact, says Jesus, there is no one alive who is greater than John! The second half of Jesus' final statement on John is also an introduction to the next scene in chapter 7: "but the least in the kingdom of God is greater than he."

The next image is a small window into the "least" Jesus just spoke of. It is a holy parenthesis. All the people, including the lowest of the low (i.e., the tax collectors), acknowledged God's way of righteousness and acknowledged the wisdom of the sermon they had heard not so long ago that spoke of loving their enemies and of a God who was kind to the ungrateful and the wicked. They were in a position to acknowledge this precisely because John the Baptist had faithfully performed in their lives the miracle of waking their consciences. John had baptized all of them, at least all of the ones who were able to understand what Jesus was talking about. But the Pharisees and experts in the law could not understand that

God's way was right because repentance had no place in their lives.

Glancing in their direction, Jesus tries to put them in perspective for his disciples. "They are just like children," he says, with a sad twinkle in his eye. "They wanted us to dance to their tune. They thought we would weep to their sad songs. But John and I don't dance."

MOVING FROM THE HEAD TO THE HEART

36 Then one of the Pharisees invited Him to eat with him. He entered the Pharisee's house and reclined at the table. 37 And a woman in the town who was a sinner found out that Jesus was reclining at the table in the Pharisee's house. She brought an alabaster flask of fragrant oil 38 and stood behind Him at His feet, weeping, and began to wash His feet with her tears. She wiped His feet with the hair of her head, kissing them and anointing them with the fragrant oil.

39 When the Pharisee who had invited Him saw this, he said to himself, "This man, if He were a prophet, would know who and what kind of woman this is who is touching Him—she's a sinner!"

40 Jesus replied to him, "Simon, I have something to say to you."

"Teacher," he said, "say it."

41 "A creditor had two debtors. One owed 500 denarii, and the other 50. 42 Since they could not pay it back, he graciously forgave them both. So, which of them will love him more?"

43 Simon answered, "I suppose the one he forgave more."

"You have judged correctly," He told him. 44 Turning to the woman, He said to Simon, "Do you see this woman? I entered your house; you gave Me no water for My feet, but she, with her tears, has washed My feet and wiped them with her hair. 45 You gave Me no kiss, but she hasn't stopped kissing My feet since I came in. 46 You didn't anoint My head with oil, but she has anointed My feet with fragrant oil. 47 Therefore I tell you, her many sins have been forgiven; that's why she loved much. But the one who is forgiven little, loves little." 48 Then He said to her, "Your sins are forgiven."

49 Those who were at the table with Him began to say among themselves, "Who is this man who even forgives sins?"

50 And He said to the woman, "Your faith has saved you. Go in peace."

*J*esus accepts the invitation of a Pharisee named Simon. They are all reclining, Roman-style, at a three-sided table, propping themselves up on their left elbows and eating with their right hands. Although Simon invited Jesus to his home, he neglected the common courtesy of providing water and a towel so Jesus could wash his tired feet. Perhaps because he was still not sure just whose side Jesus was on, he also neglected to greet him with the customary kiss. Finally, he failed to provide Jesus with refreshing oil with which to anoint his head.

At some point during the meal, a "sinful" woman makes her way to the place directly behind the reclining Jesus. Perhaps she has heard him speak, or perhaps she was the result of John's baptism of repentance; Luke apparently doesn't think we need to know how she got there. As she stands behind Jesus, caught up in the power of conviction, she begins to weep, her tears falling on his unwashed feet. Seeing what she has done, she kneels and, in an extraordinary gesture of intimacy, takes down her hair and wipes her tears away. After she has wiped her tears away, she pours an expensive bottle of perfume on Jesus' now-clean feet.

Once again in Luke's Gospel, someone who should have known better—Simon the Pharisee, who knows his Scripture better than you and I could ever hope to know it—misses the point, while the last person we might have expected—the sinful woman—understands fully her sin and need for Jesus. It would have represented a stunning reversal in Jesus' day.

Notice, however, that Jesus does not condemn Simon. Listen to the tenderness in his voice: "Simon, I have something to say to you . . ." Jesus ignores the offense. He overlooks the fact that Simon has judged him. He tells the Pharisee a parable about two debtors. By means of that wonderful story, Simon begins to see.

Luke loves to contrast religious men who don't get it with simple women who do. Here is yet another example. Simon the Pharisee is totally blind to the spiritual reality of what is going on, while a nameless "sinful woman" is able to see to the very depths of what is most spiritual and real. So what is it that they each see?

When Simon looks at the woman, all he sees is one of his theological categories: a sinner. He sees a serious violation of his rules, for the Talmud said a woman could only let down her hair in the presence of her husband.[8] In fact, rabbis considered the exposing of the hair as equal to the exposing of the bosom.

When he looks at Jesus, he tries to fit him into yet another category: a prophet. Yet according to his definition, Jesus does not neatly fit. (If you follow him long enough, you will discover that no label can define him and no category can contain him!) Jesus will also reveal that Simon had failed to see an opportunity to minister to him by providing water to wash his road-weary feet. Like many of the religious people of his day (and ours), Simon is functionally spiritually blind (compare to Mt 23:16-19).

But what about the woman? What do her eyes see? First, she has clearly seen her own sin. Perhaps she has heard John the Baptist preach about repentance, or maybe she has even heard one of Jesus' sermons. Either way, she is clearly repentant over the darkness she has seen in her own life and knows Jesus is the only person in whom she'll find forgiveness and restoration.

She also sees Jesus' feet and an opportunity to worship him by becoming, in effect, his slave. That is why she can stand "behind" Jesus and have access to his feet. She wets them with her sorrow-filled tears, then wipes them with her hair. Then, in an amazing demonstration of intimacy, she pours thousands of dollars worth of perfume on them. For the clarity of her spiritual vision, Jesus forgives her sins.

But the story does not end there. Does Jesus simply dismiss Simon for his blindness? No. Then he would be guilty of the same offense as Simon. Instead, Jesus tells a powerful little story about a man loaning different amounts of money to two people and then canceling both debts. "Which of them will love him more?" Jesus then asks.

Simon—who, after all, is no fool—gives the correct answer and so is caught in the parable's trap. Thanks to Jesus' story, Simon has begun to see. Then Luke is careful to give us the detail that Jesus *turned to the woman* and said to Simon, "Do you see this woman?" This little phrase contains the meat of the story. It is an invitation to Simon and to us to engage, to truly see those around us who have been marginalized for any and every reason.

Before this incident, Simon failed to really see anything at all; he saw neither Jesus nor the woman. He was blind to her act of repentance and love, and saw instead a serious sin. Jesus, who loves stubborn Simon as much as he loves the woman, longs for him to really see her—not as a category, not as a "sinner," but simply as a person who, above all, needs to be loved and forgiven.

When I was a boy, I was drawn to a particular picture of the crucifixion of Jesus. It seemed more realistic than any of the others I had ever seen. The expression on Jesus' face spoke not of pain but of the agonizing anticipation of pain. The painting was shrouded in shadows, with the only beam of light focused directly on Jesus. It always puzzled me that the principal person in the picture, besides Jesus, was a peculiar, non-Roman character wearing a beret cocked to one side and lifting the heavy cross into place. Later I learned the painting was by Rembrandt. He gave it the title *The Erection of the Cross,* and the solitary person struggling to raise the cross, bathed in the same spotlight with Jesus, was, in fact, himself—a self-portrait. The painting in and of itself is extremely powerful. But understanding it in the context of the painter's life lifts the painting's meaning to another dimension. It is Rembrandt's contrite confession of his own complicity in the crucifixion of Christ. It is more than the painting; it is a parable.

Jesus' brilliant parable is only two verses long, yet it can stand alone as a work of literary art. But when we see it in the frame Luke alone provides, it leaps to another quantum level. His story provides a place for all of them: the woman as the great debtor, and Simon as the one who owed less. Luke means to ask you and me to take our places in the parable. In the same instant, he invites us to find our place at Simon's banquet. Will we sit beside Jesus and acknowledge only a small debt, or will we fall down at his feet and, in tears, beg for the forgiveness we do not deserve?

This parable is the means for a miracle: the opening of Simon's blind eyes. At precisely this point in Matthew's narrative, Jesus heals the eyes of two blind men (Mt 9:27-31). Luke, a companion to another Pharisee, Paul, chooses at this point to tell the story of another kind of healing miracle. We cannot say for certain whether Simon, like so many other

Pharisees, eventually becomes a disciple of Jesus. What we can say for certain is that his blind eyes start to see, which is no less a miracle.

Part of the bottomless miracle of this simple, two-verse parable is that as he listens, Simon discovers that he is hearing the story of his own life. The gentleness of Jesus' story leads the Pharisee, like a lost sheep, to a place of understanding he could never have reached otherwise. How could he have known that the simple exchange that began with the words, "I have something to tell you," would end with the promise of a new life? The parable reveals that Simon has the answer in his head. The parable also makes it possible for the answer to move to his heart.

LUKE 8

THE WOMEN

8:1-3 The female supporters of the ministry.

THE PARABLE OF THE SOILS

8:4-8 The parable of the sower.

8:9-15 A private explanation for the disciples.

8:16-21 The appearance of Jesus' family.

A DEMONIC STORM

8:22-25 The calming of the storm.

A DEMONIZED MAN

8:26-39 The healing of the demon-possessed man of Gadara.

THE HEALING OF TWO DAUGHTERS

8:40-42 The pleas of Jairus.

8:43-48 The interruption by the woman subject to bleeding.

8:49-56 The healing of Jairus's daughter.

THE WOMEN

[1]Soon afterwards He was traveling from one town and village to another, preaching and telling the good news of the kingdom of God. The Twelve were with Him, [2]and also some women who had been healed of evil spirits and sicknesses: Mary, called Magdalene (seven demons had come out of her); [3]Joanna the wife of Chuza, Herod's steward; Susanna; and many others who were supporting them from their possessions.

When we pick up in Luke 8, Jesus is on the road once more. The ministry in the Galilee is well underway. What's more, there seems to be a focus simply on Jesus' preaching and telling the good news.

Only Luke, who is so tenderhearted toward the plight of women in general, tells us specifically of a band of women who are supporting Jesus and his disciples from their own means. This was not unusual; several rabbis had women supporters. But the fact that they are actually on the road with Jesus would have seemed scandalous, since most rabbis did not even speak to women in public—not even to their own wives!

Luke tells us in verse 3 that there are many of these women, but he only names three. The first is Mary from the village of Magdala. We are told that she had once been possessed by seven demons. She is sometimes confused with the sinful woman who washed Jesus' feet in chapter 7.

Next, Luke tells us about an extraordinary woman named Joanna. She must have been one of the wealthiest of the group. Her husband was a royal official in the court of Herod Antipas. I sometimes wonder if her husband is the same royal official we meet in John 4:46-53. I like to think he might be the same person.

Finally, Luke lists Susanna. This is the only place in the Gospels where she is named. We know absolutely nothing about her except that she has boldly identified herself with Jesus. Perhaps that is all we need to know about Susanna.

Apparently this group of women followed Jesus throughout the course of his ministry. At this moment they are surely excited about the prospect of Jesus' ministry and filled with hope with regard to the future. I can almost see the expressions on their faces: smiles, their skin tanned from the extended time out of doors. This could possibly be the happiest moment of their lives. We will not see them again until chapter 23, when they will be huddled at the foot of the cross, no doubt the most nightmarish moment of their lives.

THE PARABLE OF THE SOILS

⁴As a large crowd was gathering, and people were flocking to Him from every town, He said in a parable: ⁵"A sower went out to sow his seed. As he was sowing, some fell along the path; it was trampled on, and the birds of the sky ate it up. ⁶Other seed fell on the rock; when it sprang up, it withered, since it lacked moisture. ⁷Other seed fell among thorns; the thorns sprang up with it and choked it. ⁸Still other seed fell on good ground; when it sprang up, it produced a crop: 100 times [what was sown]." As He said this, He called out, "Anyone who has ears to hear should listen!"

⁹Then His disciples asked Him, "What does this parable mean?" ¹⁰So He said, "The secrets of the kingdom of God have been given for you to know, but to the rest it is in parables, so that

> *Looking they may not see,*
> *and hearing they may not understand.*

¹¹"This is the meaning of the parable: The seed is the word of God. ¹²The seeds along the path are those who have heard. Then the Devil comes and takes away the word from their hearts, so that they may not believe and be saved. ¹³And the seeds on the rock are those who, when they hear, welcome the word with joy. Having no root, these believe for a while and depart in a time of testing. ¹⁴As for the seed that fell among thorns, these are the ones who, when they have heard, go on their way and are choked with worries, riches, and pleasures of life, and produce no mature fruit. ¹⁵But the seed in the good ground—these are the ones who, having heard the word with an honest and good heart, hold on to it and by enduring, bear fruit.

¹⁶"No one, after lighting a lamp, covers it with a basket or puts it under a bed, but puts it on a lampstand so that those who come in may see the light. ¹⁷For nothing is concealed that won't be revealed, and nothing hidden that

*won't be made known and come to light. ¹⁸Therefore, take care how you lis-
ten. For whoever has, more will be given to him; and whoever does not have,
even what he thinks he has will be taken away from him."*

*¹⁹Then His mother and brothers came to Him, but they could not meet
with Him because of the crowd. ²⁰He was told, "Your mother and Your brothers are standing outside, wanting to see You."*

*²¹But He replied to them, "My mother and My brothers are those who hear
and do the word of God."*

*T*he crowd seems to be growing. People are flocking from everywhere. For a brief time there has been a respite from the persecution of
the religious leaders. There is no word of the seemingly ever-present
cadre of Pharisees, lurking in the shadows, waiting for Jesus to make a
ritualistic slip. This, it seems to me, is one of the safest, most open moments of the ministry.

In this context Jesus tells one of his most well-known parables, the
only one he will explain in detail. It is usually referred to as the parable
of the sower. If you listen closely, you will notice that the focus is really
on the various conditions of the soils.

It begins simply enough: "A sower went out . . ." The first piece of background that will help us in understanding the story is that in the ancient
world, sowing always preceded plowing. That is, the farmer would scatter
the seed and then work it into the ground with the plow. This is important
lest we think the sower in our story is being careless with the seed.

The seeds land in four places: on the path, in the rocks, among the
thorn bushes and finally on good ground. Lo and behold, although
only one-fourth of the seed fell onto a place where it could grow, nevertheless the crop produced one hundred times what was sown!

Jesus shouts to his listeners the closing challenge: "Anyone who has
ears to hear should listen!" I imagine him stepping out of the center of
attention and moving aside where he can have a private word with the
disciples (not necessarily just the Twelve), who ask Jesus to explain.

Once again, the power of the parable tends to be the fact that Jesus
would not explain it. But the Twelve are about to be sent out on mission

(Lk 9:1). I believe Jesus wants to fully prepare them, especially with this parable that is a picture of what they are about to go out and do on their own. They will become the sowers. Jesus wants them to know that their seed will be received in many different ways. Nevertheless, they can expect a remarkable harvest.

Jesus unpacks the parable by giving a human face to the four types of ground. The path represents those who hear, but the seed is stolen by the devil, represented earlier by the birds who consume the seed. The rocky ground represents those who initially hear the word of God with joy; when the blistering sun of testing comes, however, they leave. The thorny ground represents those in whom the seed apparently sprouts, but the thorns of life choke the young plant of their faith so that no fruit is produced. Finally, the best is saved for last. The good ground speaks of those who receive the word into hearts that are honest and good; they hold on and, because of their endurance, produce fruit.

Jesus' closing statement about the lamp on the stand appears to sum up the entire process we have just witnessed: what is obvious to some is being hidden from others. Jesus has just lit the lamp, and he intends that it be put on a stand so that everyone who comes in will see the light. Nothing is concealed that won't be revealed. Everything hidden will come to the light. That, after all, is the nature of light.

Just then, we are told, Jesus' mother Mary and his brothers appear, but the wall of people surrounding him keeps them from getting to Jesus. When Jesus is told they are standing outside, waiting to see him, he responds, "My mother and My brothers are those who hear and do the word of God."

When Mark tells this story (Mk 3), the incident with the family happens before the parable is told. But Luke tells us this incident after the parable, perhaps because he saw a connection between the two. Earlier, when he is summing up the parable, Jesus says, "take care how you listen" (Lk 8:18). It is as if their lives depend on it. Now, with his family waiting outside, Jesus emphasizes the point once more, with greater intensity. Those who do listen have become his true family. Hearers are his brothers. Doers have become like his mother. When you take into consideration the central place family occupied in the value system of Jesus' listeners, it was a shocking thing to say, placing the family of faith above the earthly family.

A DEMONIC STORM

[22]One day He and His disciples got into a boat, and He told them, "Let's cross over to the other side of the lake." So they set out, [23]and as they were sailing He fell asleep. Then a fierce windstorm came down on the lake; they were being swamped and were in danger. [24]They came and woke Him up, saying, "Master, Master, we're going to die!" Then He got up and rebuked the wind and the raging waves. So they ceased, and there was a calm. [25]He said to them, "Where is your faith?"

They were fearful and amazed, asking one another, "Who can this be? He commands even the winds and the waves, and they obey Him!"

*A*lthough they are seldom understood as such, the next two stories are linked. The portrayal of the storm functions to prepare us to meet the demonized man who dwells on the other side of the lake. In terms of engaging with the imagination, it is one of my favorite stories.

Shortly after they set sail, Jesus, apparently exhausted from ministry, falls asleep. It is one of the few nakedly human moments, not unlike the time he was tired and thirsty beside the well (Jn 4). Many commentaries resort to meteorological explanations when it comes to the storm. Long discussions concerning the weather patterns in and around the Lake of Galilee are brought up to explain the ferocity of the storm.

I would like to suggest that the storm is demonic in character. Many of the disciples are fishermen who know this lake and the kinds of storms that can blow up upon it. Yet it seems to me that they have never seen a storm like this. Second, in Mark when Jesus is rudely awakened, he deals with the storm by using precisely the same word he uses in dealing with demons: "Be muzzled" (Mk 4:39). In response to the miracle, Luke tells us the disciples are afraid, or perhaps in awe *(phobos)*. They stammer, "Who can this be?"

It is an important question, even though they seem to have uttered it out of confusion. It is a question that Luke will set about answering from this point in the narrative until the final moment when Jesus sets out for Jerusalem.

A DEMONIZED MAN

[26]Then they sailed to the region of the Gerasenes, which is opposite Galilee. [27]When He got out on land, a demon-possessed man from the town met Him. For a long time he had worn no clothes and did not stay in a house but in the tombs. [28]When he saw Jesus, he cried out, fell down before Him, and said in a loud voice, "What do You have to do with me, Jesus, You Son of the Most High God? I beg You, don't torment me!" [29]For He had commanded the unclean spirit to come out of the man. Many times it had seized him, and although he was guarded, bound by chains and shackles, he would snap the restraints and be driven by the demon into deserted places.

[30]"What is your name?" Jesus asked him.

"Legion," he said—because many demons had entered him. [31]And they begged Him not to banish them to the abyss.

[32]A large herd of pigs was there, feeding on the hillside. The demons begged Him to permit them to enter the pigs, and He gave them permission. [33]The demons came out of the man and entered the pigs, and the herd rushed down the steep bank into the lake and drowned. [34]When the men who tended them saw what had happened, they ran off and reported it in the town and in the countryside. [35]Then people went out to see what had happened. They came to Jesus and found the man the demons had departed from, sitting at Jesus' feet, dressed and in his right mind. And they were afraid. [36]Meanwhile the eyewitnesses reported to them how the demon-possessed man was delivered. [37]Then all the people of the Gerasene region asked Him to leave them, because they were gripped by great fear. So getting into the boat, He returned.

[38]The man from whom the demons had departed kept begging Him to be with Him. But He sent him away and said, [39]"Go back to your home, and tell all that God has done for you." And off he went, proclaiming throughout the town all that Jesus had done for him.

*T*he region of the Gerasenes, also known as Gadara, was one of the cities of the Decapolis, a Gentile area on the eastern shore of the Lake of Galilee. As they drop their anchor, the disciples behold a madman coming their way. He is naked, which was an especially appalling condition to their Jewish sensibilities. Equally disgusting to the disciples is the fact that he lives in the most unclean of locations: a graveyard. Mark 5 tells us that he also was known to cut himself with stones, yet another sign of demonic possession (see 1 Kings 18:28).

As he approaches, Jesus commands the demons to leave the man. In response he falls down in front of Jesus, screaming. When Jesus asks, "What is your name?" the man replies, "Legion"—a name that implies a number anywhere from four to six thousand! The demons beg Jesus not to cast them into the abyss, a specific place prepared for Satan and his demonic hosts (Rev 20:1-3).

It puzzles some readers that Jesus seems to acquiesce to the demons' demand. But nothing could be further from the truth. By allowing the demons to enter the herd of swine that is feeding on the hillside, Jesus reveals to everyone what would have eventually happened to the man, since the ultimate goal of demonic possession is always the destruction of life.

It is a remarkable picture to try to imagine: hundreds of pigs floating lifeless in the lake while the dumbfounded disciples look on. The pig herders flee the scene, spreading the news. Eventually people from town make their way toward the lake to see if what they have heard is true.

They find the former lunatic no longer naked but fully dressed. He is calm, sitting at the feet of Jesus. Something about the scene terrifies the Gerasenes, who beg Jesus to go away.

As Jesus and his disciples are climbing into the boat, the nameless man who has found deliverance begs to be taken along. If Jesus were only trying to attract a crowd, wouldn't this man's testimony be just the trick? "Behold the man of the tombs," Jesus could advertise, "who is now delivered and in his right mind!"

But Jesus is not trying to simply drum up followers. He is creating disciples and preparing to send them out on a mission. The truth is the man who was formerly demon-possessed will have his own missionary task: spreading the good news of Jesus throughout the Decapolis. When Jesus returns to this area, large crowds will be anxious to hear what he has to say.

THE HEALING OF TWO DAUGHTERS

[40]When Jesus returned, the crowd welcomed Him, for they were all expecting Him. [41]Just then, a man named Jairus came. He was a leader of the synagogue. He fell down at Jesus' feet and pleaded with Him to come to his house, [42]because he had an only daughter about 12 years old, and she was at death's door.

While He was going, the crowds were nearly crushing Him. [43]A woman suffering from bleeding for 12 years, who had spent all she had on doctors yet could not be healed by any, [44]approached from behind and touched the tassel of His robe. Instantly her bleeding stopped.

[45]"Who touched Me?" Jesus asked.

When they all denied it, Peter said, "Master, the crowds are hemming You in and pressing against You."

[46]"Somebody did touch Me," said Jesus. "I know that power has gone out from Me." [47]When the woman saw that she was discovered, she came trembling and fell down before Him. In the presence of all the people, she declared the reason she had touched Him and how she was instantly cured. [48]"Daughter," He said to her, "your faith has made you well. Go in peace."

[49]While He was still speaking, someone came from the synagogue leader's [house], saying, "Your daughter is dead. Don't bother the Teacher anymore."

[50]When Jesus heard it, He answered him, "Don't be afraid. Only believe, and she will be made well." [51]After He came to the house, He let no one enter with Him except Peter, John, James, and the child's father and mother. [52]Everyone was crying and mourning for her. But He said, "Stop crying, for she is not dead but asleep."

[53]They started laughing at Him, because they knew she was dead. [54]So He took her by the hand and called out, "Child, get up!" [55]Her spirit returned, and she got up at once. Then He gave orders that she be given something to eat. [56]Her parents were astounded, but He instructed them to tell no one what had happened.

When they return to the other side of the lake, the ever-present crowd is waiting for them. At that moment a man named Jairus, the chief organizer of the synagogue, falls at Jesus' feet with a breathless request. His only daughter is dying; will Jesus please come and heal her?

As they are making their way to the home of the desperate father, the crowd is so large and so excited that they are literally crushing Jesus. In the midst of the confusion of the mob, a pale woman elbows her way behind Jesus. This woman had been hemorrhaging for over twelve years. In a culture that both revered and abhorred blood, this would have rendered her perpetually unclean. If she can be healed, it is not simply her health that will be restored; she will get back her life.

As an observant Jew, Jesus would have worn the prayer shawl with tassels at the four corners. The woman, believing that simply touching Jesus would heal her, reaches out for one of the tassels. Immediately she senses inside herself that the bleeding has stopped. Her intention is to slip away and disappear in the crowd.

But she is not the only one who senses that a miracle has occurred. Jesus asks, "Who touched me?" Peter responds in essence: "What do you mean? Everyone is touching you!" But Jesus is insistent. It is not enough to simply give her healing. No, he wants to give her himself.

She is the third person in this chapter to be found at the feet of Jesus. First there was the demoniac, and then there was Jairus. And now this nameless woman confesses before Jesus and the crowd what she has done and what has happened in her as a result. Even though he is on an urgent mission, Jesus pauses to help a poor woman whose illness has marginalized her.

It is the only time in all the Gospels that Jesus calls a woman by this tender term. "Daughter," he says, "your faith has made you well." It is the same thing he told the sinful woman in Luke 7. In his humility, Jesus will always point away from himself and thereby win praise for God. Although few recognize it, two daughters will be healed in this story.

Pressing into the crowded circle, someone comes from the house of the synagogue leader. Jairus hears the words he has dreaded to hear: his only daughter is dead. The man who has brought the message then makes an interesting conclusion. His words reveal his level of expectation and probably the expectations of everyone in the crowd. He says, "Don't bother the Teacher anymore." This statement shows that they expected Jesus to have the power to heal the little girl but not to raise her from the dead. There's no point. You might as well let Jesus go on his way.

Jesus pulls the frightened father aside and whispers, "Do not be afraid." As they come to the house, Jesus tells them he wants only Peter, James and John, along with the child's parents, to come into the house. They pass by a group of mourners who have already gathered outside the house. I would love to know the tone of Jesus' voice when he says, "Stop crying, for she is not dead but asleep."

Perhaps it is the absurdity of what he says, or maybe it is because they are only hired mourners, but the crowd bursts into laughter. They know what death looks like. In their time they have seen too many dead children.

It's another one of those unmiraculous miracles. As simply as you or I would wake up our children on any given morning, Jesus calls out, "Child, get up!" With that, the color returns to her cheeks and her eyes open. She sits up in bed and is enveloped in the arms of her awestruck parents. As he turns to leave and pushes his way through the crowd, Jesus lowers his voice and almost pleadingly asks them not to tell anyone.

Power over the demonic and now authority over disease and death: if we have begun to ask the question "Who is this man?" then in the span of just a few verses we have come a long way.

LUKE 9

A FIRST FORAY

9:1-6 The sending of the Twelve.

9:7-9 Herod's confusion about "Who is Jesus?"

THE MIRACLE BEHIND THE MIRACLE

9:10-17 Feeding of the five thousand.

A FINAL CLARITY: WHO JESUS IS

9:18-27 "Who is Jesus?"

CONFIRMATION FROM THE FATHER

9:28-36 A dramatic answer to the question.

THE IMPOTENCE OF UNBELIEF

9:37-45 The healing of the demon-possessed boy.

9:46-50 The command to childlikeness.

THE FINAL JOURNEY BEGINS

*9:51-56 The beginning of the travel narrative,
when "Jesus resolutely set out for Jerusalem."*

9:57-62 Three would-be disciples.

A FIRST FORAY

¹Summoning the Twelve, He gave them power and authority over all the demons, and [power] to heal diseases. ²Then He sent them to proclaim the kingdom of God and to heal the sick.

³"Take nothing for the road," He told them, "no walking stick, no traveling bag, no bread, no money; and don't take an extra shirt. ⁴Whatever house you enter, stay there and leave from there. ⁵If they do not welcome you, when you leave that town, shake off the dust from your feet as a testimony against them." ⁶So they went out and traveled from village to village, proclaiming the good news and healing everywhere.

⁷Herod the tetrarch heard about everything that was going on. He was perplexed, because some said that John had been raised from the dead, ⁸some that Elijah had appeared, and others that one of the ancient prophets had risen. ⁹"I beheaded John," Herod said, "but who is this I hear such things about?" And he wanted to see Him.

*I*t is the countdown before they leave on the final journey to Jerusalem and the cross. Jesus is sending out the Twelve on what appears to be a preliminary mission, so here, in verses 3-5, he issues their marching orders. Having imparted to them his power to heal and cast out demons, Jesus' charge is simple: "to proclaim the kingdom of God and to heal the sick." His charge is simple, but not easy, and the following series of accounts will show that Jesus' command is, in fact, often impossible. The disciples will not be able to accomplish it on their own power or authority. Success in ministry will come to them in proportion to their own acknowledgment of weakness.

Every moment of the mission will be a reminder of their helplessness. They must take no provisions, no stick, no bag, no money and no clothes besides those they are wearing. They will be entirely dependent on God's grace and on Jewish hospitality. Although they will be living as beggars, Jesus does not want them going from house to house as beggars would. If they are not welcome, they are to shake off the dust from that place as "a testimony against them," effectively a sign that the place was unclean. (Compare this to Acts 13:51, in which Paul and Barnabas do the same thing in Pisidian Antioch.)

It is a time of transition as they move from a Capernaum-based outreach in the area of Galilee to an uncertain involvement in Jerusalem—uncertain for the Twelve but crystal-clear for Jesus. Twice in chapter 9 he warns them of what is awaiting him at the end of the road that leads to Jerusalem (Lk 9:21-22, 44-45). On the second occasion, Luke tells us that the disciples are afraid to ask Jesus what he means.

In Luke 9:7-9, the central question of Luke's Gospel is reintroduced. It was first asked by the Twelve in Luke 8:25, when Jesus calmed the demonic storm on the Lake of Galilee. Here it is raised once more by Herod Antipas, the son of Herod the Great. He is clearly confused as to just who Jesus is. It has been rumored that he might be John the Baptist alive again, so Herod nervously mutters to himself, "I beheaded John." There were also rumors that Jesus might be the "Elijah who is to come," or perhaps one of the other prophets. Herod concludes that he wants to see Jesus, and indeed he will. In chapter 23 Jesus will be sent as a peace offering from Pilate to Herod. They had been enemies, but after this they become friends. Herod will at first be pleased to see Jesus, hoping to be entertained by one of his miracles. When Jesus refuses, Herod's curiosity will turn vindictive. He will wrap the bruised and bleeding Jesus in an elegant robe and send him back to Pilate and the cross.

THE MIRACLE BEHIND THE MIRACLE

[10]*When the apostles returned, they reported to Jesus all that they had done. He took them along and withdrew privately to a town called Bethsaida.* [11]*When the crowds found out, they followed Him. He welcomed them, spoke to them about the kingdom of God, and cured those who needed healing.*

[12]*Late in the day, the Twelve approached and said to Him, "Send the crowd away, so they can go into the surrounding villages and countryside to find food and lodging, because we are in a deserted place here."*

[13]*"You give them something to eat," He told them.*

"We have no more than five loaves and two fish," they said, "unless we go and buy food for all these people." [14]*(For about 5,000 men were there.)*

Then He told His disciples, "Have them sit down in groups of about 50 each." *¹⁵They did so, and had them all sit down. ¹⁶Then He took the five loaves and the two fish, and looking up to heaven, He blessed and broke them. He kept giving them to the disciples to set before the crowd. ¹⁷Everyone ate and was filled. Then they picked up 12 baskets of leftover pieces.*

*T*he disciples return and report back to Jesus. Since no details are provided, we are left to assume that things went well for them. Then they retreat to the wilderness. At this same moment in Mark 6:31-32, Jesus tells them to come to a quiet place for some rest. Matthew tells us also that Jesus hears of the beheading of his cousin John at this time and seeks seclusion in the wilderness (Mt 14:13). The ever-present crowd follows, and what was supposed to be a retreat becomes a convention of between ten and fifteen thousand! Luke wants to make it clear, however, that Jesus "welcomed them."

As the day is coming to a close, the worried disciples warn Jesus that he needs to send the people away so they can find food for themselves. Jesus, perhaps turning to behold the vast crowd, looks toward the impoverished Twelve and says, "You give them something to eat."

It is an impossible command. It is one of those situations in which Jesus continually puts his disciples, both then and now. Bill Lane used to say, "You should always work at the level of your own inadequacy." That was his way of encouraging us to accept following Jesus as a life of impossible commands. The disciples have just come back from a mission on which they carried nothing for themselves to eat. It is a thoroughly hopeless situation, a perfect parallel to the starving Israelites in the wilderness (Ex 16). The disciples are able to scrounge up five loaves and two small fish. From John's Gospel we learn that it was Andrew who borrowed them from a small boy (Jn 6:9). I imagine a frantic pause just about now, as the breathless disciples look back and forth between the small supper meant to feed a small boy and the enormous crowd. Jesus breaks the silence with a simple command: "Have them sit down." Sitting down would indicate to the crowd that a meal is about to be served. The hillside is dotted with hungry, expectant groups of fifty.

It is one of the most unmiraculous of all his unmiraculous miracles.

In every account, Jesus breaks bread and pronounces a *berakah*, a blessing, that might have gone something like: "Blessed art Thou, eternal God our Father, who causes bread to come forth from the earth."

The bread and fish are passed out, and everyone eats until they are satisfied. When did the miracle occur? Where is the "amazed" response of the crowd we have come to expect from Luke? There is no waving of arms in the air, but only a simple blessing. Some commentators conclude that there was, in fact, no miracle at all but only a wave of generosity that spread through the crowd when they saw how generous the little boy was. But a miracle did indeed occur. In fact, two miracles happened. The second one, though even less miraculous, is the real point of the story.

In the second half of Luke 9:17, we read that twelve small lunch-pail-sized wicker baskets, *kophinoi*,[9] of the leftovers are picked up. The leftovers were referred to as the *peah* in Judaism and were usually left as provision for the slaves (see Mt 15:27; Mk 7:28). Wasting food was seen as an insult to God. The "miracle behind the miracle" of the feeding of the five thousand is the perfect provision that is left for the Twelve, who were in the process of learning to be servants. Out of that vast crowd, which must have covered several acres, twelve lunch pails of leftovers were gathered for the Twelve. While the miracle of the feeding of the four thousand (Mt 15:32-38) with the seven human-size baskets *(spuris)*[10] of leftovers is abundance, we need to learn to appreciate the miracle of perfect provision demonstrated by the twelve small baskets.

A FINAL CLARITY: WHO JESUS IS

[18]*While He was praying in private and His disciples were with Him, He asked them, "Who do the crowds say that I am?"*

[19]*They answered, "John the Baptist; others, Elijah; still others, that one of the ancient prophets has come back."*

[20]*"But you," He asked them, "who do you say that I am?"*

Peter answered, "God's Messiah!"

[21]*But He strictly warned and instructed them to tell this to no one,* [22]*saying, "The Son of Man must suffer many things and be rejected by the elders,*

chief priests, and scribes, be killed, and be raised the third day."

²³Then He said to [them] all, "If anyone wants to come with Me, he must deny himself, take up his cross daily, and follow Me. ²⁴For whoever wants to save his life will lose it, but whoever loses his life because of Me will save it. ²⁵What is a man benefited if he gains the whole world, yet loses or forfeits himself? ²⁶For whoever is ashamed of Me and My words, the Son of Man will be ashamed of him when He comes in His glory and that of the Father and the holy angels. ²⁷I tell you the truth: there are some standing here who will not taste death until they see the kingdom of God."

*T*he question has been waiting until this moment to be finally answered. It is important that it comes in the context of a time of prayer, for nothing happens in Luke apart from prayer. It is important that it is Jesus who finally poses the question to the Twelve, since it will be left to him to help them understand what being the Messiah entails once the question is answered. It is important that it is Peter who gives the final answer, since he will give leadership to the disciples in the months and years that follow. Most especially, it is important that the question is answered by faith before the final proof of the transfiguration occurs.

Jesus breaks the question into two parts. First, who do *people* say I am? And finally, who do *you* say I am? He is not asking because he needs the answer; it is they, the disciples, who need it. Their response to the first question echoes a lame list we've heard before (Mk 6:14). Just a few verses ago we saw Herod Antipas working his way through this list. When the second question is spoken, it is Peter, often the spokesman for the Twelve, who responds. As he does so often, Peter is saying more than he knows. In Matthew 16, Jesus blesses him for his answer but reminds Peter that it was the Father who revealed the answer.

Listen closely to what Peter says. It is not a direct answer to Jesus' question, "who do *you* say that I am?" Peter does not answer, *"We say that you are . . ."* No. Instead, he blurts out absolutely, "God's Messiah!" Peter has not spoken on his own; after all, his knowledge of Jesus' identity was a matter of revelation (Mt 16:17).

Now that the crucial question has been answered, Jesus must undeceive his followers. For them, the Messiah is the victorious conqueror of the Romans who will set up his earthly kingdom. Never could any of them have believed that the Messiah had in fact come to die for them and for the Romans as well. So before the echo of Peter's answer has died away, Jesus tells them that being the Messiah means he must "suffer many things . . . be killed, and be raised the third day." It is a statement they only selectively seem to hear. That is, they only hear parts of it—the pieces they want to hear. When the time comes, no one will seem to remember that Jesus had said he would rise on the third day. Not a single one of them is expecting it.

If suffering and death are what it means to be the Messiah, then the call to his followers must be shaped by this brutal reality. In Luke 9:23-27, Jesus defines just what their call will look like. It will look like self-denial: losing their lives in order to save them. It will look like standing, unashamed of Jesus before the world, even as one day he will stand, unashamed of us before the angels. Luke is the only Gospel that reminds us that we must take up the cross "daily" (v. 23). And then comes a remarkable promise: some of them will not die until they see the kingdom. It is a promise that has gone largely misunderstood, both then and now. The followers of John the disciple mistook this promise, thinking that John would not die until Jesus returned (Jn 21:23). But the fact is, for three of them, the promise will come true on a mountaintop in just eight days.

CONFIRMATION FROM THE FATHER

[28]*About eight days after these words, He took along Peter, John, and James, and went up on the mountain to pray. *[29]*As He was praying, the appearance of His face changed, and His clothes became dazzling white. *[30]*Suddenly, two men were talking with Him—Moses and Elijah. *[31]*They appeared in glory and were speaking of His death, which He was about to accomplish in Jerusalem.*

[32]*Peter and those with him were in a deep sleep, and when they became fully awake, they saw His glory and the two men who were standing with Him. *[33]*As the two men were departing from Him, Peter said to Jesus, "Master, it's good for us to be here! Let us make three tabernacles: one for You, one*

for Moses, and one for Elijah"—not knowing what he said.

³⁴While he was saying this, a cloud appeared and overshadowed them. They became afraid as they entered the cloud. ³⁵Then a voice came from the cloud, saying:

> *This is My Son, the Chosen One;*
> *listen to Him!*

³⁶After the voice had spoken, only Jesus was found. They kept silent, and in those days told no one what they had seen.

One of the most deliberate things Jesus did was create community. Earlier we saw him calling the Twelve; in the next chapter, he will set apart the Seventy. Here, for the second time, we see him focusing on the Three: Peter, James and his brother John. Among the Gospel writers, Luke alone emphasizes that the miracle will happen as Jesus is praying. Although he will command them to keep it secret, this is most definitely *not* one of the unmiraculous miracles.

As Jesus goes to prayer, a veil is lifted. Perhaps a veil is lifted every time anyone goes to prayer. It is important to note that Jesus was *transfigured*. Jesus' form does not change; that is, he is not transformed. This is not the transformation. No, he is transfigured: that is, the Three are only seeing to the core of what Jesus has been all along. He becomes luminous.

All at once two men appear. They are talking with Jesus. I suppose their conversation reveals that they are, in fact, Moses and Elijah. One is a saint who had died; the other was taken to heaven before he died. They are the only kind of people who will inhabit the kingdom of heaven: those who have died before his second coming and those who are still living when he appears. Only Luke tells us the fascinating detail in verse 31 that they are talking to Jesus about his literal "exodus," which was about to happen in Jerusalem. Moses, talking to Jesus about *his* exodus! It is all going to happen, once again, in Jerusalem, the very place Jesus will be determinedly leaving for in a few days.

We are always too hard on the disciples when it comes to their sleepiness, both here and in the garden of Gethsemane. The fact is that, at the moment, they are exhausted from trying to keep up. In the garden, Luke will tell us, they are exhausted "from their grief" (Lk 22:45). Here on the mountain, perhaps it is the voices that awaken them, or maybe it is the crackling and sizzling of the "glory." Whichever it is, they awake as the two visitors are turning to go, to walk back into eternity.

Luke makes it clear that Peter does not know what he is saying. Greek scholars have told me that Peter's statement can be translated two ways: as a simple statement or as a question. I hear it as the second. Peter, in the context of fear and confusion, may be asking, "Is it good for us to be here?" This helps explain his second confused statement about building the shelters. I used to think that since the Jewish Feast of Tabernacles was near, Peter wanted to make ceremonial "booths" for the three of them. This is still a popular interpretation. But given the fear that is about to envelope them as the cloud envelopes them all, I believe Peter wants to build small tabernacle-like tents to shield the three disciples from the danger of seeing the glory of God that is radiating from the other three. He needn't have minded, since at that moment God himself shields them with the cloud. It is fascinating to imagine their faces as the overshadowing cloud obscures them.

Now imagine a voice coming from inside a cloud that surrounds you. "This is My Son, the Chosen One; listen to Him!" It is the fulfillment of Jesus' word of a few days ago. In a sense, they have seen—almost entered into—the kingdom. If they had any doubts before, they should have vanished by now. The question has been answered by God himself. Who is Jesus? The Son of God, the Chosen One.

THE IMPOTENCE OF UNBELIEF

37 The next day, when they came down from the mountain, a large crowd met Him. 38 Just then a man from the crowd cried out, "Teacher, I beg You to look at my son, because he's my only [child]. 39 Often a spirit seizes him; suddenly he shrieks, and it throws him into convulsions until he foams at the mouth; wounding him, it hardly ever leaves him. 40 I begged Your disciples to drive it out, but they couldn't."

41 Jesus replied, "You unbelieving and rebellious generation! How long will

I be with you and put up with you? Bring your son here."

⁴²As the boy was still approaching, the demon knocked him down and threw him into severe convulsions. But Jesus rebuked the unclean spirit, cured the boy, and gave him back to his father. ⁴³And they were all astonished at the greatness of God.

While everyone was amazed at all the things He was doing, He told His disciples, ⁴⁴"Let these words sink in: the Son of Man is about to be betrayed into the hands of men."

⁴⁵But they did not understand this statement; it was concealed from them so that they could not grasp it, and they were afraid to ask Him about it.

⁴⁶Then an argument started among them about who would be the greatest of them. ⁴⁷But Jesus, knowing the thoughts of their hearts, took a little child and had him stand next to Him. ⁴⁸He told them, "Whoever welcomes this little child in My name welcomes Me. And whoever welcomes Me welcomes Him who sent Me. For whoever is least among you—this one is great."

⁴⁹John responded, "Master, we saw someone driving out demons in Your name, and we tried to stop him because he does not follow us."

⁵⁰"Don't stop him," Jesus told him, "because whoever is not against you is for you."

*T*he lingering inadequacies of the disciples, which first came up at the feeding of the five thousand (vv. 12-17), are brought out more forcefully here in their inability to cast the demon from the young boy. In verse 49, ironically, they will castigate someone who was able to cast out a demon using Jesus' name. Both incidents tell us that the disciples still have a long way to go.

As they are coming down—literally—from their mountaintop experience, a man from the crowd shouts to Jesus that the disciples failed to cast a demon out of his son. He begs Jesus to help his only child, who suffers from convulsions and foaming at the mouth as the demon tries to obscure the image of God in the little boy.

We can sense that a transition is coming from Jesus' frustrated state-

ment, "How long will I be with you and put up with you?" He calls
them unbelieving and rebellious. His tired anger comes from the fact
that their unbelief has rendered them impotent. Oddly enough, it is not
the demons that seem to be bothering Jesus at the moment, but the
unbelief of his own followers!

"Bring your son here," he says. As the boy is brought closer to Jesus,
the demon tries one last time to take his life by throwing him into what
Luke's medical mind tells him were "severe convulsions." All it takes is
a word from Jesus, and the demon is gone. The consistent response of
the amazed crowd is always to praise God, never Jesus. What was it
about his countenance or his posture that always pointed away from
himself and always to the Father? Notice the doublet: they were *astonished* and everyone was *amazed*.

Amid the adulation, Jesus tells his disciples for the second time that
he is about to be betrayed. But Luke tells us that they do not understand. Mysteriously, he writes that it is "concealed" from them. The
tone of their fellowship is shifting as the road to Jerusalem nears. They
are afraid because Jesus is saying fearful things. And here, for the first
time, we are told they are afraid even to ask Jesus about it. This is the
setting for the departure from the familiarity and simplicity of the Galilee to the bustle and duplicity of Jerusalem.

Before they depart, Luke paints one more scene that completes the
image of the frightened and impotent disciples. For the first time we
know of—but not the last—an argument breaks out among them concerning who is the greatest. Perhaps it is their tiredness speaking, or
maybe it is an attempt to change the subject from Jesus' frightening
predictions of suffering.

The answer from Jesus speaks once more of the radically reversed
nature of his kingdom. The way up is down. Being wise means embracing the foolishness of the gospel. To be free you must become a slave
and submit to his gentle yoke. The way to become truly rich is to give
it all away and travel with nothing, like a beggar. And here, if you want
to become great, you must be like this child. There is a tradition that
says that the child Jesus used for his illustration was Peter's crippled
daughter and that they were in his house in Capernaum. Whether or

not that legend is true, we do know that they are about to leave home and that some of them will never return.

THE FINAL JOURNEY BEGINS

⁵¹When the days were coming to a close for Him to be taken up, He determined to journey to Jerusalem. ⁵²He sent messengers ahead of Him, and on the way they entered a village of the Samaritans to make preparations for Him. ⁵³But they did not welcome Him, because He determined to journey to Jerusalem. ⁵⁴When the disciples James and John saw this, they said, "Lord, do You want us to call down fire from heaven to consume them?"

⁵⁵But He turned and rebuked them, ⁵⁶and they went to another village.

⁵⁷As they were traveling on the road someone said to Him, "I will follow You wherever You go!"

⁵⁸Jesus told him, "Foxes have dens, and birds of the sky have nests, but the Son of Man has no place to lay His head." ⁵⁹Then He said to another, "Follow Me."

"Lord," he said, "first let me go bury my father."

⁶⁰But He told him, "Let the dead bury their own dead, but you go and spread the news of the kingdom of God."

⁶¹Another also said, "I will follow You, Lord, but first let me go and say good-bye to those at my house."

⁶²But Jesus said to him, "No one who puts his hand to the plow and looks back is fit for the kingdom of God."

*T*he momentous journey begins with another story that reveals all that is lacking in the disciples. Having gone through the preparation they have received from Jesus, and having heard all they have heard and seen all they have seen, they might be expected to have more than impotent unbelief and short tempers.

Jesus adopted the strategy of sending out heralds in advance of his coming to a town. This strategy will become more formalized in the next chapter with the choosing of the Seventy. As they travel from Galilee toward Jerusalem, they must pass through Samaria, the region of the hated Samaritans. Some commentators mention that by even going through Samaria Jesus exhibits an extraordinary openness. Josephus, however, tells us that it was customary for Galileans to go through Samaria.

Whatever openness Jesus might be showing, it is not reciprocated by the Samaritans, who do not welcome the group because they are on their way to Jerusalem for Passover. Passover was a particular time of tension between the Jews and Samaritans. They took turns desecrating each other's temples. One Passover, the Samaritans dug up some graves and threw the bones into the temple court to keep the Jews from celebrating their most holy feast. The next year the Jews responded by burning the Samaritan temple on Mount Gerizim to the ground.

Jesus has already given the disciples instructions about what to do if they are not welcomed. In Luke 9:5 they were told to shake off the dust as a testimony against a town. In the face of the Samaritan insult, James and John forget Jesus' command. Reveling in their new power to heal and cast out demons, they suppose they might even be able to call fire down from heaven as Elijah had against the priests of Baal (2 Kings 1:1-17). From this episode it is believed they received the nickname *Boanerges*, or "Sons of Thunder" (Mk 3:17).

Verse 57 begins with a phrase that will become familiar to us as we travel with Jesus on this final journey. Most people read right past them, but phrases like "As they were traveling" and "as they were going up to Jerusalem" will constantly remind us that we are on the road with Jesus. As they are walking along, three different men approach, all wanting to join Jesus' group of disciples. The first makes the grandiose promise to follow wherever Jesus goes. Jesus responds that, like a fox or a bird, he has no home, not even a place to lay his head. His response hints at the notion that the man who made the offer had in mind that following Jesus would take him to some sort of sumptuous place, perhaps a palace. But it is not a palace that awaits Jesus at the end of the road to Jerusalem.

Jesus issues the call to the next man who responds with the legitimate excuse that he has to go and bury his father. I have heard it taught that, owing to the Jewish obligation to bury the parents, this man's father might not have actually been dead and that his excuse might have excused him from following Jesus for a period of years. This explanation, while perhaps credible—it has been suggested by people a lot smarter than I am!—diffuses the impact of the story. I prefer to think that his father has died. Given that burial in the first century took place on the day of death, the man's excuse would have only meant a day's delay. But Jesus will not allow even that. This passage highlights the theme of "faith before family" that appears in Luke.

Jesus says to "let the dead bury their own dead," implying that those who forsake the kingdom for perfunctory obligations are already as good as dead. They are the dead who bury the dead. If you want to really know life, Jesus would say, then die and come and follow him!

The point is reinforced with the final man, who simply wants to go and say goodbye, something that the Twelve seemed to have never done. When Elijah's servant Elisha asked for the same privilege—to go back and kiss his father and mother goodbye—the prophet let him go. Elisha was, by the way, plowing when the prophet confronted him with the call to leave home (1 Kings 19:19). But One greater than Elijah has come, and his call demands that no one who follows even looks back on their old life. The road to Jerusalem lies before us all, in one way or another, and so does the call to not look back.

LUKE 10

THE SENDING OF THE SEVENTY

10:1-3 The appointing of the Seventy.

10:4-16 Instructions for those who are on the road with Jesus.

10:17-20 The return and report of the Seventy.

THE JOY OF JESUS

10:21-24 Jesus full of joy and blessing.

A PARABLE OF UNEXPECTED MERCY

10:25-29 Setting for the parable.

10:30-35 Parable of the good Samaritan.

10:36-37 Jesus' conclusion, the lawyer's response.

A MONUMENTAL SHIFT

10:38-42 Jesus with Martha and Mary (on the road).

THE SENDING OF THE SEVENTY

[1]After this, the Lord appointed 70 others, and He sent them ahead of Him in pairs to every town and place where He Himself was about to go. [2]He told them: "The harvest is abundant, but the workers are few. Therefore, pray to the Lord of the harvest to send out workers into His harvest. [3]Now go; I'm sending you out like lambs among wolves. [4]Don't carry a money-bag, traveling bag, or sandals; don't greet anyone along the road. [5]Whatever house you enter, first say, 'Peace to this household.' [6]If a son of peace is there, your peace will rest on him; but if not, it will return to you. [7]Remain in the same house, eating and drinking what they offer, for the worker is worthy of his wages. Don't be moving from house to house. [8]When you enter any town, and they welcome you, eat the things set before you. [9]Heal the sick who are there, and tell them, 'The kingdom of God has come near you.' [10]When you enter any town, and they don't welcome you, go out into its streets and say, [11]'We are wiping off [as a witness] against you even the dust of your town that clings to our feet. Know this for certain: the kingdom of God has come near.' [12]I tell you, on that day it will be more tolerable for Sodom than for that town.

[13]"Woe to you, Chorazin! Woe to you, Bethsaida! For if the miracles that were done in you had been done in Tyre and Sidon, they would have repented long ago, sitting in sackcloth and ashes! [14]But it will be more tolerable for Tyre and Sidon at the judgment than for you. [15]And you, Capernaum, will you be exalted to heaven? No, you will go down to Hades! [16]Whoever listens to you listens to Me. Whoever rejects you rejects Me. And whoever rejects Me rejects the One who sent Me."

[17]The Seventy returned with joy, saying, "Lord, even the demons submit to us in Your name."

[18]He said to them, "I watched Satan fall from heaven like a lightning flash. [19]Look, I have given you the authority to trample on snakes and scorpions and over all the power of the enemy; nothing will ever harm you. [20]However, don't rejoice that the spirits submit to you, but rejoice that your names are written in heaven."

*B*efore we get started, let's settle this business about the Seventy or the Seventy-Two. The number comes to us from Genesis 10, a passage referred to as the "Table of Nations." The list represents all of the known nations of the world. In time the number of the nations became a symbol for the Gentile world. So Jesus' appointing of seventy (or seventy-two) disciples to be sent ahead points to the universality of the gospel, a central theme in Luke's Gospel.

Here is where the seeming discrepancy comes in. In the Hebrew Bible, the number of the nations is seventy. In the Septuagint, the ancient Greek translation of the Old Testament, the number is seventy-two. Hence, some translations of Luke have seventy and others have seventy-two. The best that scholars have come up with by way of explanation is that the original manuscript probably contained seventy, and that later scribes, who were immersed in the Septuagint, changed it to seventy-two to reflect the text as they knew it. (Incidentally, the number seventy could also reflect the seventy elders of Israel mentioned in Exodus 24:1 and other places. There are not any variant readings regarding this number, however.)

The Twelve have been chosen, appointed as "apostles," and have completed their first mission. The journey to Jerusalem has begun. Now Jesus further implements his strategy by appointing seventy "others." Like the Twelve, they are sent out two by two, so that the mouths of two witnesses can establish the truth of their message (Deut 19:15). The details of their marching orders are reminiscent of the instructions given to the Twelve in Luke 9:3-5, with a few additions. The list of the things they are allowed to take with them is slightly different. Like the Twelve, they cannot take a traveling bag or any money. The Twelve could not take a walking stick, no bread, no extra shirt. The Seventy could not take sandals. They are both commended to stay in the same house, while the Seventy are also told to eat whatever is given to them. These differences seem inconsequential.

More significant are two charges made only to the Seventy. First, Jesus tells them not to talk to anyone along the road. This is a reflection of the seriousness of their mission (see 2 Kings 4:29). Additionally, they are given the charge to speak "peace" (Hebrew *shalom)* if they find a "son of peace" there. If so, Jesus says, your peace will rest on him; if not, your peace will return to you. This authority to grant *shalom* to a particular home is connected to their identities as the *shaliakhim,* or authoritative representatives of Jesus. Although they are not specifically appointed apostles as the Twelve were, the Seventy still represent Jesus. If they are not welcomed, Jesus speaks of the most dreadful consequences for that town (v. 12). In verse 16 they are clearly included in the sanction, "whoever rejects you rejects Me."

The mention of the fate of Sodom triggers a series of woes from Jesus as he contemplates how much worse it will be for the cities of his time that refuse the gospel. The first woe is spoken to Chorazin. I have been to the ruins of this city. It contains one of the best examples of a first-century synagogue, complete with the seat of Moses. This is the only reference to Chorazin, but it implies that Jesus had done miracles there that were not well received. The next city is Bethsaida, the hometown of several of the disciples. They are compared with Tyre and Sidon, coastal pagan cities associated with Gentile paganism. Finally Capernaum, "his own city," is included in the list of condemned Jewish towns in Galilee.

It is the same language of radical reversal we have seen throughout Luke's Gospel. When Jesus spoke in the synagogue in Nazareth, the message was the same: God showed favor to the widow from Sidon and to Naaman the Syrian and not necessarily to the Israelites.

In an undisclosed period of time, the Seventy return, rejoicing that even the demons submitted to them in Jesus' name. It would seem that their first mission was more successful than that of the Twelve, who could not cast the demon from the boy after the transfiguration (Lk 9:37-40).

In response to their triumph over the demonic, Jesus shares in their joy and exults in a memory that is all his own. "I watched Satan fall from heaven," he says, referring to a moment recorded in Isaiah 14:12. Jesus reminds the disciples that they have been given authority to "trample on snakes and scorpions." He is speaking figuratively of the demons they are confronting when they are out on mission. But as great a cause for rejoicing as that is, Jesus encourages them to celebrate all the more that their names are written in heaven!

THE JOY OF JESUS

²¹In that same hour He rejoiced in the Holy Spirit and said, "I praise You, Father, Lord of heaven and earth, because You have hidden these things from the wise and the learned and have revealed them to infants. Yes, Father, because this was Your good pleasure. ²²All things have been entrusted to Me by My Father. No one knows who the Son is except the Father, and who the Father is except the Son, and anyone to whom the Son desires to reveal Him."

²³Then turning to His disciples He said privately, "The eyes that see the things you see are blessed! ²⁴For I tell you that many prophets and kings wanted to see the things you see yet didn't see them; to hear the things you hear yet didn't hear them."

*T*he successful return of the Seventy brings about a moment in the life of Jesus that is unlike any other recorded in the Gospels. If ever Jesus' joy could be said to overflow, this is the moment. It behooves those who long to bring him more joy to look more closely at it.

The successful return of the Seventy is a high point in the ministry. We are not told if the first mission of the Twelve was successful or not, but the failures that surround them before and after their first mission are not cause for hope. Also, they have begun their final journey to Jerusalem, a trip that will have precious few moments of joy. Given the flow of the ministry, this seems to be a moment when success outweighs failure. It seems to be a time when the disciples are getting it. Jesus grabs the moment while he can and returns the joy he is feeling to the Father as an act of worship.

This moment also explains the central theme of Luke: radical reversal. It helps us to see why those who should *don't*, while those who shouldn't *do*. It is because God wants it that way. Jesus is almost singing, "You have hidden these things from the wise and learned and have revealed them to infants . . . because this was Your good pleasure." This is an appropriate song coming from a man whose mother once sang, "He has satisfied the hungry with good things and sent the rich away empty" (Lk 1:53). The world is being turned upside down because the Father wants it that way, and Jesus could not be more joyful at the prospect. It is a rare moment of light on an otherwise dark journey to Jerusalem.

A PARABLE OF UNEXPECTED MERCY

25Just then an expert in the law stood up to test Him, saying, "Teacher, what must I do to inherit eternal life?"

26"What is written in the law?" He asked him. "How do you read it?"

27He answered:

> *Love the Lord your God with all your heart, with all your soul, with all your strength, and with all your mind; and your neighbor as yourself.*

28"You've answered correctly," He told him. "Do this and you will live."

29But wanting to justify himself, he asked Jesus, "And who is my neighbor?"

30Jesus took up [the question] and said: "A man was going down from Jerusalem to Jericho and fell into the hands of robbers. They stripped him, beat him up, and fled, leaving him half dead. 31A priest happened to be going down that road. When he saw him, he passed by on the other side. 32In the same way, a Levite, when he arrived at the place and saw him, passed by on the other side. 33But a Samaritan on his journey came up to him, and when he saw [the man], he had compassion. 34He went over to him and bandaged his wounds, pouring on oil and wine. Then he put him on his own animal, brought him to an inn, and took care of him. 35The next day he took out two denarii, gave them to the innkeeper, and said, 'Take care of him. When I come back I'll reimburse you for whatever extra you spend.'

36"Which of these three do you think proved to be a neighbor to the man who fell into the hands of the robbers?"

37"The one who showed mercy to him," he said.

Then Jesus told him, "Go and do the same."

So pervasive is the theme of "those who should *don't*, and those who shouldn't *do*" that it even appears in the teaching of Jesus. In the parable of the banquet, the invited refuse and the "uninvited" are dragged to the feast (Lk 14:14-24). In the parable of the lost son, the degenerate comes home, offering himself as a slave, while the older, righteous brother bitterly complains that he is the one who has been "slaving" (Lk 15:11-32). In the parable of the rich man and Lazarus, the one who had been "blessed" (by wealth) ends up in hell, while the cursed, leprous beggar ends up on Abraham's lap (Lk 16:19-31). But without a doubt, the supreme example of this theme of radical reversal is the story of the good Samaritan (Lk 10:25-37).

It seems to have been spoken in the wake of Jesus' most joyful moment, for Luke introduces the story with, "Just then . . ." Luke, who loves to show us parables at work, often tells the story of what leads up to the story, what happens in the aftermath and what effect the parable has on its hearers. The parable of the good Samaritan is one of the best examples.

We are told that the lawyer or scribe (*nomikos*) means to test Jesus with his question about eternal life. When he asks it, Jesus puts the onus back on him. How does *he* read it in the Scriptures?

As so often happens, the professional religious person who asks Jesus the question already knows the answer (see also Simon the Pharisee in Luke 7:36-50). The scribe performs right on cue. You could probably wake him in the middle of the night, press his nose and get this answer (Deut 6:5 and Lev 19:18).

"Correct," Jesus essentially says. "Now do this and you will live."

It might have been over. A question asked and answered. An affirmation granted from the rabbi. But the scribe wants more from the exchange, and so he asks a question he will later wish he had bitten his tongue off rather than asked. "And who is my neighbor?" The scribe is asking Jesus to define one of the terms from his own answer.

Just look at what Jesus does with an irritating, confrontational situation. He makes a luminous teaching moment out of it. He transforms it into a situation in which the arrogant scribe just might actually learn something!

Jesus transitions into the parable without so much as a hiccup. Someone traveling down the barren and dangerous road to Jericho is attacked, literally in the Greek, by "men of violence." He is beaten and left for dead.

A priest happens to be going down at the same time. You have to decide for yourself just what "going down" means. You have two choices. First, if it is literal, "going down" means going from Jerusalem to Jericho, which was considered the "city of priests" due to the fact that many priests chose to live there, close to Jerusalem. That would mean the priest is done with his ritual duties at the temple and should have less regard for contracting uncleanness by touching a potentially dead body. Second, "going down" could simply mean the sense in which we use it: that is, the priest is going along the road in no general direction. When the professional religious person sees the man in need, he moves over and passes by on the other side.

Then the Levite comes by. Like the priest, he would have been a descendant of Levi but not a descendant of Aaron, as the priest would be. He too assists in the temple sacrifices. He too moves over and passes by. Those who should have helped didn't.

Next comes someone who, to the Jewish way of thinking, is the last person in the world who would do the right thing: a Samaritan. The schism began when the Jews who returned from the exile refused the help of the "half-breeds": those who were the mixed descendants of the Jews who had been left behind and the pagans who had settled in the region. The animosity only grew with time. The point is that the person who shouldn't have gotten it *did*. When the Samaritan saw the suffering man, he "had compassion." If our working definition of the Hebrew word *hesed* is "when the person from whom I have a right to expect nothing gives me everything," then the Samaritan clearly exhibits *hesed*. His care for the injured man is over the top: he bandages, pours on oil to soothe the wounds and wine to disinfect them, puts him on his own donkey, takes him to the inn, cares for him there, and leaves money to cover any further care that might be needed. To top it off, he promises to come back later and check on the recovery of the nameless, wounded man.

I can see the scribe, wide-eyed, wondering where this distasteful story is going to lead, when Jesus responds to his original question with another question. It is a simple question, with an inevitable answer. "Which of these . . . proved to be a neighbor?"

Swallowing hard, the scribe cannot even bring himself to say the word "Samaritan," so he uses the circumlocution, "the one who showed mercy."

Hesed is always something you do, and so Jesus closes the interaction with the simple command, "Go and do the same." Perhaps without realizing it, the scribe's first question was just answered as well. "What must I do to inherit eternal life?"

Jesus' answer? Do *hesed*.

A MONUMENTAL SHIFT

38 While they were traveling, He entered a village, and a woman named Martha welcomed Him into her home. 39 She had a sister named Mary, who also sat at the Lord's feet and was listening to what He said. 40 But Martha was distracted by her many tasks, and she came up and asked, "Lord, don't You care that my sister has left me to serve alone? So tell her to give me a hand."

41 The Lord answered her, "Martha, Martha, you are worried and upset about many things, 42 but one thing is necessary. Mary has made the right choice, and it will not be taken away from her."

*D*on't forget that we are on the road with Jesus. Luke reminds us with the opening phrase, "While they were traveling . . ." Jesus and his disciples enter Bethany, although Luke does not give us the name of the village. This might be his first time in the home of Mary and Martha. John tells us they became friends. Lazarus is not mentioned at all. Martha, the older sister who has the responsibility of welcoming people to the home, invites Jesus in. It is a picture of the Jewish hospitality that the Twelve and the Seventy were told to depend on when they were on the road earlier.

Martha's sister, we are told, is named Miriam, or Mary. She immediately takes her place at the feet of Jesus, which is a way of saying that she becomes a pupil. Paul uses the same expression in Acts 22:3 when he speaks of being the pupil of the great rabbi Gamaliel.

It is hard to explain what a momentous paradigm shift this moment represents. In Judaism, women did not study with rabbis. Two quotes from the Mishnah, a collection of rabbinic teaching from 200 B.C. to A.D. 200, will suffice:

> If a man gives his daughter knowledge of the law it is as though he taught her lechery. (*m. Sotah* 3.4)

> He that talk much to womankind brings evil upon himself and neglects the study of the law and at last will inherit Gehenna. (*m. Abot* 1.5[7])

Martha is justifiably irritated that Mary is not lending a hand. After all, Jesus has shown up with who-knows-how-many mouths to feed. It is a legitimate complaint. Martha might have dialed back her tone a notch or two. To accuse Jesus, of all people, of not caring is a bit over the top. But clearly, he should tell Mary to get up and help out.

Jesus' response sounds gentle to me, in contrast to Martha's tense question. The double use of her name adds to the pathos. She is worried about many things, but only one is necessary, and Mary has chosen it. "[I]t will not be taken away from her," translates into, "So, no, I will not tell her to leave her place."

The notion that it is more admirable for a woman to sit and learn as opposed to working in the kitchen would have been little less than seismic in Jesus' time. This story comes under the theme of "faith before family." Mary's choice, although it goes against every conceivable standard for women in Jesus' day, is commended. This is an example of one of the most radical paradigm shifts for women in the entire Bible.

LUKE 11

A BREATH OF A PRAYER

¹He was praying in a certain place, and when He finished, one of His disciples said to Him, "Lord, teach us to pray, just as John also taught his disciples."
²He said to them, "Whenever you pray, say:

> *Father,*
> *Your name be honored as holy.*
> *Your kingdom come.*
> *³Give us each day our daily bread.*
> *⁴And forgive us our sins,*
> *for we ourselves also forgive everyone*
> *in debt to us.*
> *And do not bring us into temptation."*

⁵He also said to them: "Suppose one of you has a friend and goes to him at midnight and says to him, 'Friend, lend me three loaves of bread, ⁶because a friend of mine on a journey has come to me, and I don't have anything to offer him.' ⁷Then he will answer from inside and say, 'Don't bother me! The door is already locked, and my children and I have gone to bed. I can't get up to give you anything.' ⁸I tell you, even though he won't get up and give him anything because he is his friend, yet because of his persistence, he will get up and give him as much as he needs.

⁹"So I say to you, keep asking, and it will be given to you. Keep searching, and you will find. Keep knocking, and the door will be opened to you. ¹⁰For everyone who asks receives, and the one who searches finds, and to the one who knocks, the door will be opened. ¹¹What father among you, if his son asks for a fish, will give him a snake instead of a fish? ¹²Or if he asks for an egg, will give him a scorpion? ¹³If you then, who are evil, know how to give good gifts to your children, how much more will the heavenly Father give the Holy Spirit to those who ask Him?"

*I*f you want a window into the personal prayer life of Jesus, the Gospel of Luke is the best place to begin. When you look through the various panes of the pages of his Gospel, you will see Jesus staying up all night to pray on several occasions (for example, Lk 5:16). At every turning point, whether it was choosing the Twelve (Lk 6:12-16) or preparing for the night of the transfiguration (Lk 9:28), Luke tells us that events happened as he was praying. When Jesus angrily tears up, for the second time, in the marketplace in the temple court, Luke tells us that the real reason for Jesus' emotion is his desire that the Gentiles have a quiet place to *pray* (Lk 19:46). More than any other Gospel, Luke paints us a picture of Jesus on his knees.

You would expect, then, that we would actually get to hear Jesus praying again and again as the story of his life unfolds. But being the great storyteller that he is, Luke forces us, for eleven long chapters, to wait impatiently for that precious moment when we finally get to actually hear Jesus pray. It has been a long, long wait, and Luke understands that we, like the Twelve, simply can't wait any longer. When his disciples finally say, "Lord, teach us to pray, just as John also taught his disciples," we are so relieved and happy that they asked. Back in Luke 5:33, the Pharisees noted that Jesus' disciples do not pray like John's disciples do. Now we have a chance to witness what is different.

It is just then that we are confronted with the same "problem" with which everyone who comes close to Jesus is confronted. He always fails to meet your expectations. He almost never gives people what they expect. In fact, he almost never gives what they ask for; instead, he gives what we *should* have asked for, whether we want it or not. (He loves us so much that he is willing to risk our not liking him in order that we might learn to really love him.) The same is true when Luke finally gets around to letting us hear Jesus pray. It is not what we think we wanted to hear.

The Pharisees or other religious leaders of that day (and ours) would have provided a long, impressive prayer, filled with illusions to the Torah and to the rabbinic traditions. They would have used strictly religious language and multisyllabic words. (In fact, Jesus gives us a picture of such a person in Lk 18:9-14.) But Jesus knows that kind of prayer is not what we need.

Instead, when his disciples finally ask, Jesus provides a prayer—the shorter form of which appears only in Luke—that can be spoken in a single breath. The longer form in Matthew 6 occurs earlier in the ministry and is not spoken in response to a question from the disciples.

A child who is just learning to speak can learn to pray by means of this prayer. And if what Jesus says in Luke 10:21 is true, God will understand it as well as the prayer of someone with a Ph.D. I have always believed that the essence of profundity is simplicity, and the Lord's Prayer is the perfect expression of this.

It is a child's unique privilege to use the name "Father." Jesus, the Son, speaks to God in this way and, at the same time, gives us permission to address God that way. It has been said that praying to God as "Father" was something new. This is not strictly true. The Pharisees used the formula "our father who art in heaven," but the prayers they prayed sounded nothing like Jesus' simple prayer. What was disturbingly new was Jesus' reference to God as "Abba": the intimate name a child or sometimes even an adult uses that is much like "our papa." Unlike Mark, who uses the transliteration *abba* (Mk 14:36), Luke uses the Greek *patēr*. Scholars tend to agree, however, that it is still a translation for the more tender term.

This prayer is rooted in reality. "Give us bread for today," it asks. But in the same breath, it takes us to the extremes of "Your kingdom come." In doing so, Jesus brings together the nearness of present need and the distant hope of God breaking fully into the present, because the truth is that they are only separated by a momentary breath. The disciples have just witnessed the feeding of the five thousand, which was a lived-out fulfillment of this prayer for perfect, daily provision.

The prayer closes with the ideas of sin, forgiveness and temptation. Keeping in mind that they are the *perfect* words because Jesus chose them, we realize that they perfectly explain the correlation between these concepts. Sin must first be repented of, and so Jesus tells us to speak the words "Forgive us our sins." But forgiveness must be expressed by an appropriate response. Luke prepared us to hear this word in the story of Simon and the sinful woman (Lk 7:47). Forgiving and being forgiven are two sides of the same coin. Jesus knows that when we cannot find it in ourselves to forgive someone else, it is because we have lost sight of all for which we have been forgiven.

Jesus' closing words place our dependence back where it belongs: on the Father. Is Jesus saying that God is the cause of temptation? No, of course not (see Jas 1:13). But as in Job, he who is sovereign over everything places boundaries on just how far we can be tempted (1 Cor 10:13). Later on, Jesus will echo this same idea when he tells his disciples to pray that they will not fall into temptation (Lk 22:46).

Jesus teaches us that what we ask for in prayer is rarely what we need. We usually ask for provision, when the God who knows how to give good gifts is ready to give us his presence through the Holy Spirit. And so the prayer Jesus gives us, which can be spoken in a single breath, is rooted in the request for his breath—for his Spirit.

Jesus follows the example of prayer with the first of two parables he will tell on the topic of prayer. (The other is found in Lk 18:1-8.) It is a delightfully rustic story of two men, one who needs bread in the middle of the night and the other who is sound asleep in the family bed amid a pile of slumbering little children. It is a story based on the obligations of Jewish hospitality—the kind of hospitality Jesus and the disciples have just received from Martha and on which they depended for their lives when they were on the road.

The first man has had a surprise visitor in the middle of the night, and his cupboard is empty. After he knocks at his friend's door, he hears a sleepy voice from the inside telling him to go away: everyone is asleep. Anyone with children, especially more than one, understands his reluctance to wake them up. Without painting a detailed picture of the first man persistently knocking until the sleeper gets up to help, Jesus implies that his persistence does the trick and that he finally gets what he wants. That is by far the most popular interpretation of this parable. But there is another.

In Luke 11:8, the "his" in the phrase "because of his persistence" is normally thought to refer to the first man—the one who is knocking. But the Greek is ambiguous. It could refer to the sleeper. And the word translated "persistence" can also mean "shameless." In this version, the sleeper gets up and provides for his friend because he wants to avoid the shame of violating the law of hospitality.

I lean toward this second view. I like the idea that our confidence in prayer should come not from us "getting it right"—that is, knocking long enough for the door to open—but rather from the knowledge that the One who sometimes seems to be sleeping will answer because of his commitment to doing what he has promised. When Jesus uses the rabbinic "how much more" *(qal vahomer)* at the conclusion of this block of teaching, he places the parable within that interpretive context. That is, if the lazy, good-for-nothing neighbor will get up to avoid being shamed, then *how much more* will the Lord answer the door of prayer when we knock?

In verse 9 Jesus sums it up like this: ask, seek, knock. Be confident in prayer, not because you have gotten the words just right (hence the bald-faced simplicity of the prayer Jesus had just taught them) but because of the goodness of the One to whom you are praying.

THE FINGER OF GOD

¹⁴Now He was driving out a demon that was mute. When the demon came out, the man who had been mute, spoke, and the crowds were amazed. ¹⁵But some of them said, "He drives out demons by Beelzebul, the ruler of the demons!" ¹⁶And others, as a test, were demanding of Him a sign from heaven.

¹⁷Knowing their thoughts, He told them: "Every kingdom divided against itself is headed for destruction, and a house divided against itself falls. ¹⁸If Satan also is divided against himself, how will his kingdom stand? For you say I drive out demons by Beelzebul. ¹⁹And if I drive out demons by Beelzebul, who is it your sons drive them out by? For this reason they will be your judges. ²⁰If I drive out demons by the finger of God, then the kingdom of God has come to you. ²¹When a strong man, fully armed, guards his estate, his possessions are secure. ²²But when one stronger than he attacks and overpowers him, he takes from him all his weapons he trusted in, and divides up his plunder. ²³Anyone who is not with Me is against Me, and anyone who does not gather with Me scatters.

²⁴"When an unclean spirit comes out of a man, it roams through waterless places looking for rest, and not finding rest, it then says, 'I'll go back to my house where I came from.' ²⁵And returning, it finds [the house] swept and put in order. ²⁶Then it goes and brings seven other spirits more evil than itself, and they enter and settle down there. As a result, that man's last condition is worse than the first."

²⁷As He was saying these things, a woman from the crowd raised her voice and said to Him, "The womb that bore You and the one who nursed You are blessed!"

²⁸He said, "Even more, those who hear the word of God and keep it are blessed!"

*T*he next scene takes place before a divided crowd with mixed motives. Luke tells us that some still want to see a sign, while others are ready to say Jesus' power comes from Satan. Some are still simply amazed.

Jesus is casting out a demon from a man who is mute. When it is all over, he can speak once more. This is what amazes one segment of the divided crowd. But it causes others to accuse Jesus of casting out demons by the power of Beelzebul, the prince of demons, a name whose background can be found in 2 Kings 1:2.

Jesus' response is not so much spiritual but plain common sense. Satan wouldn't work against himself, or else his kingdom would be divided. And besides, if Jesus is doing this with Satan's help, then who must be helping the sons of the Pharisees who are likewise casting out demons? They seem to be silenced by this.

The kingdom of God must be here, Jesus says, because I am casting out demons by "the finger of God." When Pharaoh's magicians saw the plague of gnats in Exodus 8:19, they responded, "This is the finger of God." And the tablets of the commandments were said to have been written by the finger of God (Ex 31:18; Deut 9:10). Jesus appeals to a powerful image, one that would have arrested the attention of the Pharisees. He is claiming his power comes from exactly the same source. He is saying that the same finger that engraved the commandments they claim to revere is now actively working among them. And with that finger he can overpower the "strong man" who is guarding his estate. Jesus is the stronger One who is attacking and overpowering, stripping the strong man of his panoply of weapons, all with his finger. In this battle there is no neutral place, says Jesus. You are either for me or against me. It is a challenge to the Pharisees to choose.

His power and authority are clearly being demonstrated as the demonic forces are scattered. It is a clear sign that the kingdom of God has come, vested with the power of "the finger of God." When Satan's victims are freed from his power, then clearly their master is being overcome.

From the mixed crowd comes a voice. It is a woman who seeks to bless Jesus by praising his mother, a common notion in the ancient world. Jesus does not deny or push aside the blessing. He simply adds to it that those who hear and do the word of God are even more blessed. In Hebrew the word for "hear"—*shema*—also implies doing.

THE SIGN OF THE SON OF MAN

²⁹As the crowds were increasing, He began saying: "This generation is an evil generation. It demands a sign, but no sign will be given to it except the sign of Jonah. ³⁰For just as Jonah became a sign to the people of Nineveh, so also the Son of Man will be to this generation. ³¹The queen of the south will rise up at the judgment with the men of this generation and condemn them, because she came from the ends of the earth to hear the wisdom of Solomon, and look—something greater than Solomon is here! ³²The men of Nineveh will rise up at the judgment with this generation and condemn it, because they repented at Jonah's proclamation, and look—something greater than Jonah is here!

³³"No one lights a lamp and puts it in the cellar or under a basket, but on a lampstand, so that those who come in may see its light. ³⁴Your eye is the lamp of the body. When your eye is good, your whole body is also full of light. But when it is bad, your body is also full of darkness. ³⁵Take care then, that the light in you is not darkness. ³⁶If therefore your whole body is full of light, with no part of it in darkness, the whole body will be full of light, as when a lamp shines its light on you."

Luke begins this segment of the narrative by telling us that the crowds are increasing. I take this to mean that as they are traveling to Jerusalem, people are being attracted to the crowd, which is causing it to continually grow. Jesus does not see an ever-growing audience as a sign of success. He says that their frequent demands for a sign are evil (v. 16). No sign will be given except that of Jonah. In Matthew 12:40, Jesus explains that even as Jonah was in the belly of the fish for three days, so he will be in the heart of the earth for three days.

Next Jesus strings together examples of pagans who got it when the Jews, who should have gotten it, didn't. It reminds us of the lists he gave in the synagogue at Nazareth (Lk 4:25-27) and of the woes he pronounced on Chorazin and the other Jewish cities (Lk 10:13-16). The pagan queen of the south recognized the sign of Solomon and his wisdom, just as the pagan Ninevites recognized the sign of Jonah. Now someone greater than both Solomon and Jonah is here, and yet the crowd still demands miraculous signs. They don't recognize that Jesus himself is the sign!

Quoting a proverb he used before in Luke 8:16 to demonstrate that nothing will be hidden, Jesus uses the image of the lamp, either meaninglessly hidden in the crypt or put forth on a lamp stand for all to see. Your eye, which is the "lamp" of your body, will let in good light if it is good. If it is bad there will only be darkness inside you. Jesus appeals to basic physics. When a door is opened to a darkened room, the light floods in and illumines every corner. The darkness does not extinguish the light. It is always pushed back. The evil generation should simply look to the sure sign of the Light that is Jesus. Then they would stop asking for other signs, for no more signs will be coming.

THE PROPHET AT THE DINNER TABLE

37 As He was speaking, a Pharisee asked Him to dine with him. So He went in and reclined at the table. 38 When the Pharisee saw this, he was amazed that He did not first perform the ritual washing before dinner. 39 But the Lord said to him: "Now you Pharisees clean the outside of the cup and dish, but inside you are full of greed and evil. 40 Fools! Didn't He who made the outside make the inside too? 41 But give to charity what is within, and then everything is clean for you.

42 "But woe to you Pharisees! You give a tenth of mint, rue, and every kind of herb, and you bypass justice and love for God. These things you should have done without neglecting the others.

43 "Woe to you Pharisees! You love the front seat in the synagogues and greetings in the marketplaces.

44 "Woe to you! You are like unmarked graves; the people who walk over them don't know it."

45 One of the experts in the law answered Him, "Teacher, when You say these things You insult us too."

46 Then He said: "Woe also to you experts in the law! You load people with burdens that are hard to carry, yet you yourselves don't touch these burdens with one of your fingers.

47 "Woe to you! You build monuments to the prophets, and your fathers killed them. 48 Therefore you are witnesses that you approve the deeds of your fathers, for they killed them, and you build their monuments. 49 Because of this, the wisdom of God said, 'I will send them prophets and apostles, and some of them they will kill and persecute,' 50 so that this generation may be held responsible for the blood of all the prophets shed since the foundation of the world; 51 from the blood of Abel to the blood of Zechariah, who perished between the altar and the sanctuary.

"Yes, I tell you, this generation will be held responsible.

52 "Woe to you experts in the law! You have taken away the key of knowledge! You didn't go in yourselves, and you hindered those who were going in."

53 When He left there, the scribes and the Pharisees began to oppose Him fiercely and to cross-examine Him about many things; 54 they were lying in wait for Him to trap Him in something He said.

*Y*ou should always be careful about inviting a prophet to dinner. This is the second of three times Jesus is seen sharing meal fellowship with a Pharisee (Lk 7:36; 14:1). All three of these incidents are found only in Luke, although Matthew will repeat some of these woes in 23:13-33. Being the long-time traveling companion of Paul, the Pharisee of the Pharisees, no doubt caused Luke to be sensitive to stories about this influential religious order that so dominated Jesus' time.

In chapter 5 we learned that Jesus and his disciples did not fast or pray according to what was deemed orthodox by the Pharisees. In chapter 6 we saw that they were not strictly "observant" when it came to working on the Sabbath. We have seen an almost continuous stream of healings by Jesus on the Sabbath, which was also interpreted as a violation of their oral tradition. In chapter 7 he actually touched the coffin of a dead boy, which was a clear violation of the laws of clean and unclean. Now we will learn that Jesus is similarly "lax" when it comes to the minute requirements of ritual washing.

As they all settle into their places on the triclinium, a couch extending around three sides of a dining table, the host notices, to his amusement, that Jesus has not ritually washed his hands. This does not mean that he failed to scrub them with soap so as to avoid the spread of infection. No, Jesus simply neglected to pour some water over his hands as a ritual gesture.

In Jesus' time there were two schools of Pharisaic thought. First was the school of Hillel the Great. He had been a woodcutter by profession and was known for his gentleness and concern for the poor. The other, far more severe group was the house of Shammai. Shammai was a contemporary of Hillel's who was famous for the most severe interpretation of the law. After Hillel died around A.D. 20, his influence waned and the school of Shammai took control of the Sanhedrin. The Pharisees with whom Jesus continually locked horns, like the host of this meal, were the house of Shammai. On any given point of conflict, Jesus almost always sided with Hillel. Shammai taught that the outside of the cup must be clean but not necessarily the inside. Hillel taught that the inside should be washed first.

Jesus, realizing what they are thinking, goes into full prophetic mode. With disturbing clarity he cites the hypocrisy of the Pharisees, who, like one of their cups, are clean on the outside but inside are full of greed. The only way to turn things around, according to Jesus, would be for them to give the food inside their plates to the poor. (This is a very Hillelite thing to say!)

Then, in pure prophetic form, the woes begin to come forth. Woe to they who fastidiously tithe their spices while forgetting about justice and loving God. They only want the best seats in the synagogue and formal greetings in the marketplace. Just as if they had walked over an unmarked grave, people become unclean without even knowing it every time they come in contact with the Pharisees. As Jesus stops to catch his breath, one of the scribes or lawyers interrupts to ask whether Jesus realizes that, when he says such things, he is insulting them too.

With that, Jesus turns on the scribes with an equal prophetic fury. They are placing a tremendous burden on the people with all their exacting legal demands and yet they won't lift a finger to help.

It is ironic, Jesus points out, that they are currently building monuments to the prophets their forefathers killed! They will be held responsible for all of it, from the blood from Abel (Gen 4:8) to Zechariah (2 Chron 24:20-21). Genesis was the first book in the Old Testament canon, while in their Scriptures, 2 Chronicles was the very last book. So, from the first murder to the last, they will all pay at the judgment!

Jesus reserves one final shot for the scribes, who should have kept their mouths shut. The key of knowledge, which they are supposed to possess, they have taken away from the people. The door remains locked. They don't care to go in, and, in the process, they keep out those who want to enter.

Does a silent, tense meal follow all these fireworks, or is it simply a matter of a slamming door? Luke does not tell us, perhaps because he thinks we don't need to know. From this point the heat is applied. The Pharisees, who before were simply the naysayers, begin to actively oppose Jesus, cross-examining him every chance they get, lying in wait to trap Jesus with every one of his luminous words.

LUKE 12

WHAT TO FEAR AND WHAT NOT TO FEAR

12:1-12 Encouragements and warnings.

I'LL SAY TO MYSELF, "SELF . . ."

12:13-21 Parable of the rich fool.

12:22-31 Parables of the ravens and the lilies.

12:32-34 "Don't be afraid, little flock . . ."

THE SLAVING SAVIOR

12:35-40 Parable of Jesus' coming and service at the banquet.

12:41-48 Application (to Peter).

FIRE ON THE EARTH

12:49-53 The divisiveness of the gospel.

12:54-59 The hypocrisy of failing to interpret the signs.

WHAT TO FEAR AND WHAT NOT TO FEAR

¹In these circumstances, a crowd of many thousands came together, so that they were trampling on one another. He began to say to His disciples first: "Be on your guard against the yeast of the Pharisees, which is hypocrisy. ²There is nothing covered that won't be uncovered, nothing hidden that won't be made known. ³Therefore whatever you have said in the dark will be heard in the light, and what you have whispered in an ear in private rooms will be proclaimed on the housetops.

⁴"And I say to you, My friends, don't fear those who kill the body, and after that can do nothing more. ⁵But I will show you the One to fear: Fear Him who has authority to throw [people] into hell after death. Yes, I say to you, this is the One to fear! ⁶Aren't five sparrows sold for two pennies? Yet not one of them is forgotten in God's sight. ⁷Indeed, the hairs of your head are all counted. Don't be afraid; you are worth more than many sparrows!

⁸"And I say to you, anyone who acknowledges Me before men, the Son of Man will also acknowledge him before the angels of God, ⁹but whoever denies Me before men will be denied before the angels of God. ¹⁰Anyone who speaks a word against the Son of Man will be forgiven, but the one who blasphemes against the Holy Spirit will not be forgiven. ¹¹Whenever they bring you before synagogues and rulers and authorities, don't worry about how you should defend yourselves or what you should say. ¹²For the Holy Spirit will teach you at that very hour what must be said."

*T*he temptation is to say that Jesus and his disciples have passed the point of no return on their journey to Jerusalem and that the momentum from now on will propel them up to the holy city. In one sense, perhaps, a case could be made for this idea, but the truth is that, at any point, Jesus could say "no" to the Father's will and simply disappear. The possibility has to be there. I can imagine the words from Hebrews 10:7 echoing through his mind, sometimes encouragingly and sometimes terrifyingly: "I have come . . . to do Your will, O God." No, it is not any sort of imagined momentum that Jesus is riding; it is his own desire for radical obedience.

The crowd has grown to many thousands. This must be not only because the fame of Jesus is growing but also because Passover is near. That means that the population of Jerusalem will grow by tens of thousands as pilgrims from all over the country come to the city to celebrate the most important feast of the year.

In the midst of the noise and confusion, Jesus turns to the disciples and warns them to guard against hypocrisy, which is like the yeast that is a part of the Passover observance. Every trace of yeast had to be removed from the home for the celebration to go on. Yeast is a perfect metaphor for sin: the tiniest thimble-full will eventually work its way through an entire batch of bread dough. Sin is like that—particularly the sin of hypocrisy, of which the Pharisees are particularly guilty. Jesus knows the coercive pressure of the crowd. The disciples, who are already arguing about which one of them is the greatest, will be easy targets for hypocrisy. The best guard against such sin is the reminder that every one of their whispered conceits will be shouted from the rooftops. This is becoming a persistent part of Jesus' message to them. Twice already he has spoken about the light that cannot be hidden. It is all going to be revealed, he says again and again. Everything that people have tried to hide will be uncovered.

The pressure will increase proportionately as they near Jerusalem. As it does, Jesus' teaching will become concentrated. There will be more maxims—shortened sayings that are easy to remember. And, as he does here, Jesus will tell them what they should and should not fear. If you listen with your imagination fully engaged, taking into account the flow of the ministry, you will detect this note of urgency that will only grow with time. You should fear this . . . but don't fear that. Don't fear the one who can kill your body; fear the one who can throw you into hell! Don't worry about what you will say when you are dragged before rulers. Don't worry; you are precious to God, who knows the number of hairs on your head. Don't fear humans; fear blasphemy. Luke 12:4-12 provides the overture for a block of teaching that will extend to Luke 20. Here is a partial list of Jesus' maxims:

- Don't be afraid; you are worth more than many sparrows! (Lk 12:7)

- One's life is not in the abundance of his possessions. (Lk 12:15)

- For life is more than food and the body more than clothing. (Lk 12:23)

- But seek His kingdom, and these things will be provided for you. (Lk 12:31)

- For where your treasure is, there your heart will be also. (Lk 12:34)

- Much will be required of everyone who has been given much. And even more will be expected of the one who has been entrusted with more. (Lk 12:48)

- Note this: some are last who will be first, and some are first who will be last. (Lk 13:30)

- For everyone who exalts himself will be humbled, and the one who humbles himself will be exalted. (Lk 14:11; see also Phil 2:6-11)

- Whoever does not bear his own cross and come after Me cannot be My disciple. (Lk 14:27)

- Now, salt is good, but if salt should lose its taste, how will it be made salty? (Lk 14:34)

- I tell you, in the same way, there will be more joy in heaven over one sinner who repents than over 99 righteous people who don't need repentance. (Lk 15:7)

- I tell you, in the same way, there is joy in the presence of God's angels over one sinner who repents. (Lk 15:10)

- But we had to celebrate and rejoice, because this brother of yours was dead and is alive again; he was lost and is found. (Lk 15:32) (This maxim is contained within a parable.)

- No household slave can be the slave of two masters. . . . You can't be slaves to both God and money. (Lk 16:13)

- For what is highly admired by people is revolting in God's sight. (Lk 16:15)

- If they don't listen to Moses and the prophets, they will not be persuaded if someone rises from the dead. (Lk 16:31) (This maxim is contained within a parable.)

- Where the corpse is, there also the vultures will be gathered. (Lk 17:37)

- Maxim from Luke 14:11 repeated in Luke 18:14.

- I assure you: Whoever does not welcome the kingdom of God like a little child will never enter it. (Lk 18:17)

- What is impossible with men is possible with God. (Lk 18:27)

- Everyone who falls on that stone will be broken to pieces, and if it falls on anyone, it will grind him to powder! (Lk 20:18)

- Give back to Caesar the things that are Caesar's and to God the things that are God's. (Lk 20:25)

Past the middle section of chapter 20, these kinds of sayings virtually disappear from the narrative. From this point on there will be precious little time for teaching. These final sayings of Jesus demand that we tune our ears to recognize the distilled statements, the encapsulated lessons on what to fear and what not to fear, on what is valuable and what is not. The disciples are going to need this clarity.

I'LL SAY TO MYSELF, "SELF . . ."

[13] Someone from the crowd said to Him, "Teacher, tell my brother to divide the inheritance with me."

[14] "Friend," He said to him, "who appointed Me a judge or arbitrator over you?" [15] He then told them, "Watch out and be on guard against all greed because one's life is not in the abundance of his possessions."

[16] Then He told them a parable: "A rich man's land was very productive. [17] He thought to himself, 'What should I do, since I don't have anywhere to store my crops? [18] I will do this,' he said. 'I'll tear down my barns and build bigger ones, and store all my grain and my goods there. [19] Then I'll say to myself, "You have many goods stored up for many years. Take it easy; eat, drink, and enjoy yourself."'

[20] "But God said to him, 'You fool! This very night your life is demanded of you. And the things you have prepared—whose will they be?'

[21] "That's how it is with the one who stores up treasure for himself and is not rich toward God."

²²*Then He said to His disciples: "Therefore I tell you, don't worry about your life, what you will eat; or about the body, what you will wear.* ²³*For life is more than food and the body more than clothing.* ²⁴*Consider the ravens: they don't sow or reap; they don't have a storeroom or a barn; yet God feeds them. Aren't you worth much more than the birds?* ²⁵*Can any of you add a cubit to his height by worrying?* ²⁶*If then you're not able to do even a little thing, why worry about the rest?*

²⁷*"Consider how the wildflowers grow: they don't labor or spin thread. Yet I tell you, not even Solomon in all his splendor was adorned like one of these!* ²⁸*If that's how God clothes the grass, which is in the field today and is thrown into the furnace tomorrow, how much more will He do for you—you of little faith?* ²⁹*Don't keep striving for what you should eat and what you should drink, and don't be anxious.* ³⁰*For the Gentile world eagerly seeks all these things, and your Father knows that you need them.*

³¹*"But seek His kingdom, and these things will be provided for you.* ³²*Don't be afraid, little flock, because your Father delights to give you the kingdom.* ³³*Sell your possessions and give to the poor. Make money-bags for yourselves that won't grow old, an inexhaustible treasure in heaven, where no thief comes near and no moth destroys.* ³⁴*For where your treasure is, there your heart will be also.*

*T*he next section begins with another person shouting from the crowd. Someone wants Jesus, the rabbi, to do what rabbis were often asked to do: make a decision on a point of Jewish law. (Compare with John 8, where Jesus is asked to decide the fate of the woman taken in adultery.) It is almost as if Jesus shouts back over his shoulder, "Man, who appointed me a judge between you?" He does not, will not engage the man. Instead, Jesus turns back to the disciples and gives them one more thing to add to the list of what to fear: greed. Jesus takes what might have otherwise been an irritating intrusion—someone shouting at him from the mob—and turns it into a valuable lesson for the disciples.

As he launches into his story, Jesus paints the image of an exceedingly rich man who, unfortunately, is also a buffoon. His vast property has yielded a bountiful crop. He thinks to himself (and remember: anyone in Luke who thinks to themselves is bad!), *I'll tear down my old barns and build bigger newer ones, to hold all my crops and all my stuff.* For the words he speaks to himself like a fool, the Greek literally and clumsily says, "I'll say to my *self*, '*Self*, take it easy, eat, drink and be merry." "Eat, drink and be merry" is the chief motto of a worldly value system (Is 22:13; 1 Cor 15:32).

Just as the rich fool leans back, admiring all of this stuff, God appears and his illusion is shattered. "You fool," God thunders, "this very night your life [self or psyche, which is also translated "soul"] is demanded of you."

As the impact of the parable is soaking in, Jesus proceeds with his list of what to fear and what not to fear. Don't worry about food or clothes, he tells his listeners. Considering the fact that they have already been sent out on a mission with no food or extra clothes, this should be a lesson they are beginning to understand. Before it was sparrows he alluded to; now it is ravens. God provides for them and they do not sow or reap. They have no storerooms (unlike the idiot in the parable he had just told), and yet God feeds them. The sparrows, the ravens: they are all parables to the person who has the eyes to see and the ears to hear.

Lilies . . . they are parables too. Just look at them. They didn't spin or sew their beautiful adornment, and yet they outshine Solomon on his best day. So why worry about clothes? Don't worry about what you will eat or drink. Instead, seek the kingdom of God and all the rest will come. By not worrying about the wrong things, Jesus' disciples will be free to worry about the right things.

Luke 12:32 sounds to me like the finale of this beautifully illustrated and orchestrated sermon on what to and what not to fear. The final note is, "Don't be afraid, little flock." They have already been given all that they could be given: the kingdom. They should simply let everything else go. Finally comes the maxim, that memorable phrase: "For where your treasure is, there your heart will be also."

THE SLAVING SAVIOR

³⁵ *"Be ready for service and have your lamps lit.* ³⁶ *You must be like people waiting for their master to return from the wedding banquet so that when he*

comes and knocks, they can open [the door] for him at once. *37 Those slaves the master will find alert when he comes will be blessed. I assure you: He will get ready, have them recline at the table, then come and serve them. 38 If he comes in the middle of the night, or even near dawn, and finds them alert, those slaves are blessed. 39 But know this: if the homeowner had known at what hour the thief was coming, he would not have let his house be broken into. 40 You also be ready, because the Son of Man is coming at an hour that you do not expect."*

41 "Lord," Peter asked, "are You telling this parable to us or to everyone?"

42 The Lord said: "Who then is the faithful and sensible manager his master will put in charge of his household servants to give them their allotted food at the proper time? 43 That slave whose master finds him working when he comes will be rewarded. 44 I tell you the truth: he will put him in charge of all his possessions. 45 But if that slave says in his heart, 'My master is delaying his coming,' and starts to beat the male and female slaves, and to eat and drink and get drunk, 46 that slave's master will come on a day he does not expect him and at an hour he does not know. He will cut him to pieces and assign him a place with the unbelievers. 47 And that slave who knew his master's will and didn't prepare himself or do it will be severely beaten. 48 But the one who did not know and did things deserving of blows will be beaten lightly. Much will be required of everyone who has been given much. And even more will be expected of the one who has been entrusted with more.

Once the lesson about not being afraid begins to take hold in the lives of the disciples, they will be ready for the next step: learning to be watchful. Jesus draws his parable from a tradition in Judaism that would have had powerful associations with the disciples: the wedding feast.

In their culture, as the wedding feast was winding down, a special friend of the bridegroom known as the *shoshabin* would slip out with the bride and escort her to the bridal chamber. Once she was safely deposited inside, he would stand outside and guard the door of the bridal chamber, because sometimes brides had actually been stolen. The *shoshabin* would then wait in the darkness for the sound of the bridegroom's familiar voice. Only when he was positively identified would the bridegroom be allowed inside to consummate the wedding vows. In John 3:29, John the Baptist presents himself as "the groom's friend."

In this passage it is not so much an individual friend of the bridegroom but his slaves who are in view. They are not standing outside but rather waiting faithfully inside. When he knocks, they leap to their feet and open the door. They do not leave him standing outside in the dark. To the servants who are found ready, something remarkable, something unthinkable is going to happen, says Jesus. The master is going to dress himself as a slave, invite them to recline around the banquet table and wait on them! It is the height of radical reversal. The master becomes the slave, and the slaves become the objects of his service. But, says Jesus, as he comes to the end of this image, they should be ready to wait even until the early hours of dawn.

Abruptly, Jesus shifts the image from a wedding banquet to a break-in. Still, the point is watchfulness. The disciples need to be watching for the return of the bridegroom, but they also need to keep an eye peeled for the coming of the thief, for he also breaks in when you least expect it. So whether Jesus comes as the master or as the thief (Rev 16:15), the disciples must be watching and waiting. This will be the true indication of their faithfulness to him.

If the feast in the parable is literally the feast that occurs upon Jesus' second coming (Is 25:6; Rev 19:9), then it sounds as if something is going to occur that none of us could possibly expect. It sounds as if Jesus, who is the same yesterday, today and forever (Heb 13:8), is going to do at that final feast exactly what he did in John 13, when he washes his disciples' feet. He gets up from the table, dresses himself to serve and waits on them as a slave (Phil 2:7). In Jesus we should come to expect the unexpected. And when we are seated at that glorious feast, we should not be surprised if he comes to our place at the table and asks if there is anything else he can do.

Given the thousands that are flocking around them, Peter is not sure just who Jesus has been addressing: everyone around them or just the disciples? At first Jesus seems to ignore Peter's question, but in fact, as we follow the rest of the discussion, we find he is talking to his servants, the disciples, after all.

When Jesus refers in verse 42 to the "manager" who is in charge of the servants, I wonder if he doesn't have Peter in mind. He will become the chief servant of the Twelve, the slave who becomes responsible in many ways for the care and feeding of the other sheep (especially in light of Jn 21:15-17).

Jesus extends the original parable to fully answer Peter's question. The servants who continue to faithfully watch will be generously rewarded. But those who begin to doubt the master's return and to abuse the ones with whose care they were entrusted will be punished with unimaginable severity. Perhaps Peter has been hoping that Jesus wasn't talking to them, but, truth be told, they have no choice. If they follow Jesus, not simply to Jerusalem but for the rest of their lives, they have no choice but to become the faithful servants of Jesus.

FIRE ON THE EARTH

⁴⁹*"I came to bring fire on the earth, and how I wish it were already set ablaze! ⁵⁰But I have a baptism to be baptized with, and how it consumes Me until it is finished! ⁵¹Do you think that I came here to give peace to the earth? No, I tell you, but rather division! ⁵²From now on, five in one household will be divided: three against two, and two against three.*

> ⁵³*They will be divided, father against son,*
> *son against father,*
> *mother against daughter,*
> *daughter against mother,*
> *mother-in-law against her daughter-in-law,*
> *and daughter-in-law against mother-in-law."*

⁵⁴*He also said to the crowds: "When you see a cloud rising in the west, right away you say, 'A storm is coming,' and so it does. ⁵⁵And when the south wind is blowing, you say, 'It's going to be a scorcher!' and it is. ⁵⁶Hypocrites! You know how to interpret the appearance of the earth and the sky, but why don't you know how to interpret this time?*

⁵⁷"Why don't you judge for yourselves what is right? ⁵⁸As you are going with your adversary to the ruler, make an effort to settle with him on the way. Then he won't drag you before the judge, the judge hand you over to the bailiff, and the bailiff throw you into prison. ⁵⁹I tell you, you will never get out of there until you have paid the last cent."

*I*f you have been sensitive to Jesus' tone for the last several verses, you notice here that it is becoming more heated. In this last block of Luke 12, it begins to boil over.

All around him is a crowd of people who are nurturing all sorts of misinformed aspirations about Jesus and his ministry. In verse 49, he does his best to undeceive them. Those of us today who cherish our own one-dimensional view of the uncontroversial "gentle Jesus, meek and mild" should sense this rebuke directed our own way.

His voice modulating, Jesus speaks of bringing the fire of judgment on the earth. He says that he longs even now for it to be kindled. But in Jerusalem it is Jesus who will be consumed by that fire, what he refers to here as his "baptism."

It is not peace he has come to bring but division. Here Luke uses one of the seven hundred words that are found nowhere else in the New Testament. It is the Greek word *diamerismos* and is normally translated "division." But it is a strong word that indicates "diametric opposition." People won't simply be divided up because of Jesus; they will fight against one another on account of him. So Jesus does the math: a household of five will be divided, three against two and two against three. In contrast to John the Baptist's ministry, which turned the hearts of the fathers back to their children (Lk 1:17), Jesus will become a wedge between father and son, between mother and daughter, even between the in-laws. We bristle at these words, as well we should, but the reality is that in the rest of the world, more believers are dying at the hands of their own family members than ever before.

Jesus turns to the massive crowd. He finds it unforgivable that they understand that an eastern wind coming off the Mediterranean carries rain while a southern wind, from the desert, brings heat. They have become remarkably good at forecasting the winds that bring their weather, yet they are oblivious to the wind that is howling around them this very moment. His voice rising to crescendo, Jesus calls them "hypocrites," the very sin he had just warned the disciples about.

Although I imagine the volume of Jesus' voice coming down for this final parable, the intensity in his voice must have remained strong. Jesus warns the people that as they are on their way to be judged, they need to settle their differences with their adversary. This is not practical advice about avoiding lawsuits. It is a parable about coming into agreement with God before the judgment. It strikes me how different Jesus' tone is now from what it was earlier, when he spoke to his disciples about not being afraid (Lk 12:32). It is a reminder to us to remain sensitive both to tone as well as the flow of the narrative as we engage with Scripture with our imaginations.

LUKE 13

A COMMENTARY ON THE "JOB EQUATION"

¹At that time, some people came and reported to Him about the Galileans whose blood Pilate had mixed with their sacrifices. ²And He responded to them, "Do you think that these Galileans were more sinful than all Galileans because they suffered these things? ³No, I tell you; but unless you repent, you will all perish as well! ⁴Or those 18 that the tower in Siloam fell on and killed—do you think they were more sinful than all the people who live in Jerusalem? ⁵No, I tell you; but unless you repent, you will all perish as well!"

⁶And He told this parable: "A man had a fig tree that was planted in his vineyard. He came looking for fruit on it and found none. ⁷He told the vineyard worker, 'Listen, for three years I have come looking for fruit on this fig tree and haven't found any. Cut it down! Why should it even waste the soil?'

⁸"But he replied to him, 'Sir, leave it this year also, until I dig around it and fertilize it. ⁹Perhaps it will bear fruit next year, but if not, you can cut it down.'"

¹⁰As He was teaching in one of the synagogues on the Sabbath, ¹¹a woman was there who had been disabled by a spirit for over 18 years. She was bent over and could not straighten up at all. ¹²When Jesus saw her, He called out to her, "Woman, you are free of your disability." ¹³Then He laid His hands on her, and instantly she was restored and began to glorify God.

¹⁴But the leader of the synagogue, indignant because Jesus had healed on the Sabbath, responded by telling the crowd, "There are six days when work should be done; therefore come on those days and be healed and not on the Sabbath day."

¹⁵But the Lord answered him and said, "Hypocrites! Doesn't each one of you untie his ox or donkey from the feeding trough on the Sabbath, and lead it to water? ¹⁶Satan has bound this woman, a daughter of Abraham, for 18 years—shouldn't she be untied from this bondage on the Sabbath day?"

¹⁷When He had said these things, all His adversaries were humiliated, but the whole crowd was rejoicing over all the glorious things He was doing.

¹⁸He said therefore, "What is the kingdom of God like, and what can I compare it to? ¹⁹It's like a mustard seed that a man took and sowed in his garden. It grew and became a tree, and the birds of the sky nested in its branches."

20 Again He said, "What can I compare the kingdom of God to? 21 It's like yeast that a woman took and mixed into 50 pounds of flour until it spread through the entire mixture."

The "Job equation" is a simple formula that says if you are bad, you will suffer, while if you are good, you will prosper. On one hand, it represents the fundamental tenet of the law. If you are obedient, God blesses you; if you are disobedient, God disciplines you. On the other hand, there is more going on in the world that renders the equation not quite as simple as it may seem.

Job discovered that even though he was innocent, great suffering came into his life. His friends were the eloquent proponents of the equation (Job 4:7). Likewise Asaph discovered, to his dismay, that those who disobeyed were actually healthy and prosperous while he suffered almost continually for no reason (Ps 73). The Wisdom writings resonate with these kinds of questions regarding the inadequacy of the equation. The best answer, as far as I can understand it, is that God uses suffering to save the world and that the connection between sin and suffering is never as simple as we want it to be.

Since Jesus recently talked about fire and judgment, someone in the crowd brings up an incident in which Pilate murdered a group of Galileans who were offering sacrifices. No one knows specifically which event is in view here; Pilate was guilty of so much bloodletting that it is hard to know. The implication from the crowd seems to be that the Galileans who were killed only suffered what their sins deserved. Jesus won't hear of it. Were these particular Galileans any less guilty than *all* Galileans? He brings the focus away from benign theological discussion and pointedly back to personal repentance. Jesus brings up another indeterminate incident, involving the collapse of a tower in Siloam that killed eighteen people. Again the point is made: they did not suffer because they were more sinful than any other particular eighteen people. "Unless *you* repent," Jesus says, "you will all perish as well."

The conflict gives birth to a parable involving a worker in a vineyard, the owner of the vineyard and a fruitless fig tree. For three years, roughly the same period of time as Jesus' ministry, the owner had been looking for fruit from the tree but finding none. So he tells the worker to cut the tree down. The worker becomes an advocate for the fruitless tree. He asks if he might cultivate it for one more year as best he can. If the tree still proves to be fruitless, then it can be cut down.

The story is left open. There is no closure. We are left wondering about the fate of the tree. That is where the power of the parable lies. The crowd is left in silence to determine if their fruitlessness might have anything to do with the fig tree. Or if the advocate who saves the tree from destruction until it might bear fruit could possibly be Jesus himself. As readers of Luke's Gospel, we too are left in that same silent place, to determine if we also might be, in some sense, like the fruitless tree and if Jesus just might become our Advocate.

The parable reveals that there is more going on than the simple equation. Fruitlessness isn't always the fault of the tree, nor is fruitfulness only the achievement of the tree. There is more at work behind the equation—perhaps a throne-room scene like that from the book of Job, in which an accuser and an Advocate are at work behind the scenes.

The next story provides another illustration of the hidden complexity behind the Job equation. It is Sabbath and Jesus is teaching in a synagogue of an undisclosed location. A woman who has been crippled for more than eighteen years by a demonic spirit is in attendance. Luke, with his concern for women, is the only Gospel writer who records this story. As a physician, he lists the details of her condition for us: she is bent over and she cannot straighten up.

According to the equation, she is in this state because she must have done something wrong. Also according to the equation, she is required to do something good—perhaps many good things—in order to correct the situation and possibly be healed. But then Jesus sees her and simply calls out that she is free. When he touches her, she straightens up for the first time in eighteen long years. Jesus wins praise for the Father, and the woman begins to "glorify God."

The official in charge of the services at this particular synagogue responds, not by confronting Jesus directly, but by telling the crowd to come on the other six days of the week for healing, not the Sabbath. He exhibits the same spiritual blindness we have witnessed before from the synagogue leadership. He cannot see a messianic miracle because it breaks one of his rules.

Once again the name "hypocrites" comes to Jesus' lips. Can't they see the hypocrisy? Can't they see that their law permits them to untie their livestock to be watered on the Sabbath but not this human being, who is bound by Satan? Shouldn't she also be "untied" on the Sabbath?

In a rare moment, Jesus' adversaries show themselves to be humiliated. They can come up with no argument, no cross-reference to refute Jesus' words. The crowd, on the other hand, rejoices. More than once since they set out on the road to Jerusalem, Jesus has spoken about the Light that cannot be hidden. This day in the synagogue, on the road to Jerusalem, it is shining for everyone to see. It is a small victory, but a victory all the same. In the flush of this minor triumph, Jesus speaks a rhetorical question to the crowd: "What is the kingdom of God like?"

He responds to his own question with the parable of the mustard seed, which is one of the shortest parables. A man took a tiny mustard seed and planted it in his garden, and it grew so large that the birds nested in its branches.

Jesus follows up with a similarly short and simple parable about the yeast and the dough: a woman put yeast in a large amount of flour and it spread throughout the entire lump of dough.

We are almost stunned by the simplicity of these parables. In our culture, unless you are a gardener or a baker, your imagination will probably not resonate with these simple images. But once you have planted a tiny seed and over time witnessed the enormous plant that grows from it, or once you have placed a small pinch of yeast in a large lump of dough and seen it rise and expand over the sides of the bowl—then you will begin to understand how a series of small encounters two thousand years ago between religious leaders and an obscure itinerant rabbi has resulted in a kingdom whose reign extends across the universe.

THE UNEXPECTEDLY CLOSED DOOR

²²He went through one town and village after another, teaching and making His way to Jerusalem. ²³"Lord," someone asked Him, "are there few being saved?"

He said to them, ²⁴"Make every effort to enter through the narrow door, because I tell you, many will try to enter and won't be able ²⁵once the homeowner gets up and shuts the door. Then you will stand outside and knock on the door, saying, 'Lord, open up for us!' He will answer you, 'I don't know you or where you're from.' ²⁶Then you will say, 'We ate and drank in Your presence, and You taught in our streets!' ²⁷But He will say, 'I tell you, I don't know you or where you're from. Get away from Me, all you workers of unrighteousness!' ²⁸There will be weeping and gnashing of teeth in that place, when you see Abraham, Isaac, Jacob, and all the prophets in the kingdom of God but yourselves thrown out. ²⁹They will come from east and west, from north and south, and recline at the table in the kingdom of God. ³⁰Note this: some are last who will be first, and some are first who will be last."

*V*erse 22 is one of those markers reminding us that we are on the road to Jerusalem. Along the way we have heard questions from the crowd regarding repentance and judgment. We have heard Jesus respond so far that the judgment will come unexpectedly and that his hearers should repent. In that same vein, someone walking along with Jesus asks if only a few are going to be saved. (The disciples ask the same question in Mt 19:25.)

Jesus answers that the way is narrow and the time will come when the One who owns the house will get up and shut the door. Then those who could not enter will be left standing outside, knocking. They will ask him to open up, to which he will respond, "I don't know you." They will remind him that at one time they ate and drank together, that he taught in their streets. Still, from the other side of the unexpectedly closed door, the voice will say, "Get away from Me."

It is akin to the image in Luke 12:35-40, only now the people are on the outside and the master is on the inside. Outside there will be tremendous mourning, weeping and teeth-grinding sorrow. As severe as that torment is, it will get worse when they see their patriarchs, Abraham, Isaac and Jacob, in whom their national identity is found, reclining at the table with people from the four points of the compass—that is, the Gentiles. They will all recline together at the great messianic banquet and celebrate the glory of the Father. The Jews will not be saved by their Jewishness, even as the Gentiles will not be condemned for not belonging to Israel. So many of those who were considered first will end up being last. Likewise, some of those who were last will end up taking first place. It will be an unexpected, upside-down inauguration for an unexpected, upside-down kingdom.

THREE DAYS OUT

31At that time some Pharisees came and told Him, "Go, get out of here! Herod wants to kill You!"

32He said to them, "Go tell that fox, 'Look! I'm driving out demons and performing healings today and tomorrow, and on the third day I will complete My work.' 33Yet I must travel today, tomorrow, and the next day, because it is not possible for a prophet to perish outside of Jerusalem!

34"Jerusalem, Jerusalem! The city who kills the prophets and stones those who are sent to her. How often I wanted to gather your children together, as a hen gathers her chicks under her wings, but you were not willing! 35See, your house is abandoned to you. And I tell you, you will not see Me until the time comes when you say, Blessed is He who comes in the name of the Lord!"

*D*ue to an almost universal bias against the Pharisees, this story is almost always viewed with a negative slant. I would like to believe, however, that these particular Pharisees are showing a genuine concern for Jesus' safety. We will see Jesus in the home of a Pharisee one last time in chapter 14, and it will not necessarily be a negative encounter. In fact, Jesus will even heal a man with dropsy on that occasion, and yes, it will be on a Sabbath. So perhaps this is a friendly warning.

Neither is Jesus' response to the Pharisees directed against them. He sends a challenge back to Herod, whom he derides as a "fox." He will continue on with his work of healing and casting out demons for the next three days. Then he will presumably arrive at Jerusalem. He *must* travel, says Jesus, for no prophet can die outside the walls of Jerusalem. Three days out and already a confrontation with Herod.

Jesus looks back in his imagination and remembers all of the innocent blood that has been shed within those walls: all of the priests who have been stoned there, everyone God had sent who has been brutally killed. In his prophetic imagination, he sees ahead some forty years, to the thousands who will starve or be murdered and crucified by the Romans when they destroy the city.

If Herod is the fox, then Jesus is the hen who longs to extend his gracious loving protection to the city. But the city is not willing!

It is no wonder that Jesus is so frequently thought to be the prophet Jeremiah come to life again. Here he prophesies the desolation of Jerusalem, as Jeremiah had done so long ago (Jer 9:11; 23:14). And here he laments like Jeremiah for the heartbreaking city of peace that, from the beginning, has been drenched in so much innocent blood (Lk 13:34; 19:41-44; compare to Jer 22:5).

LUKE 14

A NOT UNFRIENDLY DINNER

14:1 Jesus dines with a Pharisee.

14:2-6 Healing of the man with dropsy.

14:7-11 Parable of the seats at the banquet.

14:12-14 Advice to invite the poor.

THE HEART OF THE
MASTER OF THE BANQUET

14:15 A blessing from one of the guests.

14:16-24 Parable of the banquet.

FAITH OVER FAMILY

14:25-27 Cost of following Jesus.

14:28-30 Parable of the tower.

14:31-33 Parable of the king going to war.

14:34-35 "Salt is good."

A NOT UNFRIENDLY DINNER

¹One Sabbath, when He went to eat at the house of one of the leading Pharisees, they were watching Him closely. ²There in front of Him was a man whose body was swollen with fluid. ³In response, Jesus asked the law experts and the Pharisees, "Is it lawful to heal on the Sabbath or not?" ⁴But they kept silent. He took the man, healed him, and sent him away. ⁵And to them, He said, "Which of you whose son or ox falls into a well, will not immediately pull him out on the Sabbath day?" ⁶To this they could find no answer.

⁷He told a parable to those who were invited, when He noticed how they would choose the best places for themselves: ⁸"When you are invited by someone to a wedding banquet, don't recline at the best place, because a more distinguished person than you may have been invited by your host. ⁹The one who invited both of you may come and say to you, 'Give your place to this man,' and then in humiliation, you will proceed to take the lowest place.

¹⁰"But when you are invited, go and recline in the lowest place, so that when the one who invited you comes, he will say to you, 'Friend, move up higher.' You will then be honored in the presence of all the other guests. ¹¹For everyone who exalts himself will be humbled, and the one who humbles himself will be exalted."

¹²He also said to the one who had invited Him, "When you give a lunch or a dinner, don't invite your friends, your brothers, your relatives, or your rich neighbors, because they might invite you back, and you would be repaid. ¹³On the contrary, when you host a banquet, invite those who are poor, maimed, lame, or blind. ¹⁴And you will be blessed, because they cannot repay you; for you will be repaid at the resurrection of the righteous."

Chapter 14 opens with Jesus attending his third and last dinner in the home of a Pharisee. From beginning to end this will be a different experience, both for Jesus and for his hosts. The last time he broke bread with the Pharisees, he ended up pronouncing "woes" upon them and the scribes who were also present (Lk 11:37-54). His first meal with a Pharisee was with Simon in Luke 7:36. This occasion was far less fractious than the meal in chapter 11, although Jesus was still subjected to Simon's judgmental attitudes.

Luke tells us that it is a prominent Pharisee who has extended this invitation to Jesus. In Luke 17:11 they will still be on the border between Samaria and Galilee, while in Luke 18:35 they will be in the city of Jericho. I would love to posit that this might be the home of Nicodemus, but it seems to me that we are still too far from Jerusalem.

At the dinner is a man suffering from severe edema, a disease that causes the body to retain fluids and can be very painful. He does not seem to be one of the guests, since he eventually leaves before the party is over. It is Jesus who posits the question to the group, "Is it lawful to heal on the Sabbath or not?" There is no indication that their response is adversarial; they simply keep silent. Jesus heals the man and sends him on his way. He follows the healing with the rhetorical question that is reminiscent of the synagogue dispute in Luke 13:15—although, once again, this discussion is amazingly civil. The group simply can "find no answer."

In Luke 14:7, things are reversed. Here it is Jesus who is observing the behavior of the Pharisees; usually they are scrutinizing him. He notices that they are careful to choose the best seats at the table—that is, the highest places that their ranks will allow. What follows is a friendly lesson, which is apparently openly received. It is best, Jesus advises them, to take the lowest seat. From there you can only move up. If you presumptuously take the best seat, you might face the humiliating prospect of being asked to move down. The concluding maxim rings of radical reversal: "For everyone who exalts himself will be humbled, and the one who humbles himself will be exalted."

In preparation for the parable he is about to tell, Jesus turns to the prominent Pharisee who is hosting the meal and offers more friendly advice. The Pharisee should avoid inviting friends and family, Jesus says; the reason is that they can repay him. Instead he should invite the poor, who have no hope of paying him back. This is a source of blessing, and at the "resurrection of the righteous"—a term with which the Pharisee's heart would have resonated—he will be repaid.

THE HEART OF THE MASTER OF THE BANQUET

15 When one of those who reclined at the table with Him heard these things, he said to Him, "The one who will eat bread in the kingdom of God is blessed!"

¹⁶Then He told him: "A man was giving a large banquet and invited many. ¹⁷At the time of the banquet, he sent his slave to tell those who were invited, 'Come, because everything is now ready.'

¹⁸"But without exception they all began to make excuses. The first one said to him, 'I have bought a field, and I must go out and see it. I ask you to excuse me.'

¹⁹"Another said, 'I have bought five yoke of oxen, and I'm going to try them out. I ask you to excuse me.'

²⁰"And another said, 'I just got married, and therefore I'm unable to come.'

²¹"So the slave came back and reported these things to his master. Then in anger, the master of the house told his slave, 'Go out quickly into the streets and alleys of the city, and bring in here the poor, maimed, blind, and lame!'

²²"'Master,' the slave said, 'what you ordered has been done, and there's still room.'

²³"Then the master told the slave, 'Go out into the highways and lanes and make them come in, so that my house may be filled. ²⁴For I tell you, not one of those men who were invited will enjoy my banquet!'"

*J*esus' teaching is clearly a "hit," because one of the partygoers responds to it with a *berakah*. It sounds almost like a toast: "Blessed is the one who will eat bread in the kingdom of God." Imagine that: Jesus is sharing a meal with a group of men who actually want to talk about and celebrate the kingdom!

He responds with another parable. Jesus uses his imagination to weave together observations he has made throughout the evening. Someone with the means to do so invites everyone in the village to a banquet. In Near Eastern culture, those who responded to the first invitation (we would call it an R.S.V.P.) would then be notified days or weeks later when the meal was actually ready.

Incredibly, everyone who is invited makes excuses—insulting excuses. The first man asks to be excused so he can go examine a field he has just bought (as if anyone would buy a field without looking at it first).

Likewise, a second man asks to be excused so he can try out five yoke of oxen (as if anyone would make such a huge purchase without trying them out first).

The third man does not even ask to be excused. He just rudely responds that he is not coming because he has just gotten married. This excuse is the most suspicious for two reasons. First, in a village where everyone would know if a marriage was planned, no one would throw a large banquet that might conflict with the wedding. Second, anyone who has just been married would not receive an invitation in the first place.

When the slave reports back with the list of insulting excuses, the master blows his top. He acts out the advice Jesus has earlier given his host—namely, he invites the poor to his extravagant feast. Even after they have gathered, the slave reports back that there is still room.

The final order comes: he is to go out to the highways and lanes and invite strangers and foreigners. They should be made to come in and enjoy the feast and fill the house.

This final image is a reflection of the heart of the master of the banquet. Above all, he is determined that his feast be full, no matter what the social station or class or pedigree of the persons who come. He wants his house to be full, like his heart.

FAITH OVER FAMILY

25Now great crowds were traveling with Him. So He turned and said to them: 26"If anyone comes to Me and does not hate his own father and mother, wife and children, brothers and sisters—yes, and even his own life—he cannot be My disciple. 27Whoever does not bear his own cross and come after Me cannot be My disciple.

28"For which of you, wanting to build a tower, doesn't first sit down and calculate the cost to see if he has enough to complete it? 29Otherwise, after he has laid the foundation and cannot finish it, all the onlookers will begin to make fun of him, 30saying, 'This man started to build and wasn't able to finish.'

31"Or what king, going to war against another king, will not first sit down and decide if he is able with 10,000 to oppose the one who comes against him with 20,000? 32If not, while the other is still far off, he sends a delega-

tion and asks for terms of peace. ³³In the same way, therefore, every one of you who does not say good-bye to all his possessions cannot be My disciple.

³⁴"Now, salt is good, but if salt should lose its taste, how will it be made salty? ³⁵It isn't fit for the soil or for the manure pile; they throw it out. Anyone who has ears to hear should listen!"

*I*n the last scene from chapter 14, we are on the road with Jesus once more. As the crowd comes nearer and nearer to Jerusalem, the intensity of his call and message increases. Although the group that is following him is clearly growing, Jesus' words are not designed to attract followers—especially not these next words.

Jesus tells the crowd that they cannot become his disciples unless they hate their family and their own lives. This is clearly hyperbole, since in Luke 6:27 and Luke 6:35, Jesus commanded that they love their enemies. But even though it is hyperbolic, it is no less severe a call because it includes the cross, which for Jesus and his followers is no hyperbole. It is a painful reality that awaits them in Jerusalem. He will never call his followers to take up their crosses unless he is ready to take up his own. The cost of following Jesus could not be higher. And anyone, then or now, who is truly serious needs to count the cost.

Jesus follows this costly call with two parables of counting the cost. The first is a picture of a man who begins building a tower without calculating the total cost. Eventually he is only able to finish the foundation. Who builds a tower without first counting the cost? If someone tries and cannot finish, the onlookers will see the unfinished stump of the tower and ridicule the man as someone who can't finish what he starts.

The next parable concerns a king who goes to war without determining beforehand whether his army can match his enemies. What kind of king goes to war with only ten thousand when he's fighting an army of twenty thousand? If he does, he better call it quits and seek terms of surrender. Anyone who wants to follow Jesus must first determine whether they are ready to pay the price for being engaged in such a war.

Jesus' closing statement about salt seems abrupt. But it is perfectly in keeping with all that has gone before. The salt in Jesus' area came from the Dead Sea and could contain impurities that would cause it to become rancid. This explains the notion of how salt could "lose its saltiness." It must remain pure to fulfill its purpose. Likewise, if anyone who follows Jesus falters in their allegiance to him, they lose their purpose and their reason for being is gone.

LUKE 15

THE SHEPHERD
WITH THE LOST SHEEP

15:1-2 Composition of the crowd (mixed).

15:3-7 Parable.

THE WOMAN
WITH THE LOST COIN

15:8-10 Parable.

THE FATHER
WITH THE LOST SON(S)

15:11-32 Parable.

THE SHEPHERD WITH THE LOST SHEEP

¹All the tax collectors and sinners were approaching to listen to Him. ²And the Pharisees and scribes were complaining, "This man welcomes sinners and eats with them!"

³So He told them this parable: ⁴"What man among you, who has 100 sheep and loses one of them, does not leave the 99 in the open field and go after the lost one until he finds it? ⁵When he has found it, he joyfully puts it on his shoulders, ⁶and coming home, he calls his friends and neighbors together, saying to them, 'Rejoice with me, because I have found my lost sheep!' ⁷I tell you, in the same way, there will be more joy in heaven over one sinner who repents than over 99 righteous people who don't need repentance.

*T*he three parables in Luke 15 are obviously interrelated. The first two provide an overture to the significantly longer third. They contain the same four-part structure: something (or someone) is lost; it is sought after; it is found; there is great rejoicing as a result.

Verse 1 establishes the fact that Jesus is telling the stories to a mixed crowd. It is important to know the composition of the crowd. It allows you to ask better questions, since identification is important to understanding most of the parables. Luke tells us that there are the "sinners" and tax collectors, and there are the Pharisees and scribes, or the "righteous." As Jesus weaves his parables, we need to engage with our imaginations and ask which group would identify with each character. To whom would the Pharisees have gravitated? With whom would the tax collectors have identified? Jesus' stories ask them to identify with two groups with whom they would have never imagined identifying: women and shepherds.

The first story is about a shepherd who loses one of the sheep out of his flock of one hundred. "Who wouldn't leave the ninety-nine and go look for the one?" Jesus basically asks. It might not seem so obvious until you learn that shepherds always worked in teams; leaving the ninety-nine wouldn't have presented a problem, since there would have been others to keep watch.

When the lost sheep is found, it is carried home on the shoulders of the joyful shepherd. This was a favorite theme in early Christian art, especially in paintings in the catacombs (see Ps 28:9 and Is 40:11). The story closes with everyone rejoicing over the return of the lost sheep.

Jesus concludes the first story by saying, "There will be more joy in heaven over one sinner who repents than over 99 righteous people who don't need repentance." At first it is a puzzling statement. What did the first story have to do with repentance? Did the sheep repent?

THE WOMAN WITH THE LOST COIN

[8] "Or what woman who has 10 silver coins, if she loses one coin, does not light a lamp, sweep the house, and search carefully until she finds it? [9] When she finds it, she calls her women friends and neighbors together, saying, 'Rejoice with me, because I have found the silver coin I lost!' [10] I tell you, in the same way, there is joy in the presence of God's angels over one sinner who repents."

*I*n the second parable, the numbers come down and the relative value goes up: from one hundred sheep to ten coins. In this story it is a woman who has lost the coin. In the past, some have speculated that perhaps it was part of her dowry. But this is not even implied in Jesus' story. The structure is identical to the first parable. The coin is lost; it is sought for; it is found; all is followed by a statement of rejoicing.

Although Jesus modifies the conclusion, the structure remains. This time he speaks of the angels rejoicing over one sinner who repents. But again the questions nag at us. Who sinned: the woman? Who repented: the coin?

Jesus' conclusion is supposed to leave any listener feeling the disconnect. He has deliberately told the first two stories with missing pieces. We are left wondering about repentance and sin, two topics that occupy most of the discussion as the group travels on the road to Jerusalem.

THE FATHER WITH THE LOST SON(S)

[11] He also said: "A man had two sons. [12] The younger of them said to his

father, 'Father, give me the share of the estate I have coming to me.' So he distributed the assets to them. ¹³*Not many days later, the younger son gathered together all he had and traveled to a distant country, where he squandered his estate in foolish living.* ¹⁴*After he had spent everything, a severe famine struck that country, and he had nothing.* ¹⁵*Then he went to work for one of the citizens of that country, who sent him into his fields to feed pigs.* ¹⁶*He longed to eat his fill from the carob pods the pigs were eating, but no one would give him any.* ¹⁷*When he came to his senses, he said, 'How many of my father's hired hands have more than enough food, and here I am dying of hunger!* ¹⁸*I'll get up, go to my father, and say to him, Father, I have sinned against heaven and in your sight.* ¹⁹*I'm no longer worthy to be called your son. Make me like one of your hired hands.'* ²⁰*So he got up and went to his father. But while the son was still a long way off, his father saw him and was filled with compassion. He ran, threw his arms around his neck, and kissed him.* ²¹*The son said to him, 'Father, I have sinned against heaven and in your sight. I'm no longer worthy to be called your son.'*

²²*"But the father told his slaves, 'Quick! Bring out the best robe and put it on him; put a ring on his finger and sandals on his feet.* ²³*Then bring the fattened calf and slaughter it, and let's celebrate with a feast,* ²⁴*because this son of mine was dead and is alive again; he was lost and is found!' So they began to celebrate.*

²⁵*"Now his older son was in the field; as he came near the house, he heard music and dancing.* ²⁶*So he summoned one of the servants and asked what these things meant.* ²⁷*'Your brother is here,' he told him, 'and your father has slaughtered the fattened calf because he has him back safe and sound.'*

²⁸*"Then he became angry and didn't want to go in. So his father came out and pleaded with him.* ²⁹*But he replied to his father, 'Look, I have been slaving many years for you, and I have never disobeyed your orders, yet you never gave me a young goat so I could celebrate with my friends.* ³⁰*But when this son of yours came, who has devoured your assets with prostitutes, you slaughtered the fattened calf for him.'*

³¹*"'Son,' he said to him, 'you are always with me, and everything I have is yours.* ³²*But we had to celebrate and rejoice, because this brother of yours was dead and is alive again; he was lost and is found.'"*

*I*f you read the parables of Jesus long enough, you will come to expect the fact that nothing is as it seems. In fact, the world of his listeners is about to be turned upside down. If you listen with your imagination, your world will be turned upside down as well.

The case of the younger brother is a relatively simple one. He has blown it all and forfeited everything. Upon realizing this, he returns home to ask for forgiveness. He rehearses a lame little speech along the way. Realizing that he is no longer worthy to be called a son, he is willing to be a servant. That will be his plea. Only the prodigal never gets the chance to finish his rehearsed speech, because his father envelopes him with hugs and kisses and gifts, breathlessly dragging him off to a party given in his honor.

The case of the older brother is much more complex and much more interesting. It is too bad we so rarely even take a look at him. He is standing in the shadows most of the time. He is bitter, envious and angry. He hates his brother's sin but he also hates his father's loving forgiveness. Keeping in mind the confession of his brother, listen to his bitter words in verse 29. Literally he says, "I have been slaving many years for you." Do you see the irony Jesus intended the mixed crowd to see? The prodigal (or "sinner") returns in repentance and says essentially, "I will be your slave." The older son (the Pharisee) retorts in bitterness, "I have been a slave all along!"

Whenever someone is pictured as repentant and receiving grace, Luke paints someone in the shadows who simply hates the fact that God acts in such ways. Mercy is the salvation of some and, inexplicably, the damnation of others. The older brother in the parable is a hater of *hesed*.

But once more I want you to exercise your imagination and try to understand that the older brother is really right. The first hearers of Jesus' parable would have sooner sided with him than the prodigal. Why don't you try it yourself?

After all, he stayed home and was obedient and hard-working. He didn't demand anything at all—not his inheritance, not even, it seems, his father's love. No, he would earn that. After his brother's selfish exit, he continued to labor in the father's field, savoring the day the prodigal would return and get his comeuppance.

When that day finally comes, imagine his disappointment when the father acts the way he does. He does not respond in justice but in the mercy that the older son is beginning to hate. Do you see that he has every right to be disappointed? But, when you think about it, so does his father. It seems apparent that he has given up his rights, along with his retirement. He does not seem to know how to hold on to things, only to let them go.

Between Jesus' ingenious lines, there is a subtle shift. The prodigal returns, begging only to be made a hired hand—an arrangement which, of course, the father will hear nothing of. Then the older brother exposes himself. "I have been slaving many years for you," he whines. It is the kind of radical reversal Luke loves most. The hopeless son, who deserves slavery, is mercifully restored to full sonship, while the stunning revelation comes that it is the older son who has really been a slave all along—a slave to his hatred for the lovingkindness of his generous and noble father.

If you think you're finished with this parable, try looking at the old man as a fool, for that is what most of the first hearers would have thought. He is a fool to divide his fortune and give the share to the younger brother before his death. In fact, by dividing his estate, he is giving away a big part of his own retirement. He is a fool to linger in the road, looking for the prodigal to come back. He is a fool to come running, believing the lame little speech the boy had practiced all the way home. And to add to what he has already thrown away on the boy, the old man pulls out all the stops and throws a party, giving him the treasure of a ring.

If you are able to shift in your imagination to seeing the old man as a fool, you will then be more fully shocked: the foolish old man in Jesus' story is clearly God. This is a parable of *hesed*. Remember *hesed*? "When the one from whom I have a right to expect nothing gives me everything."

The wayward boy has no right whatsoever to expect anything except perhaps a door slammed in his face upon arriving back home. The best he could reasonably hope for is a stern lecture, a beating and then *maybe* a second chance. To extend anything more would be supremely foolish. This is not a boy who deserves a second chance.

But there stands the foolish father in the middle of the road. There's no telling how long he's been there, straining toward the horizon. When he sees the familiar silhouette, limping home, he sprints toward him. There is a robe over his arm and a ring in his pocket. The boy who has a right to expect nothing is about to receive everything. He is hopeless and hungry. He is you and me. And the foolish, doting old man . . .

LUKE 16

THE PARABLE OF
THE DESPERATE MANAGER

16:1-2 The dishonest manager is caught.

16:3-7 He initiates the "fix."

*16:8-13 A new value system
in regard to money.*

THE LINE HAS BEEN CROSSED

16:14-15 The problem with the Pharisees.

*16:16-17 The line between
the old and the new.*

*16:18 A new value system
in regard to marriage.*

A PARABLE OF
RADICAL REVERSAL

16:19-21 The rich man and Lazarus.

16:22-30 They go their separate ways.

16:31 "If they don't listen to Moses . . ."

THE PARABLE OF THE DESPERATE MANAGER

¹He also said to the disciples: "There was a rich man who received an accusation that his manager was squandering his possessions. ²So he called the manager in and asked, 'What is this I hear about you? Give an account of your management, because you can no longer be [my] manager.'

³"Then the manager said to himself, 'What should I do, since my master is taking the management away from me? I'm not strong enough to dig; I'm ashamed to beg. ⁴I know what I'll do so that when I'm removed from management, people will welcome me into their homes.'

⁵"So he summoned each one of his master's debtors. 'How much do you owe my master?' he asked the first one.

⁶"'A hundred measures of oil,' he said.

"'Take your invoice,' he told him, 'sit down quickly, and write 50.'

⁷"Next he asked another, 'How much do you owe?'

"'A hundred measures of wheat,' he said.

"'Take your invoice,' he told him, 'and write 80.'

⁸"The master praised the unrighteous manager because he had acted astutely. For the sons of this age are more astute than the sons of light [in dealing] with their own people. ⁹And I tell you, make friends for yourselves by means of the unrighteous money so that when it fails, they may welcome you into eternal dwellings. ¹⁰Whoever is faithful in very little is also faithful in much, and whoever is unrighteous in very little is also unrighteous in much. ¹¹So if you have not been faithful with the unrighteous money, who will trust you with what is genuine? ¹²And if you have not been faithful with what belongs to someone else, who will give you what is your own? ¹³No household slave can be the slave of two masters, since either he will hate one and love the other, or he will be devoted to one and despise the other. You can't be slaves to both God and money."

Chapter 16 opens with Jesus telling this parable to his disciples. We will discover in verse 14 that the Pharisees are listening in and "scoffing"—literally turning up their noses at him. With the opening of this chapter, the focus of Jesus' teaching shifts toward the new value system of the kingdom: what is valuable and what is not. We have come to expect, given that radical reversal is part and parcel of the kingdom, that everything will be turned upside down. And that is precisely what we find. Money, which the world regards as the ultimate measure of value, is put in its proper place as merely a tool to be used to facilitate relationship with people, who are now to be highly valued.

The scene opens with a wealthy man discovering that he is being cheated by the manager of his household (*oikonomos,* from *oikos* or "house"). In Jesus' day, this person was generally given great responsibility and was sometimes regarded as a trusted member of the family.

This manager is accused of "squandering" the possessions of his master. We are left to read between the lines to determine the exact nature of his crime. It appears that he had been adding a percentage to his master's collections and pocketing the added money for himself. He stands accused and guilty. There is no opportunity to defend his action. He is defenseless.

In verse 3 of Luke 16 he begins talking to himself—again, always a bad sign in Luke. He is a genuinely desperate man. He is losing his livelihood and, in many ways, his identity. Out of desperation he calls in those who owe his master and "scrubs" the books, subtracting from each bill the percentage he had nefariously added on for himself and asking the debtor to write out a new bill. Eight hundred gallons of olive oil would be worth about one thousand denarii. He lowers that bill by 50 percent. One thousand bushels of wheat would have been worth roughly 2,500 denarii. He lowers that bill by 25 percent. In both cases, then, he has subtracted five hundred denarii, the illicit fee he had tacked on for himself.

Out of desperation, the dishonest manager has actually done the right thing in spite of himself. His motivation—to be able to sponge off his master's debtors—is wrong. But, incredibly, he has righted the wrong and probably improved his master's relationship with the debtors to boot. For this he is praised by the master in verse 8 (although he is still fired!).

I don't believe Jesus means this story to become a prescription for our behavior. His conclusion in verses 8-9 is tongue in cheek. "Isn't it ironic," Jesus might have said, "that the people of this world are more astute than the people of the light? They do the right thing for the wrong reasons."

Money has a limited purpose. It might just open the door to relationships in this world. Spend it now, so that when it is gone, eternal dwellings might be opened to you.

In verses 10-13, Jesus broadens the scope of his conclusion with regard to money in general. Those who can be trusted are faithful whether the amount is small or great. Those who cannot be trusted will be unfaithful regardless of the amount.

In the ancient world, two owners sometimes had mutual shares in a single slave (see Acts 16:19). In verse 13, Jesus is not saying two people cannot own one slave. Rather, he says that a slave can only be devoted to one master. In those situations in which a slave does have two owners, he will inevitably love one and hate the other. But the second half of verse 13 reveals that Jesus has been speaking metaphorically. *We* are the slaves who must decide if our devotion will be solely placed in God or in worldly things. In the end, it is a matter of which value system you accept. Things are of minimal importance. People matter more. Our devotion to God matters most.

THE LINE HAS BEEN CROSSED

14 The Pharisees, who were lovers of money, were listening to all these things and scoffing at Him. 15 And He told them: "You are the ones who justify yourselves in the sight of others, but God knows your hearts. For what is highly admired by people is revolting in God's sight.

16 "The Law and the Prophets were until John; since then, the good news of the kingdom of God has been proclaimed, and everyone is strongly urged to enter it. 17 But it is easier for heaven and earth to pass away than for one stroke of a letter in the law to drop out.

18 "Everyone who divorces his wife and marries another woman commits adultery, and everyone who marries a woman divorced from her husband commits adultery.

*W*hether overtly or covertly, the Pharisees are listening in on these teachings of Jesus. When their scoffing makes Jesus aware of their presence, he turns on them. They might fool the crowds by justifying themselves, but they haven't fooled God, who knows their hearts. Then comes another value system statement from Jesus: what the crowd values, God detests.

By way of warning, Jesus wants the scoffing Pharisees to know that a line has been crossed and that John the Baptist was the boundary. On one side are the law and the prophets—the old world that the Pharisees still occupied. On the other side is the new world that has been inaugurated by the good news of God's kingdom. All people, including them, are being urged to enter, to step over the line.

This does not mean that the law has been done away with. Heaven and earth will pass away before the smallest stroke of the law passes away. No, the law, which will be fulfilled in Jesus, is in fact being magnified and clarified in him. To illustrate, Jesus gives one example: marriage.

In the law, provision for divorce was made (Deut 24:1-4), although Jesus will explain elsewhere that it was because of the hardness of people's hearts (Mt 19:8). On this side of the line, however, here in the kingdom of God, a new standard applies.

Jesus' statement on marriage in verse 18 of Luke 16 is best understood in light of a more lengthy statement he makes in Matthew 5:17-48. There he provides a list of other examples of the law being fulfilled, or superseded, in the kingdom. Matthew 5:18 mirrors Luke 16:17. It provides a link between the two: "For I assure you: Until heaven and earth pass away, not the smallest letter or one stroke of a letter will pass from the law until all things are accomplished" (Mt 5:18).

Jesus begins by pointing out that while the law says, "Do not murder" (Ex 20:13), he says that anyone who is angry with his brother will be subject to judgment. While the law says, "Do not commit adultery" (Ex 20:14), he says that when a man looks at a woman with lust in his heart, adultery has already been committed.

Then comes the pronouncement we are looking for. Finally, Jesus tells them that while the law makes provision for divorce by allowing a man to give his wife a written notice (Deut 24:1), he says that if a man divorces his wife, except for marital unfaithfulness, he causes her to commit adultery. In essence, he is saying that even though the ritual of the law was observed by handing her the divorce document, according to the kingdom value system, they are still one flesh. She is committing adultery as well as any man who marries her. If God has bound them together, then people cannot separate them (Mt 19:6).

With this as a background, when we return to Luke 16:18 we see that, given that the kingdom value system fulfills and supersedes the value system of the old world, "everyone who divorces his wife and marries another woman commits adultery, and everyone who marries a woman divorced from her husband commits adultery." In the radical new value system of the kingdom of God, a document—even one that finds sanction in the law—cannot undo God's intention if he has made them one.

A PARABLE OF RADICAL REVERSAL

[19] "There was a rich man who would dress in purple and fine linen, feasting lavishly every day. [20] But a poor man named Lazarus, covered with sores, was left at his gate. [21] He longed to be filled with what fell from the rich man's table, but instead the dogs would come and lick his sores. [22] One day the poor man died and was carried away by the angels to Abraham's side. The rich man also died and was buried. [23] And being in torment in Hades, he looked up and saw Abraham a long way off, with Lazarus at his side. [24] 'Father Abraham!' he called out, 'Have mercy on me and send Lazarus to dip the tip of his finger in water and cool my tongue, because I am in agony in this flame!'

[25] "'Son,' Abraham said, 'remember that during your life you received your good things, just as Lazarus received bad things, but now he is comforted here, while you are in agony. [26] Besides all this, a great chasm has been fixed between us and you, so that those who want to pass over from here to you cannot; neither can those from there cross over to us.'

[27] "'Father,' he said, 'then I beg you to send him to my father's house—[28] because I have five brothers—to warn them, so they won't also come to this place of torment.'

[29] "But Abraham said, 'They have Moses and the prophets; they should listen to them.'

[30] "'No, father Abraham,' he said. 'But if someone from the dead goes to them, they will repent.'

[31] "But he told him, 'If they don't listen to Moses and the prophets, they will not be persuaded if someone rises from the dead.'"

*T*his section comes to a close with the parable of the rich man and Lazarus. Again we see Luke's delight in showing us how the supposedly blessed are missing out while those apparently cursed are, quite literally, closest to the heart of God.

Two individuals could not be more different. One is fabulously wealthy, dressed in his finest clothes and eating the finest food every day. He is not even given a name in the story. The other is pitifully poor, covered with festering sores and left abandoned at the gate. We are told by Jesus that his name is Lazarus, the only character in any of his parables to merit a name. The poor man dreams of catching the crumbs from the table of the rich man. Invariably he wakes up, day after day, only to find the unclean dogs licking his sores.

But death comes one day for both men. Lazarus is transported immediately to heaven. The angels escort him to the most privileged place beside Abraham. The rich man is unceremoniously buried.

The rich man looks up from the fiery pit only to see the beggar at Abraham's side. Even in hell he only regards Lazarus as his errand boy, the flunky who can dip his finger in water and cool his tongue. But this won't be possible because there is a great chasm between them.

If it is not possible for Lazarus to make his way to him, the rich man begs, then could he warn his five brothers so they don't also end up in "this place of torment"? But Abraham will not allow this either. He shouts across the chasm that the man's brothers have access to the books of Moses and the prophets. That should be more than enough for them.

"But if someone from the dead goes to them, they will repent," the rich man answers back.

The powerful conclusion of the parable in verse 31 of Luke 16 will set the tone for the remaining ministry of Jesus. It is a statement that takes your breath away and in the same instant sends chills down your spine. It is ironic and sadly self-evident. If the words of Moses and the prophets are not enough to inspire repentance, the miraculous appearance of someone raised from the dead will meet with the same stubborn disbelief. In real life, there will be two men raised from the dead. One, of course, will be Jesus. The other, oddly enough, is also named Lazarus.

LUKE 17

SIMPLE, TRUSTING OBEDIENCE

17:1-4 An impossible command.

17:5-10 The master and the slaves.

THE PERFECT PRAYER

17:11-19 Ten lepers cleansed.

THE COMING(S)
OF THE KINGDOM

17:20-21 The kingdom that is here.

17:22-30 The kingdom that is coming.

*17:31-37 Something from which
you cannot run away.*

SIMPLE, TRUSTING OBEDIENCE

¹He said to His disciples, "Offenses will certainly come, but woe to the one they come through! ²It would be better for him if a millstone were hung around his neck and he were thrown into the sea than for him to cause one of these little ones to stumble. ³Be on your guard. If your brother sins, rebuke him, and if he repents, forgive him. ⁴And if he sins against you seven times in a day, and comes back to you seven times, saying, 'I repent,' you must forgive him."

⁵The apostles said to the Lord, "Increase our faith."

⁶"If you have faith the size of a mustard seed," the Lord said, "you can say to this mulberry tree, 'Be uprooted and planted in the sea,' and it will obey you.

⁷"Which one of you having a slave plowing or tending sheep, will say to him when he comes in from the field, 'Come at once and sit down to eat'? ⁸Instead, will he not tell him, 'Prepare something for me to eat, get ready, and serve me while I eat and drink; later you can eat and drink'? ⁹Does he thank that slave because he did what was commanded? ¹⁰In the same way, when you have done all that you were commanded, you should say, 'We are good-for-nothing slaves; we've only done our duty.'"

Chapter 17 takes a somewhat ominous turn. Jesus begins with still more radical demands that his disciples extend forgiveness, even seven times a day, to those who sin against them. "You *must* forgive him," Jesus insists. The Twelve, recognizing that they do not possess enough faith to meet such an enormous demand for forgiveness, ask Jesus to increase their faith.

His response reflects the truth that, when it comes to faith, quantity does not matter. If they had only the tiniest speck of faith, they could uproot an enormous mulberry tree and cast it into the sea. When Jesus says "this" mulberry tree, I imagine him pointing to an actual living tree. He often uses nearby objects to illustrate whatever point he is making (Jn 4:13, 21, 35).

In verse 7, he tells a parable to illustrate still more demands. In stark contrast to the master who acted like a slave by serving his servants at the table (Lk 12:37), Jesus paints a picture of a master acting like a master.

The key to understanding this seemingly harsh statement is once again to read it in context—to look at it not as an isolated saying, but as a response to a request made by the disciples. In verse 5 of Luke 17 they make the dangerous request of Jesus, "Lord, increase our faith." Jesus has just made the enormous demand that they should forgive their repentant brother seven times a day if he asks forgiveness.

The disciples initially believed that being followers of the Messiah would mean that they would execute punishment and vengeance, not extend forgiveness. At one point they saw themselves justified in calling down fire from heaven (Lk 9:54). This new, troubling demand for forgiveness makes them realize that they are going to need more faith.

But Jesus dismisses the myth that what they need is *more* faith. In verse 6, he tells them that all they need is a speck (a mustard-seed-sized amount) of faith to do incredible things. They thought his command for forgiveness was a demand for more faith, when all along it is actually an invitation to obedience. Jesus has already made clear that the heart of a slave is undivided—that is, that he can only serve one master. Now that Master has made an impossible request: to offer forgiveness on an enormous scale.

Jesus employs an image the disciples would find easy to imagine: a slave doing his daily work. Forgiveness will be their new yoke. Their servitude will be to the One who offers forgiveness on a truly unimaginable scale to the entire world through them. Their response, as Jesus paints the picture in his parable, is not one of breathless demands for more faith to do the task, but rather the image of the slave who comes to the end of the day—or the end of a lifetime—and simply says, "I have only done my duty."

THE PERFECT PRAYER

[11]While traveling to Jerusalem, He passed between Samaria and Galilee. [12]As He entered a village, 10 men with serious skin diseases met Him. They stood at a distance [13]and raised their voices, saying, "Jesus, Master, have mercy on us!"

¹⁴When He saw them, He told them, "Go and show yourselves to the priests." And while they were going, they were healed.

¹⁵But one of them, seeing that he was healed, returned and, with a loud voice, gave glory to God. ¹⁶He fell facedown at His feet, thanking Him. And he was a Samaritan.

¹⁷Then Jesus said, "Were not 10 cleansed? Where are the nine? ¹⁸Didn't any return to give glory to God except this foreigner?" ¹⁹And He told him, "Get up and go on your way. Your faith has made you well."

In Luke 17:11-19, we are reminded of the journey once again, but finally we are given an actual location: the border between Galilee and Samaria, an area we've seen Jesus pass through more than once. As the crowd enters a village, they encounter ten lepers. The diseased men keep their distance to avoid rendering Jesus and his disciples "unclean" (Lev 13:46; Num 5:2). People in that era would have assumed that the ten contracted their skin disease as a result of personal sin. These men would have naturally seen themselves as unworthy. Nevertheless, there they stand, crying out for Jesus' help, whether they deserve it or not.

Their cry is really a prayer. It is the perfect prayer: "Master, have *mercy . . .*" It is a cry from men who, although they have a right to expect nothing, are asking for everything. This makes it a cry for *hesed*.

It will be another one of Jesus' unmiraculous miracles. Notice that there are no words of healing, no pronouncements that the ten are forgiven or clean—only Jesus' command that they go and show themselves to the priest. The only reason for someone with a skin disease to submit to examination by a priest would be to determine whether they had been healed or not. In this case, they discover on their way that they have been completely healed.

Out of the ten only one returns, shouting his praises to God. He comes back and falls at the feet of Jesus, giving thanks for what he has done. Luke wants us to know that the sole person who comes back is a Samaritan. The implication is that the other nine are Jewish. The one person who should not have gotten it, did. The other nine who should have, didn't.

THE COMING(S) OF THE KINGDOM

²⁰Being asked by the Pharisees when the kingdom of God will come, He answered them, "The kingdom of God is not coming with something observable; ²¹no one will say, 'Look here!' or 'There!' For you see, the kingdom of God is among you."

²²Then He told the disciples: "The days are coming when you will long to see one of the days of the Son of Man, but you won't see it. ²³They will say to you, 'Look there!' or 'Look here!' Don't follow or run after them. ²⁴For as the lightning flashes from horizon to horizon and lights up the sky, so the Son of Man will be in His day. ²⁵But first He must suffer many things and be rejected by this generation.

²⁶"Just as it was in the days of Noah, so it will be in the days of the Son of Man: ²⁷people went on eating, drinking, marrying and giving in marriage until the day Noah boarded the ark, and the flood came and destroyed them all. ²⁸It will be the same as it was in the days of Lot: people went on eating, drinking, buying, selling, planting, building. ²⁹But on the day Lot left Sodom, fire and sulfur rained from heaven and destroyed them all. ³⁰It will be like that on the day the Son of Man is revealed. ³¹On that day, a man on the housetop, whose belongings are in the house, must not come down to get them. Likewise the man who is in the field must not turn back. ³²Remember Lot's wife! ³³Whoever tries to make his life secure will lose it, and whoever loses his life will preserve it. ³⁴I tell you, on that night two will be in one bed: one will be taken and the other will be left. ³⁵Two women will be grinding grain together: one will be taken and the other left. [³⁶Two will be in a field: one will be taken, and the other will be left."]

³⁷"Where, Lord?" they asked Him.

He said to them, "Where the corpse is, there also the vultures will be gathered."

*T*here is a clear pattern every time Jesus talks about the second coming. He begins by focusing on near-future events and then transitions to apocalyptic language. He will first describe an event from which a person can escape, and then he will abruptly begin talking about the end of the world.

In this passage, the Pharisees ask him when the kingdom will come. Jesus responds with its present fulfillment. It is the answer they need to hear, since they have not yet accepted or entered into his kingdom. It is not something you can see, Jesus tells these men, who are anticipating an event in which the stars will fall from the sky. It is not something about which people will be able to say, "Look here," or point to and say, "Over there!" Behold, it is among you. This kingdom is already here. Jesus is referring to his first, present coming.

Later, Jesus gives different instructions to the disciples. According to the pattern, he begins with the near future. A time is coming when they will long to see one of the days of the first coming of the kingdom, one of the "days of the Son of Man." Again, just as he told the Pharisees, people will try to point it out and say "look here or there." Don't pay them any attention, says Jesus. When the Son of Man returns, you will all know. It will be like lightning flashing across the sky. It will be cataclysmic and apocalyptic. But before that can take place, Jerusalem is waiting at the end of the road, and Jesus must suffer.

Then, as it always does, his language shifts to the end time, to the apocalypse. He describes an event from which no one will be able to run away. As in the days of Noah and Lot, it will be both completely unexpected and totally destructive. When it comes, anyone on the roof should not go down to retrieve his or her belongings, because this is something from which you cannot run away. Two will be in bed, and one will be taken. Two women will be grinding together, and suddenly there will only be one left.

When the stunned disciples ask, "Where?"—as if such a worldwide cataclysm could be reduced to one isolated location—Jesus answers that the location will be indicated by signs, just as a dead body will attract vultures. The question will come up again after they reach Jerusalem in chapter 21. Jesus will follow the same pattern: beginning with a near-future event, then talking about the destruction of Jerusalem and concluding with the end of the world.

LUKE 18

PERSISTENCE AND JUSTICE

18:1–8 Parable of the persistent widow.

THE PERFECT PRAYER, 2

18:9–14 The Pharisee and the tax collector.

18:15–17 Jesus blesses the children.

ONE BROKEN LINK

18:18–30 The rich young ruler.

18:31–34 Jesus predicts his death.

THE PERFECT PRAYER, 3

18:35–43 The healing of the blind man.

PERSISTENCE AND JUSTICE

[1] He then told them a parable on the need for them to pray always and not become discouraged: [2] "There was a judge in one town who didn't fear God or respect man. [3] And a widow in that town kept coming to him, saying, 'Give me justice against my adversary.'

[4] "For a while he was unwilling, but later he said to himself, 'Even though I don't fear God or respect man, [5] yet because this widow keeps pestering me, I will give her justice, so she doesn't wear me out by her persistent coming.'"

[6] Then the Lord said, "Listen to what the unjust judge says. [7] Will not God grant justice to His elect who cry out to Him day and night? Will He delay [to help] them? [8] I tell you that He will swiftly grant them justice. Nevertheless, when the Son of Man comes, will He find that faith on earth?"

*T*he time for parables is rapidly coming to an end as they approach Jerusalem. Jesus will tell just two more here in chapter 18, and only one in chapter 19, as they near the gates of the city. Once he has entered, there will only be time for two more. So we should savor them while we can.

These two parables are introduced with an opening sentence that explains why Jesus told them. The reason for the first parable, according to verse 1, is that they need help in not being discouraged in prayer.

Irresponsible authority is one of my own personal phobias. One of the most frightening things I can imagine is to be under the authority of a judge who is negligent with his or her power. The judge in Jesus' story is just that sort of person.

Judges have two principal motivations to show justice. The first is a healthy fear of God. The knowledge that one day you will stand before his judgment seat is a marvelous incentive for worldly judges to take their calling seriously. The second is a deep respect and concern for humanity. According to Jesus, this judge has neither of these qualities. In other words, he has no reason to "do justice." But the persistent widow is about to help him find a new reason.

She persistently comes to his court saying, "Give me justice against my adversary." She has no menfolk who might take justice into their own hands in order to help her. As a widow, she has nowhere else to go.

Without allowing the story to drag on, Jesus says that for a time the unjust judge is unwilling to give her the justice she so persistently seeks. But eventually, even though he still does not fear God or respect people, he relents and settles the case in her favor.

Jesus' conclusion in Luke 18:7 is based on a rabbinic rule of interpretation known as *qal vahomer*, or "easy and hard." It is an argument from minor to major based on the "how much more" principle. Hillel, the rabbi Jesus most frequently favored, first formulated it. Hillel called it his first rule. If the unjust judge gave justice to the persistent widow, then *how much more* will God, that great Judge, give justice to those who persistently seek him? The parable closes with a note of challenge as Jesus wonders out loud if, when he returns, he will find this sort of persistent faith on the earth. As long as we live in a fallen world, the need for persistence in order to receive justice is not going to go away.

THE PERFECT PRAYER, 2

⁹He also told this parable to some who trusted in themselves that they were righteous and looked down on everyone else: ¹⁰"Two men went up to the temple complex to pray, one a Pharisee and the other a tax collector. ¹¹The Pharisee took his stand and was praying like this: 'God, I thank You that I'm not like other people—greedy, unrighteous, adulterers, or even like this tax collector. ¹²I fast twice a week; I give a tenth of everything I get.'

¹³"But the tax collector, standing far off, would not even raise his eyes to heaven but kept striking his chest and saying, 'God, turn Your wrath from me —a sinner!' ¹⁴I tell you, this one went down to his house justified rather than the other; because everyone who exalts himself will be humbled, but the one who humbles himself will be exalted."

¹⁵Some people were even bringing infants to Him so He might touch them, but when the disciples saw it, they rebuked them. ¹⁶Jesus, however, invited them: "Let the little children come to Me, and don't stop them, because the kingdom of God belongs to such as these. ¹⁷I assure you: Whoever does not welcome the kingdom of God like a little child will never enter it."

The first time we heard this perfect prayer it came from ten diseased men (Lk 17:12). Now we find that Jesus has incorporated it into one of his final parables. Verse 9 tells us the story is specifically directed toward those who are confident in their own self-righteousness. Perhaps, trying to maintain his moderately pro-Pharisee position, Luke cannot bring himself to tell us if they were the targets.

Two men are going to the temple for prayer. The first is, in fact, a Pharisee; the other is one of the tax collectors who are so despised by the people. This tax collector despises himself as well.

The Pharisee stands proud and erect, praying about himself. He thanks God that he is not like the tax collector with whom he entered the temple. He provides a short list of his meticulous observances, assuming God will be as impressed with him as he is with himself. He does not really seem to need God at all. Even his coming to the temple feels a bit perfunctory.

Before we move on, let's stop and realize that as different as he might seem from you and me, the odds are the Pharisee is the person most of us should probably identify with in this parable. We can probably camouflage our self-righteousness better, but every day we look around and thank God that we are not like some of the people we meet. And we all make our little lists, hoping to impress.

The tax collector keeps well back. His self-loathing can be seen in his body language. His eyes are lowered, and he repeatedly pounds his chest. His prayer is for mercy, but the Greek word Luke uses reflects a desire for atonement. Darrell Bock, in his marvelous commentary, translates it "mercy through atoning forgiveness."[11] He seems to intuit that a sacrifice is demanded for his sin and that he cannot hope to offer it himself. It is a cry for *hesed*. Jesus says that he goes home justified.

If you have remained sensitive to the big picture of the ministry of Jesus, you will recognize here a conclusion he has made before in Luke 14:11 (I find it interesting that Jesus repeats himself): "Everyone who exalts himself will be humbled, but the one who humbles himself will be exalted." It is radical reversal at the level of the human soul.

Some of the Passover pilgrims who are traveling along with Jesus and his disciples to Jerusalem have brought their young children with them. They ask Jesus to do a very rabbinic thing: to lay his hands on the children and impart a blessing, a *berakah*, which sometimes also contained a prophetic message regarding the future of the child. His disciples, who already seem to have forgotten his last lesson about humility, try to prod the parents away. Their rabbi is too important for such trivial things.

Jesus, always himself, says those words we've repeated a thousand times. They are repeated at the graves of little children and during a thousand children's sermons. If the disciples cannot learn to welcome the kingdom of God like a little child, says Jesus, they will never be able to enter. The children themselves are parables that need to be listened to. People will not be allowed to enter the kingdom of God unless they can enter innocently and unashamed to receive it freely.

ONE BROKEN LINK

¹⁸A ruler asked Him, "Good Teacher, what must I do to inherit eternal life?"
¹⁹"Why do you call Me good?" Jesus asked him. "No one is good but One—God. ²⁰You know the commandments:

> *Do not commit adultery;*
> *do not murder;*
> *do not steal;*
> *do not bear false witness;*
> *honor your father and mother."*

²¹"I have kept all these from my youth," he said.
²²When Jesus heard this, He told him, "You still lack one thing: sell all that you have and distribute it to the poor, and you will have treasure in heaven. Then come, follow Me."
²³After he heard this, he became extremely sad, because he was very rich.

²⁴Seeing that he became sad, Jesus said, "How hard it is for those who have wealth to enter the kingdom of God! ²⁵For it is easier for a camel to go through the eye of a needle than for a rich person to enter the kingdom of God."
²⁶Those who heard this asked, "Then who can be saved?"

²⁷He replied, "What is impossible with men is possible with God."

²⁸Then Peter said, "Look, we have left what we had and followed You."

²⁹So He said to them, "I assure you: There is no one who has left a house, wife or brothers, parents or children because of the kingdom of God, ³⁰who will not receive many times more at this time, and eternal life in the age to come."

³¹Then He took the Twelve aside and told them, "Listen! We are going up to Jerusalem. Everything that is written through the prophets about the Son of Man will be accomplished. ³²For He will be handed over to the Gentiles, and He will be mocked, insulted, spit on; ³³and after they flog Him, they will kill Him, and He will rise on the third day."

³⁴They understood none of these things. This saying was hidden from them, and they did not grasp what was said.

We don't know just what this "ruler" (*archōn*) was ruler of. Perhaps he was some sort of secular official, or maybe he was a synagogue ruler. Apparently Luke doesn't think we need to know. He comes to Jesus with the same question the scribe asked in Luke 10:25: "What must I do to inherit eternal life?" It is a flawed question, based on a misunderstanding that eternal life is inherited based on something *we do*.

Jesus seems a bit put-off at being called "good" teacher. I get the feeling that he wants the ruler to know just who he really is. Or perhaps he senses that the ruler is expecting to be addressed with some corresponding honorific title. On the other side of the line, the side of the law and prophets, eternal life was the reward for those who kept the commandments. So Jesus provides a brief list for the ruler.

The ruler responds without a blink. He has kept them all—or at least he has redefined them all so as to make them "keepable." He's not being conspicuously self-righteous. Many people in Jesus' time would have answered the same way.

"There's just one thing left," Jesus basically says. "Sell everything and give it to the poor. Then come and follow me" (see Lk 14:33). Jesus is inviting the ruler to cross the line he laid out in Luke 16:16 when he announced that "the Law and the Prophets were until John; since then, the good news of the kingdom of God has been proclaimed." The ruler is an uncomfortable resident of the old world. Something is telling him there is more. By inviting him to let go of his wealth and to transfer it into heavenly treasure, Jesus is pointing out his personal pathway to the other side of the line: a new world, a new value system, a radically reversed kingdom.

Apparently not another word is spoken. The rich man simply walks away, extremely sad.

Sometimes it is difficult for the wealthy to cross the line into the new world. Jesus says it is easier for a camel to go through the eye of a needle. (In my opinion, we don't need any of the complicated explanations that have been proposed for this passage—the ones about a gate called the "eye of the needle," or the word *camel* actually meaning *rope*. It is what it is: a ridiculously impossible image!) When Jesus asks the ruler to sell his possessions, he is revealing the fact that the ruler hasn't kept all the commandments after all. In fact, he has broken the very first one: he has made money his god (Deut 5:7). There is an ancient tradition that says the ruler eventually came back and became a follower of Jesus. We can only hope that it is true.

Bill Lane, who lived out so well this lifestyle of "letting go," used to say that the commandments are like a chain that is suspending you over an alligator pit. It does not matter which link of the chain breaks: "Either way," Bill would laugh, "you are going down!" The chain on which the ruler had depended had been broken all along. Yet he never even knew it.

All of our attention has been focused on Jesus and the ruler. We have neglected to notice how visibly shaken the disciples are. In their old-world value system, a person was rich because they had been blessed by God . . . case closed. Hearing Jesus say that it is hard for the wealthy to enter the kingdom has caused the disciples to wonder if anyone can be saved.

Jesus' response is in verse 27: "What is impossible with man is possible with God." Men and women don't save themselves. Saving is God's business.

Peter, particularly shaken, looks for a reassuring pat on the back. He reminds Jesus that they have left everything. And truth be told, they have. And so a reassuring pat on the back is exactly what Jesus gives him (Lk 18:29-30).

Twice so far Jesus has taken the Twelve aside and told them, in frightening detail, what awaits him in Jerusalem (Lk 9:22, 44). They are never quite able to understand. In Luke 9:44-45, they are even afraid to ask him. This is the last time he will tell them. Once again, they cannot understand. Somehow, mysteriously, Luke says, it "was hidden from them." I cannot help but think that the hiddenness of it all was a blessing. How could they take another step if they understood what was waiting for Jesus?

THE PERFECT PRAYER, 3

35 As He drew near Jericho, a blind man was sitting by the road begging. 36 Hearing a crowd passing by, he inquired what this meant. 37 "Jesus the Nazarene is passing by," they told him.

38 So he called out, "Jesus, Son of David, have mercy on me!" 39 Then those in front told him to keep quiet, but he kept crying out all the more, "Son of David, have mercy on me!"

40 Jesus stopped and commanded that he be brought to Him. When he drew near, He asked him, 41 "What do you want Me to do for you?"

"Lord," he said, "I want to see!"

42 "Receive your sight!" Jesus told him. "Your faith has healed you." 43 Instantly he could see, and he began to follow Him, glorifying God. All the people, when they saw it, gave praise to God.

The last time we heard this perfect prayer, the tax collector in Jesus' parable spoke it. Now we will hear it in real life one last time. Jerusalem is awfully close now. They are coming to Jericho, known also as the "City of Palms," the last major stop before the holy city. Jesus' followers will cut the palm branches here that they will wave before him as he enters Jerusalem.

Beggars, then and now, tend to gather where the crowds are entering the city. This beggar is blind. He is poor. He wonders daily what he did to deserve this terrible punishment. If someone could be found on the extreme opposite of the scale from the rich ruler, it would be this nameless man.

The blind man's stubborn insistence to keep on crying out to Jesus is what makes me love this little man so much. I believe it's why Jesus also seems to have been delighted by him as well. He sits there in his own personal darkness, crying out for a gift he knows he does not deserve. He cries out for mercy, for *hesed*. It is the perfect prayer. It is the simplest request for what is most critical. It asks from God what is most essential. It is a plaintive cry for a piece of God's own heart. It is a prayer that Christians have whispered for centuries.

Healing the blind was one of the great messianic miracles in Isaiah (Is 35:5; 61:1). It is the final miracle on the road to Jerusalem. Once he has reached the city, there will be precious little time for miracles. He will heal the ear of Malchus (Lk 22:51). It will be one of those unmiraculous miracles, since no one will even recognize that it occurred. The opening of the eyes of the blind man will set the tone for the so-called triumphal entry.

Jesus is about to enter Jerusalem and the Passion. There, on the cross, he will perfectly demonstrate what mercy is all about. He will show the world what the *hesed* of God looks like. He will offer the world an unimaginable alternative. To those who have a right to expect nothing, Jesus will offer everything. It is a door to an infinite store of mercy. The door can be opened by seven simple words: "Son of David, have mercy on me."

LUKE 19

A PARADIGM FOR
A NEW VALUE SYSTEM

19:1–10 Zacchaeus.

A BLUEPRINT FOR
CENTURIES TO COME

19:11–27 The parable of the minas.

A TEARFUL ENTRY

19:28–44 Jesus enters Jerusalem.

THE SECOND
TEMPLE CLEANSING

*19:45–48 Jesus confronts
the moneychangers.*

A PARADIGM FOR A NEW VALUE SYSTEM

[1]He entered Jericho and was passing through. [2]There was a man named Zacchaeus who was a chief tax collector, and he was rich. [3]He was trying to see who Jesus was, but he was not able because of the crowd, since he was a short man. [4]So running ahead, he climbed up a sycamore tree to see Jesus, since He was about to pass that way. [5]When Jesus came to the place, He looked up and said to him, "Zacchaeus, hurry and come down, because today I must stay at your house."

[6]So he quickly came down and welcomed Him joyfully. [7]All who saw it began to complain, "He's gone to lodge with a sinful man!"

[8]But Zacchaeus stood there and said to the Lord, "Look, I'll give half of my possessions to the poor, Lord! And if I have extorted anything from anyone, I'll pay back four times as much!"

[9]"Today salvation has come to this house," Jesus told him, "because he too is a son of Abraham. [10]For the Son of Man has come to seek and to save the lost."

Luke 19 opens with Jesus finally reaching the city of Jericho, just twenty-three miles from Jerusalem. It was known as "the city of priests," and yet when Jesus arrives, he breaks bread in the home of a chief tax collector.

In Zacchaeus, all the teaching concerning the new value system will come together. Of the hated group of tax collectors, he is a cut above. Zacchaeus is a "chief" tax collector (*architelōnēs)*. This means he is in charge of an entire cadre of lesser tax collectors. This means that he would have been the object of particular scorn among the Jews. It is best to get beyond the "wee little man" image we sang about in Sunday school. The simple fact is that the crowd has grown exponentially since Jesus left Galilee. Just to catch a glimpse of Jesus walking in the midst of the churning mass would have required that someone find an elevated place. Zacchaeus found a sycamore tree.

Looking up, Jesus calls him by name and tells him that he intends to stay at his house. Zacchaeus seems fairly unruffled that the celebrity knows his name and has invited himself for dinner. He simply climbs down and happily leads Jesus to what is most likely a large and well-furnished house. Usually it is the Pharisees who comment on Jesus' unorthodox choice of company. Now it is the people at large who complain that he is staying with a "sinful man."

Let me state the obvious: Zacchaeus is not misunderstood. He is not the victim of circumstance. He is a genuinely bad man. He has chosen to work for the Romans, to bilk his own people. So successful is he at this job that he has risen in the ranks to become a chief tax collector. The people don't despise him because they are close-minded and judgmental; they despise him because he is a slimy, good-for-nothing thief. And he knows he is.

In verse 8 Zacchaeus stands up before Jesus, presumably now at the meal in his home, and makes the announcement that, first, he will give half his possessions to the poor and, second, he will restore anything he has extorted from the taxpayers four times over. The "four times" figure is the required restoration a thief was commanded to make in the Torah (Ex 22:1). It is a vivid (and expensive!) confession of his thievery.

Compared to the sad story of the rich ruler from the preceding chapter, Zacchaeus is a happy contrast. He is the poster child, the paradigm for the radically reversed value system Jesus has been teaching from the very beginning. The fact that it is Zacchaeus who meets Jesus on this last stop before Jerusalem—Zacchaeus, the short, gleeful, reformed, tree-climbing con man—must be a thoroughly satisfying moment for the tired, footsore rabbi from Galilee.

A BLUEPRINT FOR CENTURIES TO COME

11As they were listening to this, He went on to tell a parable because He was near Jerusalem, and they thought the kingdom of God was going to appear right away.

12Therefore He said: "A nobleman traveled to a far country to receive for himself authority to be king and then return. 13He called 10 of his slaves, gave them 10 minas, and told them, 'Engage in business until I come back.'

14"But his subjects hated him and sent a delegation after him, saying, 'We don't want this man to rule over us!'

15"At his return, having received the authority to be king, he summoned those slaves he had given the money to so he could find out how much they had made in business. *¹⁶The first came forward and said, 'Master, your mina has earned 10 more minas.'*

¹⁷"Well done, good slave!' he told him. 'Because you have been faithful in a very small matter, have authority over 10 towns.'

¹⁸"The second came and said, 'Master, your mina has made five minas.'

¹⁹"So he said to him, 'You will be over five towns.'

²⁰"And another came and said, 'Master, here is your mina. I have kept it hidden away in a cloth ²¹because I was afraid of you, for you're a tough man: you collect what you didn't deposit and reap what you didn't sow.'

²²"He told him, 'I will judge you by what you have said, you evil slave! [If] you knew I was a tough man, collecting what I didn't deposit and reaping what I didn't sow, ²³why didn't you put my money in the bank? And when I returned, I would have collected it with interest!' ²⁴So he said to those standing there, 'Take the mina away from him and give it to the one who has 10 minas.'

²⁵"But they said to him, 'Master, he has 10 minas.'

²⁶"I tell you, that to everyone who has, more will be given; and from the one who does not have, even what he does have will be taken away. ²⁷But bring here these enemies of mine, who did not want me to rule over them, and slaughter them in my presence.'"

When you first read the parable of the minas, coming at such a crucial moment in the flow of the ministry, you have to wonder, "What's up?" It is unusually long and filled with detail, there are so many characters, and all the coming and going can be confusing. And finally, the grisly scene at the end . . . it is enough to confuse and distract anyone. I must confess that it bothered me for some time. Then, as I read and reread the story, the pieces began to fit together. As I kept asking myself, "Why here?" the answer finally clicked.

This is a parable that is also a blueprint. It is an imaginative map of the centuries that will stretch between the cross and the second coming. More than any other parable, this one weaves in Jesus' own life situation. It has to be here in this narrative, not a chapter before or after, or else it would lose some of its timely significance.

In verse 11 Luke gives us one of the one-sentence introductions we have come to expect and depend on. The key phrase in the sentence is "because . . . they thought the kingdom of God was going to appear right away." The evidence is clear that many in the crowd think Jesus is going to Jerusalem to stage some kind of "holy coup." The disciples are bickering about thrones and who is the greatest. Jesus tells the parable as a subtle way to undeceive them.

A nobleman (Jesus) comes to a far country to be made king. He calls ten of his slaves (disciples) and entrusts them with the relatively small sum of ten minas, or about three months' worth of wages. The people who were to become the subjects revolt, refusing to have him as their king (the ultimate rejection of Jesus). When he returns (the second coming) he calls the slaves together and asked for an accounting. What have they done with the little that was entrusted to them? Some have done quite well and hear "well done." In proportion to their fruitfulness, they are assigned entire towns. Then we come to the final slave, who took the mina and foolishly hid it in a "sweat cloth." He explains that he was afraid that the king would try to collect where he hadn't even deposited anything.

The response of the king could not be less compassionate. He judges the slave according to his own words. Taking away the single mina, he gives it to the one with ten, to which the crowd responds with a degree of incredulity. They still haven't completely accepted the king's radical new value system. And so he explains in verse 26, "To everyone who has, more will be given; and from the one who does not have, even what he does have will be taken away." Jesus is repeating himself again; it is the same maxim he used after explaining the parable of the sower (Lk 8:18).

The gruesome sentence that is passed in verse 27 does not extend to the slaves. It is reserved for the enemies of the king, who refused his rule over them.

This is a parable designed to prepare Jesus' followers for what will become a most unexpected absence—two thousand years and counting! It is also the most severe warning to those who refuse to acknowledge him now as Lord and King.

A TEARFUL ENTRY

28When He had said these things, He went on ahead, going up to Jerusalem. 29As He approached Bethphage and Bethany, at the place called the Mount of Olives, He sent two of the disciples 30and said, "Go into the village ahead of you. As you enter it, you will find a young donkey tied there, on which no one has ever sat. Untie it and bring it here. 31If anyone asks you, 'Why are you untying it?' say this: 'The Lord needs it.'"

32So those who were sent left and found it just as He had told them. 33As they were untying the young donkey, its owners said to them, "Why are you untying the donkey?"

34"The Lord needs it," they said. 35Then they brought it to Jesus, and after throwing their robes on the donkey, they helped Jesus get on it. 36As He was going along, they were spreading their robes on the road. 37Now He came near the path down the Mount of Olives, and the whole crowd of the disciples began to praise God joyfully with a loud voice for all the miracles they had seen:

> *38Blessed is the King*
> *who comes in the name of the Lord.*
>
> *Peace in heaven*
> *and glory in the highest heaven!*

39Some of the Pharisees from the crowd told Him, "Teacher, rebuke Your disciples."

40He answered, "I tell you, if they were to keep silent, the stones would cry out!"

41As He approached and saw the city, He wept over it, 42saying, "If you knew this day what [would bring] peace—but now it is hidden from your eyes. 43For the days will come on you when your enemies will build an embankment against you, surround you, and hem you in on every side. 44They will crush you and your children within you to the ground, and they will not leave one stone on another in you, because you did not recognize the time of your visitation."

At long last, the goal of the journey is reached. The Mount of Olives is only a good bowshot from Jerusalem. Today it is one of the most popular overlooks for the Temple Mount. From here Jesus sends two of his disciples to fetch the donkey, which he has prearranged. This fact is indicated by his instructions to them to answer, "The Lord needs it," if they are challenged by its owners.

Though Luke does not quote Zechariah 9:9, it is clearly the backdrop for the next few verses: "Rejoice greatly, Daughter Zion! Shout in triumph, Daughter Jerusalem! See, your King is coming to you; He is righteous and victorious, humble and riding on a donkey."

As the crowd begins to descend the Mount of Olives, just a few hundred yards remain to cross the Kidron Valley and ascend the hill to Jerusalem. Here the disciples of Jesus, amid the much larger Passover throng, begin singing, first a psalm (Ps 118:26). Then, remarkably, they sing a fragment of the very song the angels sang at Jesus' birth (Lk 2:14). They are exuberant, owing to all the miracles they have witnessed along the way.

Some of the Pharisees, who seem to be moving along with the crowd, chastise Jesus, telling him to silence the disciples. Jesus answers that the stones would cry out if the disciples were silenced. As the enormous walls of the city loom before them, Jesus, overcome by his own prophetic insight, begins to weep. In horrifying detail, he paints a picture of what Titus and the Romans will do to the city in A.D. 70. It is an image he will not be able to erase from his mind (see Lk 21:20-24).

This moment is traditionally called the triumphal entry. This refers to the adulation that surrounds Jesus as he enters the city. More significant, I think, is the fact that as he enters the gates of the city, he is still wiping the tears from his eyes.

THE SECOND TEMPLE CLEANSING

[45] He went into the temple complex and began to throw out those who were selling, [46] and He said, "It is written, My house will be a house of prayer, but you have made it a den of thieves!"

[47] Every day He was teaching in the temple complex. The chief priests, the scribes, and the leaders of the people were looking for a way to destroy Him, [48] but they could not find a way to do it, because all the people were captivated by what they heard.

*T*he second temple cleansing is the first hiccup in the chronology of Passion Week. According to some reconstructions, it occurs immediately upon Jesus' arrival. In others, it happens the next day. Whichever it was, its significance is connected to Luke's major theme of prayer. The temple market was normally located on the Mount of Olives. This is the second time it was ever said to have been located in the temple complex (see Jn 2:14). This area was as close as Gentile believers (known as "God-fearers") could come to the heart of the temple complex. When Jesus sees, for the second time, that the market has been set up here, he is filled with righteous anger and drives the merchants from the area. The purpose, according to Luke's Gospel, is to reestablish a quiet place so the Gentiles can pray.

With Luke 19:47, we settle into what will be Jesus' final week. A part of every remaining day will be spent teaching in the temple area, while the Jewish authorities look for a way to destroy him.

LUKE 20

Six Trick Questions

1. BY WHOSE AUTHORITY?

20:1-2 The question of the second temple expulsion.

2. JOHN'S BAPTISM: FROM HEAVEN OR HUMANS?

20:3-8 Jesus questions the Jewish leaders.

3. WHAT WILL THE OWNER DO?

20:9-15a Parable of the talents.
20:15b Jesus concludes with a question.
20:16-19 Aftermath.

4. PAY TAXES OR NOT?

20:20-22 Another trick question for Jesus.
20:23-26 Jesus' answer.

5. WHOSE WIFE WILL SHE BE?

20:27-32 The Sadducees' unlikely story.
20:33 Yet another trick question for Jesus.
20:34-38 Jesus' answer.
20:39-40 Aftermath.

6. HOW CAN CHRIST BE DAVID'S SON?

20:41-44 Jesus poses his most unanswerable question.
20:45-47 "Beware the teachers of the law."

1. BY WHOSE AUTHORITY?

¹One day as He was teaching the people in the temple complex and proclaiming the good news, the chief priests and the scribes, with the elders, came up ²and said to Him: "Tell us, by what authority are You doing these things? Who is it who gave You this authority?"

Luke 20 turns on six major questions. If we were looking for an example of Luke functioning in an editorial way, this chapter is a great one. He has grouped the questions that were asked to and by Jesus during the Passion Week. Here we see that questions, as they so often do, can tell us more than answers.

Luke 19:47 left us with the image of Jesus going to the temple to teach. Here in verse 1 of chapter 20, we see him doing just that. Notice that Luke does not specifically refer to the Pharisees when he describes the group that is coming together to persecute and trap Jesus. The chief priests, who we are meeting here for the first time, oversaw all of the activities of the temple. They possessed a large measure of authority within the religious arenas. The scribes might have come from anywhere. Some, no doubt, arrived in the crowd along with Jesus. Many lived in and around Jerusalem. The elders have been described as "a type of collegial religious and civil authority over Israel. They comprised what amounted to the supreme court of Israel, the Sanhedrin."[12]

This first confrontational question probably relates to Jesus casting the merchants out of the court of the Gentiles the day before. Notice here that no one ever says that what Jesus did was actually wrong. It is only a matter of authority: "Who gave you the authority to do these things?" Luke does not indicate whether this question is a trap. The only two answers Jesus could possibly offer, however, will pose problems for him. If he answers that his authority comes from humans, then they can denounce him as a disturber of the peace, or *Pax Romana*. If Jesus says his authority is from God, this will open up a more serious charge of blasphemy.

2. JOHN'S BAPTISM: FROM HEAVEN OR HUMANS?

³He answered them, "I will also ask you a question. Tell Me, ⁴was the baptism of John from heaven or from men?"

⁵They discussed it among themselves: "If we say, 'From heaven,' He will say, 'Why didn't you believe him?' ⁶But if we say, 'From men,' all the people will stone us, because they are convinced that John was a prophet."

⁷So they answered that they did not know its origin.

⁸And Jesus said to them, "Neither will I tell you by what authority I do these things."

$\mathcal{A}$s he so often does, Jesus answers their question with another, harder question. He leaves them with the same list of possible answers that was left to him. Was John's baptism of *heaven* or of *humanity?* Verse 5 tells of their whispered discussion. Both answers are potentially dangerous. If they acknowledge it was from heaven, then the people will denounce them for not giving John their support. If they say it was from humans, they will face the even more serious charge of blasphemy. In the next verse we hear this group say something that I would assume they rarely, if ever, said: "We don't know." Since they cannot give an answer to Jesus' question, they have lost the intellectual capital to coerce Jesus to answer their question. It is a stalemate.

3. WHAT WILL THE OWNER DO?

⁹Then He began to tell the people this parable: "A man planted a vineyard, leased it to tenant farmers, and went away for a long time. ¹⁰At harvest time he sent a slave to the farmers so that they might give him some fruit from the vineyard. But the farmers beat him and sent him away empty-handed. ¹¹He sent yet another slave, but they beat that one too, treated him shamefully, and sent him away empty-handed. ¹²And he sent yet a third, but they wounded this one too and threw him out.

¹³"Then the owner of the vineyard said, 'What should I do? I will send my beloved son. Perhaps they will respect him.'

¹⁴"But when the tenant farmers saw him, they discussed it among themselves and said, 'This is the heir. Let's kill him, so the inheritance will be ours!' ¹⁵So they threw him out of the vineyard and killed him.

"Therefore, what will the owner of the vineyard do to them? ¹⁶He will come and destroy those farmers and give the vineyard to others."

But when they heard this they said, "No—never!"

¹⁷But He looked at them and said, "Then what is the meaning of this Scripture:

> *The stone that the builders rejected—*
> *this has become the cornerstone?*

¹⁸Everyone who falls on that stone will be broken to pieces, and if it falls on anyone, it will grind him to powder!"

¹⁹Then the scribes and the chief priests looked for a way to get their hands on Him that very hour, because they knew He had told this parable against them, but they feared the people.

*T*his is now the second parable Jesus has told that is actually a veiled story of his own experience (see Lk 19:11-27). He draws the images for the parable from the prophetically charged song of the vineyard in Isaiah 5:1-7 (NIV):

> ¹I will sing for the one I love
> > a song about his vineyard:
> My loved one had a vineyard
> > on a fertile hillside.
> ²He dug it up and cleared it of stones
> > and planted it with the choicest vines.
> He built a watchtower in it
> > and cut out a winepress as well.
> Then he looked for a crop of good grapes,
> > but it yielded only bad fruit.
>
> ³"Now you dwellers in Jerusalem and men of Judah,
> > judge between me and my vineyard.
> ⁴What more could have been done for my vineyard
> > than I have done for it?
> When I looked for good grapes,
> > why did it yield only bad?
> ⁵Now I will tell you
> > what I am going to do to my vineyard:

I will take away its hedge,
    and it will be destroyed;
I will break down its wall,
    and it will be trampled.
⁶I will make it a wasteland,
    neither pruned nor cultivated,
    and briers and thorns will grow there.
I will command the clouds
    not to rain on it."

⁷The vineyard of the LORD Almighty
    is the house of Israel,
and the men of Judah
    are the garden of his delight.
And he looked for justice, but saw bloodshed;
    for righteousness, but heard cries of distress.

The problem with Jesus' parable is not its obscurity. Who the characters represent is all too clear. A man who owns a vineyard (God) leases it to some tenant farmers (Israel). When the harvest comes, he sends slaves (the prophets) to collect his portion of the fruit. The farmers beat the slaves and send them away (just as Israel routinely persecuted the prophets).

The farmer sends more of his slaves, but they are all beaten and sent back empty-handed. Finally the owner (God) decides to send his son (Jesus), incorrectly assuming that the farmers will respect him.

When the farmers see the son coming, they falsely assume that the owner has died. If they kill the son, they believe the vineyard will be theirs. So they brutally kill the beloved son.

Jesus concludes the parable with this question: "What will the owner do?" I believe he tells the story so convincingly that the crowd is caught up in the sad drama. Then, when they hear Jesus answer his own question with, "He will come and destroy those farmers, . . ." they erupt, "No—never!" They're like moviegoers who get so caught up in the story that they shout at the screen.

Jesus quotes Psalm 118:22 as his conclusion. It is the image of the *skandalon:* the Messiah as the great Stumbling Stone. The image in the psalm comes from a tradition that one of the stones intended for the temple, which was initially rejected, ended up being used as the chief cornerstone, the most visible stone in the structure.

In verse 18 Jesus lists the only two possibilities of encountering this messianic Stone. The first possibility is that a person can stumble over it and be broken—a metaphor of what happens to all Jesus' disciples. Brokenness is foundational to becoming a follower. The second possibility speaks of the judgment that will fall, like a stone, on those who refuse to accept Jesus' saving grace. It is an image of complete, grinding destruction.

The response of the priests and scribes in Luke 20:19 is predictable. This is not a veiled conundrum of a parable. Its message is all too obvious, and they receive it loud and clear.

4. PAY TAXES OR NOT?

20 They watched closely and sent spies who pretended to be righteous, so they could catch Him in what He said, to hand Him over to the governor's rule and authority. 21 They questioned Him, "Teacher, we know that You speak and teach correctly, and You don't show partiality, but teach truthfully the way of God. 22 Is it lawful for us to pay taxes to Caesar or not?"

23 But detecting their craftiness, He said to them, 24 "Show Me a denarius. Whose image and inscription does it have?"

"Caesar's," they said.

25 "Well then," He told them, "give back to Caesar the things that are Caesar's and to God the things that are God's."

26 They were not able to catch Him in what He said in public, and being amazed at His answer, they became silent.

*T*he next confrontational question comes from a group of "spies." It is the only time this term appears in the New Testament. It comes from a Greek verb that means "to send in." The word paints the image of someone being sent in to covertly reconnoiter an enemy town. The very next word also only appears here in the New Testament. This reminds us of Luke's massive vocabulary. It means "to feign." It comes from the same root as "hypocrite." Luke sees them as "hypocritical spies." They are charged with the clandestine mission of pretending to be righteous in order to trick Jesus into some kind of a political misstep. If they are successful, they intend to hand him over to Pilate, who is in residence in Jerusalem to help keep the peace during Passover. This should be seen as a secular trap.

The introduction to their question, even two thousand years later, still drips with insincerity. It is another trap. No matter if Jesus answers "yes" or "no," he will be caught. If he answers, "Yes, pay Caesar's taxes," the Jews—and in particular the Zealots—will immediately put him on the top of their hit list. If he answers, "No, don't pay Caesar's taxes," he will be clearly infringing on the absolute authority of Rome and subject to immediate arrest.

Jesus asks for a Roman denarius, the type of coin used to pay the tax. If the coin was current, it would have displayed the image of Tiberius on one side (see Lk 3:1). Remember Tiberius Claudius Nero, the reluctant, lecherous emperor who came to power through the machinations of his mother Livia? By this time he had already retired to the isle of Capri. Suetonius tells us that he lived there in debauchery until his death in A.D. 37.

Jesus' question really has two sides, like the coin he is holding up. Whose "image" and whose "inscription" does it contain? Whether the image is of Tiberius or Octavius makes little difference. It is the inscription that offers the key to understanding this passage. Beneath the picture of the emperor would have been an inscription that contained either the words "divine Caesar" or "Caesar our Savior."

Jesus answers them with a maxim that I believe is often misinterpreted and misused. He says, "Give back to Caesar the things that are Caesar's and to God the things that are God's." So often this verse is quoted to support the notion of a Christian's duty to support the state. This principle is indeed supported elsewhere in Scripture (see Rom 13:1) but not here. Behind Jesus' veiled answer is the conviction that nothing belongs to an emperor who claims to be divine.

It is not the answer they were hoping for. It is not an answer they would have even anticipated. Now for the second time, Jesus has silenced his opponents.

5. WHOSE WIFE WILL SHE BE?

[27]Some of the Sadducees, who say there is no resurrection, came up and questioned Him: [28]"Teacher, Moses wrote for us that if a man's brother has a wife, and dies childless, his brother should take the wife and produce offspring for his brother. [29]Now there were seven brothers. The first took a wife and died without children. [30]Also the second [31]and the third took her. In the same way, all seven died and left no children. [32]Finally, the woman died too. [33]Therefore, in the resurrection, whose wife will the woman be? For all seven had married her."

[34]Jesus told them, "The sons of this age marry and are given in marriage. [35]But those who are counted worthy to take part in that age and in the resurrection from the dead neither marry nor are given in marriage. [36]For they cannot die anymore, because they are like angels and are sons of God, since they are sons of the resurrection. [37]Moses even indicated [in the passage] about the burning bush that the dead are raised, where he calls the Lord the God of Abraham and the God of Isaac and the God of Jacob. [38]He is not God of the dead but of the living, because all are living to Him."

[39]Some of the scribes answered, "Teacher, You have spoken well." [40]And they no longer dared to ask Him anything.

*T*he Sadducees were an aristocratic party formed in the first century B.C. According to Josephus, they were not looking for the Messiah, as the Pharisees so adamantly were. The only Scriptures the Sadducees regarded as authoritative were the books of Moses. They rejected the existence of angelic beings and, above all, they denied the reality of resurrection, or, more precisely, life after death. It was indeed duplicitous of them to pose a question based on a concept in which they did not believe.

At first, it seems to be a question on marriage—levirate marriage, to be precise (see Deut 25:5-10). If a man died without leaving an heir, the law provided that his brother could have children by his widow, thus assuring the deceased man would have offspring and his name would not die with him. In reality, however, the Sadducees' question is about the resurrection.

They are hoping that in the course of giving an answer, Jesus will affirm the resurrection, thereby allowing them to prosecute him.

Jesus' answer indeed affirms the reality of the resurrection. Their dilemma is that he uses a reference from the Torah, their own Scripture, to demonstrate it. Jesus alludes to the story of the burning bush in Exodus. There God refers to himself as "the God of Abraham, the God of Isaac, and the God of Jacob" (Ex 3:6). Jesus reasons that God is not the God of the dead but of the living, because all are living to him. This is a statement with which the Sadducees would be forced to agree.

In an instant, the argument is over. Luke assumes we will follow Jesus' rabbinic logic and understand the implications of his last assertion. Since Abraham, Isaac and Jacob are "alive" to God, even after their death they still "live." Then the resurrection, which speaks of someone coming to life after they have died, must be a reality.

No doubt with a smile on his face, Luke records a response from some of the scribes. They would have been Pharisees who believed vehemently in the resurrection. "Well said!" they call out to Jesus. For a third time, Jesus' opponents are silenced by his brilliant questions and answers.

6. HOW CAN CHRIST BE DAVID'S SON?

⁴¹Then He said to them, "How can they say that the Messiah is the Son of David? ⁴²For David himself says in the Book of Psalms:

> *The Lord declared to my Lord,*
> *'Sit at My right hand*
> *⁴³until I make Your enemies Your footstool.'*

⁴⁴David calls Him 'Lord'; how then can the Messiah be his Son?"

⁴⁵While all the people were listening, He said to His disciples, ⁴⁶"Beware of the scribes, who want to go around in long robes and who love greetings in the marketplaces, the front seats in the synagogues, and the places of honor at banquets. ⁴⁷They devour widows' houses and say long prayers just for show. These will receive greater punishment."

*J*esus' interrogative coup de grâce comes in verses 41-44. He poses a dilemma so obscure that once more there isn't a word of response from the religious leaders. One of the favorite rabbinic titles for the Messiah was "son of David." This comes from the promise that from David's line, the Messiah would be born (2 Sam 7:11-16). Yet Jesus goes on to say, "David calls Him [the Messiah] 'Lord'" (see Ps 110:1). If David calls him "Lord," a term that affirms David's subordination to the Messiah, then how can the Messiah be called David's "son"?

At this point in the narrative, you must imagine the scribes grasping for biblical or rabbinic references to help them out of the cul-de-sac in which Jesus has abandoned them. Luke leaves Jesus' opponents speechless in the text. There is not a word of response. This could well be Luke's invitation to you and me to engage with our imaginations.

With scribes, Sadducees, spies and Pharisees left "bruised and bleeding" all around, Jesus turns back to the crowd and issues his final warning. He tells them the scribes are in this for the pomp, the grandiose greetings and the important seats of honor. They say long prayers "just for show." Jesus accuses them of devouring widows' houses. The scribes have exploited the most helpless members of the community they are responsible to serve. This last condemnation prepares for the next scene.

LUKE 21

A WIDOW OFFERS HER LIFE

¹He looked up and saw the rich dropping their offerings into the temple treasury. ²He also saw a poor widow dropping in two tiny coins. ³"I tell you the truth," He said. "This poor widow has put in more than all of them. ⁴For all these people have put in gifts out of their surplus, but she out of her poverty has put in all she had to live on."

Luke 20 closes with a word about widows directed at the Pharisees who "devour widows' houses." Apparently these religious teachers were taking advantage of the hospitality of poor widows. Luke 21 opens with a touching story of a poor but generous widow, revealing how marvelously Luke's narrative is woven together.

We have seen before that Luke loves to contrast religious (and usually wealthy) people who should get it but don't with marginalized (and usually poor) people who should not get it but do. Imagine the scene: Jesus leans against the wall across from the temple treasury as a line of the faithful drop their monetary gifts into the metal, trumpet-shaped receptacles. The wealthy dump in their money bags with a presumptuous, prolonged clatter. At the end of the line a widow, who lives at the level of poverty, quietly drops in two *lepta*, the smallest copper coins. The tiny wisps of metal would have barely made a sound as they fell into the treasury chest.

Jesus' intuition tells him that these two coins were all she had to live on. Since there were two coins, she might have kept one for herself, to stave off starvation for a few more days. But her heart is one that cannot hold anything back. In Jesus' eyes, her two tiny coins are more precious than the other bags of gold.

There is an ancient rabbinic story found in *Leviticus Rabbah* 3:107a about a presumptuous priest who refused the offering of a handful of meal offered by another poor widow. He did not see any value in such a small gift. That night in a dream he was told, "Do not despise her. It is as if she offered her very life."

TWO QUESTIONS, TWO ANSWERS
(The First Question)

⁵As some were talking about the temple complex, how it was adorned with beautiful stones and gifts dedicated to God, He said, ⁶"These things that you see—the days will come when not one stone will be left on another that will not be thrown down!"

⁷"Teacher," they asked Him, "so when will these things be? And what will be the sign when these things are about to take place?"

⁸Then He said, "Watch out that you are not deceived. For many will come in My name, saying, 'I am He,' and, 'The time is near.' Don't follow them. ⁹When you hear of wars and rebellions, don't be alarmed. Indeed, these things must take place first, but the end won't come right away."

¹⁰Then He told them: "Nation will be raised up against nation, and kingdom against kingdom. ¹¹There will be violent earthquakes, and famines and plagues in various places, and there will be terrifying sights and great signs from heaven. ¹²But before all these things, they will lay their hands on you and persecute you. They will hand you over to the synagogues and prisons, and you will be brought before kings and governors because of My name. ¹³It will lead to an opportunity for you to witness. ¹⁴Therefore make up your minds not to prepare your defense ahead of time, ¹⁵for I will give you such words and a wisdom that none of your adversaries will be able to resist or contradict. ¹⁶You will even be betrayed by parents, brothers, relatives, and friends. They will kill some of you. ¹⁷You will be hated by everyone because of My name, ¹⁸but not a hair of your head will be lost. ¹⁹By your endurance gain your lives.

²⁰"When you see Jerusalem surrounded by armies, then recognize that its desolation has come near. ²¹Then those in Judea must flee to the mountains! Those inside the city must leave it, and those who are in the country must not enter it, ²²because these are days of vengeance to fulfill all the things that are written. ²³Woe to pregnant women and nursing mothers in those days, for there will be great distress in the land and wrath against this people. ²⁴They will fall by the edge of the sword and be led captive into all the nations, and Jerusalem will be trampled by the Gentiles until the times of the Gentiles are fulfilled.

*J*esus has surprisingly little to say with regard to specifics about the end times. He is more interested, I believe, in our faithfulness here and now than how informed we are regarding the intimate details of the end of the world as we know it. In Matthew he says that even *he* does not know when it will occur, an amazingly mystifying confession (Mt 24:36). When it happens, says Jesus, it will be obvious to all, like lightning flashing from horizon to horizon (Lk 17:24). In order to be "ready," in the meantime, we are to be found serving him.

We have seen that he tends to follow a pattern. First Jesus explains events in the near future—events from which a person can run away. Then his language becomes apocalyptic and he describes a cataclysm with cosmic images from which no one can run.

Jesus' alarming statement in Luke 21:6 comes in response to the disciples calling attention to the beautiful stones that adorned the walls of the temple. Mark 13:1 speaks of the disciples pointing out the "massive" stones of the foundation, a few of which are larger than the stones in the pyramids of Egypt. Jesus seems tense, perhaps even angry. His disciples are stunned by his words and respond with two questions that are really only in regard to one event. First they ask, "When will these things be?" and second, "What will be the sign when these things are about to take place?"

Jesus understands that his statement concerning the stones being thrown down might have sounded to them like the end of the world, and so he provides his first answer (Lk 21:8-24) concerning near-future events of persecution and finally of the destruction of the temple. The first answer is filled with concrete images: wars, earthquakes, Jerusalem being surrounded by an army. Jesus is describing an event that you might run away from. "Flee to the mountains," he says (v. 21). With prophetic clarity, Jesus describes the siege of Jerusalem by Titus in A.D. 70.

In verse 8, Jesus warns his disciples not to be fooled by people who might come in his name. "Don't follow them," he says. In a passage that is frequently misinterpreted, Jesus tells them *not* to be alarmed by "wars and rumors of wars." Before any of these things occur, they will be brought before kings and governors, something we will see literally fulfilled in Luke's second volume, Acts. The disciples will be hated, even killed for Jesus' name.

Verse 20 jumps ahead to A.D. 70, when Titus surrounded the city with three legions for an entire year. The suffering inside the walls was unimaginable. Some people even resorted to cannibalism. These horrific images in Jesus' imagination are what caused him to weep when he entered Jerusalem.

When you see these things, he warns them, "Flee to the mountains." Shortly after he laid siege to the city, Titus surrounded it with a low wall, marking the boundary, the line past which no one could go. He built the same sort of low wall around Masada, the remains of which can still be seen today.

In book 5 of his *War of the Jews*, Josephus describes specifically the suffering of the women in the besieged city. After it was all over, the Romans crucified those left alive until they literally ran out of wood for making crosses. In verse 23 Jesus mentions pregnant women and nursing mothers, who provide some of the most ghastly images in Josephus's account. The few who survived were dispersed. Many were sold as slaves. From the proceeds of the sacking of the city, Titus was able to construct the well-known Colosseum. This Jesus refers to as the fulfillment of the "times of the Gentiles."

(The Second Question)

^{25} *"Then there will be signs in the sun, moon, and stars; and there will be anguish on the earth among nations bewildered by the roaring sea and waves.* ^{26} *People will faint from fear and expectation of the things that are coming on the world, because the celestial powers will be shaken.* ^{27} *Then they will see the Son of Man coming in a cloud with power and great glory.* ^{28} *But when these things begin to take place, stand up and lift up your heads, because your redemption is near!"*

Luke gives us the disciples' first question in verse 7. He also provides both of Jesus' answers: the near-future answer that deals with persecutions and the fall of Jerusalem (Lk 21:8-24) as well as the second apocalyptic answer here in Luke 21:25-28. What is not provided in Luke is the second question. We need to turn to Matthew 24:3 to retrieve this one. In addition to the first question we have already read in Luke 21:7, the Twelve ask: "And what is the sign of Your coming and of the end of the age?" (Mt 24:3).

This is a very different question indeed, and the shift in verse 25 as Jesus begins to answer it is no less startling. The impact, says Jesus, will be astronomical: signs in the sun and moon and stars: "Celestial powers will be shaken." This is the same event he described for us in Luke 17:31, in which he warned those on the rooftops not to go down to retrieve their belongings. At the moment at which things seem most helpless, Jesus encourages the disciples (and us) to "lift up your heads." When we do, we will behold a second coming that could not be more different than the first so-called triumphal entry we read about in Luke 19:28-40. Jesus will come in a cloud, "with power and great glory." Later Paul, Luke's companion, will say that Jesus will be "marveled at among all who have believed" (2 Thess 1:10 ESV).

A LESSON FROM THE LEAVES

29 Then He told them a parable: "Look at the fig tree, and all the trees. 30 As soon as they put out [leaves] you can see for yourselves and recognize that summer is already near. 31 In the same way, when you see these things happening, recognize that the kingdom of God is near. 32 I assure you: This generation will certainly not pass away until all things take place. 33 Heaven and earth will pass away, but My words will never pass away.

34 "Be on your guard, so that your minds are not dulled from carousing, drunkenness, and worries of life, or that day will come on you unexpectedly 35 like a trap. For it will come on all who live on the face of the whole earth. 36 But be alert at all times, praying that you may have strength to escape all these things that are going to take place and to stand before the Son of Man."

37 During the day, He was teaching in the temple complex, but in the evening He would go out and spend the night on what is called the Mount of Olives. 38 Then all the people would come early in the morning to hear Him in the temple complex.

*I*t seems as if, to make a point real, Jesus feels the desire to fictionalize it. Perhaps a parable reaches us more broadly and more deeply than mere didactic information. He can list the signs, both concrete and apocalyptic, but they are too big for our minds to contain. But the feeling of looking for a lost coin or waiting for a wayward child or anticipating the change in the trees when spring is here: those things we can understand with all of our hearts and minds.

In contrast to the over-the-top images with which he has startled them, Jesus directs their attentions to a simple fig tree. I imagine him pointing out an actual, living fig tree, although he implies that it could be any tree. It is spring, after all, and the trees around Jerusalem, especially the heavily wooded Mount of Olives, would just be leafing out.

The appearance of leaves is a certain sign that summer is near, says Jesus. You can sense the disciples calming down and starting to focus. In the same way, he suggests to them, know that when you see the things I have spoken of beginning to appear, the kingdom is near.

The promise in verse 32—that this generation would not pass away until all these things take place—has been interpreted two ways. First, "this generation" could refer to everyone who was alive in Jesus' day. They would not pass away until "all these things" (Lk 21:32 NIV)—namely, the concrete predictions of the near-future persecutions and the fall of Jerusalem—occur. The other interpretation understands "generation" to represent the entire human race. In other words, the race of humankind will not die out before "all these things"—meaning the entire range of Jesus' prophetic utterance, including the end of the world—take place. I prefer the first approach. It connects to the first answer, while the final charge is connected to the second. This last pronouncement (vv. 33-36) clearly applies to the second, apocalyptic answer, since Jesus says it will come on "all who live on the face of the whole earth."

Notice that none of Jesus' advice includes scrutinizing the signs or making calculations. He simply says, "Be on your guard." No matter when the kingdom finally breaks in, the way to truly be ready is to be faithful and found serving when he comes. And he *will* come, as surely as spring turns into summer; just look at the leaves.

LUKE 22

FOR THE PRICE OF A SLAVE

¹The Festival of Unleavened Bread, which is called Passover, was draw-
ing near. ²The chief priests and the scribes were looking for a way to put Him
to death, because they were afraid of the people.

³Then Satan entered Judas, called Iscariot, who was numbered among the
Twelve. ⁴He went away and discussed with the chief priests and temple police
how he could hand Him over to them. ⁵They were glad and agreed to give
him silver. ⁶So he accepted [the offer] and started looking for a good opportu-
nity to betray Him to them when the crowd was not present.

It seems as if some dark gravitational force is drawing people together
to the plot to have Jesus crucified. Here we read that the chief priests
and the scribes have banded together. The priests were, by and large,
Sadducees, while the scribes were part of the Pharisaic movement. The
first group, wealthy and aristocratic, brokered a deal with Rome and
bought the priesthood. They were well known for their scornful atti-
tude toward the ʿam haʾarets, the "mob" or "people of the land" (see Jn
7:49). The Pharisees, on the other hand, were the party of the people.
They were the back-to-the-Bible movement that Israel had been waiting for. They were blue-collar, working-class men. Hillel had been a
woodcutter. Shammai was in construction. Paul, that most celebrated
of Pharisees, worked in leather. The Sadducees and the Pharisees were
so radically different, yet they were woven together by their fear of and
hatred for Jesus of Nazareth.

Even Judas, one of the Twelve, was pulled into the plot. He will
forever be a dark cipher in the story of Jesus. The disciples, the authors
of the four Gospels and most of us today still ask ourselves how he
could have done it. How could someone spend almost three years with
a man who perfectly lived a life of love and servanthood—and then
hand him over to his enemies? Perhaps we should add Judas's name to
the list of those who hate *hesed*. Luke says in verse 4 that Judas discussed with the temple guards and priests how he could place Jesus into
their hands. Matthew says that he first approached them by simply
asking, "What are you willing to give me if I hand Him over to you?"

(Mt 26:15). Here, in Luke 22:5, Luke says they were glad to give him silver. Matthew tells us it was thirty pieces of silver—which is, ironically, the price that Exodus 21:32 places on the life of a slave. I often wonder if Judas, scornful of the way Jesus would humiliate himself by serving the disciples and acting as if he were a slave, decided that thirty pieces of silver was the perfect price. Experts in ancient coins have calculated that thirty pieces of these particular silver coins from the temple treasury would have been worth about five thousand dollars in today's money, although valuing ancient currency is tricky at best.

Verse 6 states that, after the meeting, Judas begins looking for an opportune time to hand over Jesus. Since they have arrived in Jerusalem, Jesus has been spending the evenings on the Mount of Olives (Lk 21:37), where the garden of Gethsemane is located. I can imagine Judas filing the location away in his mind as one of the best possible places, because Jesus would be most vulnerable there.

THE SERVANT SAVIOR

[7] Then the Day of Unleavened Bread came when the Passover lamb had to be sacrificed. [8] Jesus sent Peter and John, saying, "Go and prepare the Passover meal for us, so we can eat it."

[9] "Where do You want us to prepare it?" they asked Him.

[10] "Listen," He said to them, "when you've entered the city, a man carrying a water jug will meet you. Follow him into the house he enters. [11] Tell the owner of the house, 'The Teacher asks you, "Where is the guest room where I can eat the Passover with My disciples?"' [12] Then he will show you a large, furnished room upstairs. Make the preparations there."

[13] So they went and found it just as He had told them, and they prepared the Passover.

[14] When the hour came, He reclined at the table, and the apostles with Him. [15] Then He said to them, "I have fervently desired to eat this Passover with you before I suffer. [16] For I tell you, I will not eat it again until it is fulfilled in the kingdom of God." [17] Then He took a cup, and after giving thanks, He said, "Take this and share it among yourselves. [18] For I tell you, from now on I will not drink of the fruit of the vine until the kingdom of God comes."

¹⁹And He took bread, gave thanks, broke it, gave it to them, and said, "This is My body, which is given for you. Do this in remembrance of Me." ²⁰In the same way He also took the cup after supper and said, "This cup is the new covenant [established by] My blood; it is shed for you. ²¹But look, the hand of the one betraying Me is at the table with Me! ²²For the Son of Man will go away as it has been determined, but woe to that man by whom He is betrayed!"

²³So they began to argue among themselves which of them it could be who was going to do this thing.

²⁴Then a dispute also arose among them about who should be considered the greatest. ²⁵But He said to them, "The kings of the Gentiles dominate them, and those who have authority over them are called 'Benefactors.' ²⁶But it must not be like that among you. On the contrary, whoever is greatest among you must become like the youngest, and whoever leads, like the one serving. ²⁷For who is greater, the one at the table or the one serving? Isn't it the one at the table? But I am among you as the One who serves. ²⁸You are the ones who stood by Me in My trials. ²⁹I bestow on you a kingdom, just as My Father bestowed one on Me, ³⁰so that you may eat and drink at My table in My kingdom. And you will sit on thrones judging the 12 tribes of Israel.

Passover has finally arrived, and Jesus assigns Peter and John the task of making the elaborate preparations for the ceremonial meal. I suppose Jesus could have asked a couple of the women who were traveling with them to make the preparations, but I wonder whether he is trying to instill in Peter and his young friend John a lesson about servanthood. It is going to be a long day and night for Simon. Every time he tries to do the right thing, Jesus will rebuke him for it. He will pledge his loyalty, and Jesus will respond by telling him that he's going to deny him three times. When he approaches Peter to wash his feet, out of respect for Jesus, Peter will try to refuse; yet then Jesus will tell him that unless he submits, they have nothing in common. He alone will have the courage to draw his sword in the garden, and yet Jesus will rebuke him and tell him to put it away.

For now the two disciples set out to buy the essentials for the Passover meal: the bitter herbs, the unleavened bread, the wine and most especially the lamb. They are told to look for a man carrying a water jar. That will be easy to spot, since men don't normally carry water; that is a job for women. It is another one of those prearranged signals, like finding the donkey for Jesus to ride into Jerusalem (Lk 19:30). Perhaps it is even the same person, a family acquaintance of Jesus who lives in Jerusalem.

I can see Peter and John, perhaps a bit frazzled by the work of preparation, welcoming the other disciples and Jesus into the upstairs room where they have spent a busy day preparing the meal. As everyone reclines around the banquet table, Jesus begins by telling the Twelve how he has longed to spend this time with them before he suffers. He tells them this will be the last time he will eat this meal until it is fulfilled in the kingdom. It will be the last time he will drink this cup until the kingdom comes. He can only mean that their little meal in the upper room in Jerusalem is just a shadow of the fulfillment of the meal that they will celebrate as the wedding supper of the Lamb (Is 25:6-9; Rev 19:7). The prescribed toast at this point in the traditional meal was, "This year in Jerusalem; next year the kingdom!"

Next, Jesus takes the unleavened bread of Passover and hands it out to the Twelve, saying, "This is My body, which is given for you." He asks that they remember him every time they celebrate the meal. Later, after the resurrection, a few of them will have their eyes opened when the risen Lord breaks the bread (Lk 24:30-35). After supper, he takes the final cup of the meal and passes it around, saying, "This cup is the new covenant . . . it is shed for you" (see Jer 31:31-34).

As the shadows begin to gather around the table, the disciples seem confused and dazed by all the talk of his broken body and poured-out blood. In stunned silence they recline around the low table and try to come up with something meaningful to talk about. Just then Jesus breaks the uncomfortable silence with still more bad news. One of them is going to betray him—someone whose hand is on the table (Ps 41:9). Da Vinci tried to capture this moment of confusion in his famous painting of the Last Supper. But even as great a painter as him could not hope to have portrayed the scene.

In verse 23 they begin to argue about which one it might be. Clearly, Judas is not the obvious choice. He has not been a shadowy figure, lurking in the background for the last three years. John tells us he was, in fact, regarded so highly that the others had made him treasurer, that trusted person who kept track of the money bag. When he leaves in a few moments to go and meet with the temple guards and the high priest, no one will think anything about it. The disciples assume he is going to give something to the poor. If anyone had had an inkling of what he was about to do, Judas would have never left the room alive.

The argument about who the betrayer might be quickly transitions into a dispute about which one of them is the greatest. This is not the first time they have argued about this (Lk 9:46). It is precisely this argument that causes Jesus to do the unthinkable. In fact, it is such a bizarre thing to do that Luke cannot bring himself to tell us the story. Only John, decades later, is able to tell the heartbreaking account of Jesus washing their feet. But Luke gives us something that John does not. Only Luke provides Jesus' explanation after the foot washing.

It must have happened somewhere around verse 25. Jesus is wordlessly responding to their argument about who is greatest with a living parable of servanthood. (Perhaps at this point he has given up on words.) Now, after the silent lesson is over, Jesus settles back into his place at the table and begins to explain what he has just done. It must be during this discourse that Judas slips out.

He begins by trying to appeal to their identity as Jewish men. Don't be like the Gentiles, Jesus tells them—people who simply use good works to gain the social position of "benefactor."

In the Roman world, aspiring politicians would climb the social ladder (the *cursus honorum*) by acts of public generosity and donations for temples, public works projects or lavish civic meals. Julius Caesar began his climb to power through such acts of "charity" to the point of virtual bankruptcy.

But you, says Jesus, should not be like them. You should never give something to get something in return. This is an upside-down kingdom where little children are the greatest, where the last will be first and where the Lord of all becomes the servant of all. Jesus is repeat-

ing himself again (Lk 9:48; 10:21; 18:16). Then comes the pronouncement that most certainly is a commentary on what he has just done.
Listen for yourself and see if these are not the words of someone who
has just washed their feet: "For who is greater, the one at the table or
the one serving? Isn't it the one at the table? But I am among you as
the One who serves."

THE SIFTING OF SIMON

*31"Simon, Simon, look out! Satan has asked to sift you like wheat. 32But I
have prayed for you that your faith may not fail. And you, when you have
turned back, strengthen your brothers."*

*33"Lord," he told Him, "I'm ready to go with You both to prison and to
death!"*

*34"I tell you, Peter," He said, "the rooster will not crow today until you
deny three times that you know Me!"*

*35He also said to them, "When I sent you out without money-bag, travel-
ing bag, or sandals, did you lack anything?"*

"Not a thing," they said.

*36Then He said to them, "But now, whoever has a money-bag should take
it, and also a traveling bag. And whoever doesn't have a sword should sell his
robe and buy one. 37For I tell you, what is written must be fulfilled in Me:
And He was counted among the outlaws. Yes, what is written about Me is
coming to its fulfillment."*

38"Lord," they said, "look, here are two swords."

"Enough of that!" He told them.

The abrupt focus on Peter is hard to explain. It seems clear that Peter
has said or done something that has caused Jesus to single him out. If
you remember from John's Gospel, only moments before Peter refused
to allow Jesus to wash his feet. In light of this, Jesus' words sound like
a solemn warning to Peter.

"Satan has asked to sift you [all]." The first "you" is plural and refers
to all the disciples. "But I have prayed for you [singular—Simon] . . ."

We know the story. Peter, the rock, will crack, denying that he even knows Jesus. But in the end he will "turn around" and become one of the keystones in the building of the church. Not because of his courage or faith or intestinal fortitude, but simply because his best Friend has prayed for him. Luke, who shows so much concern for the prayer life of Jesus, has taught us this: nothing happens without prayer.

There is another time in the Bible when Satan is required to ask permission to "sift" someone. In the first two chapters of Job, Satan clearly must receive some sort of permission from God before his attack on Job begins. The same is true here in Luke. "Satan has asked . . ." says Jesus. He *must* ask, for God is sovereign. This is why later on Paul promises that we will never be tempted beyond what we are able to bear (1 Cor 10:13). The God who knows our frame would never allow it.

For those of us who are being "sifted" right now, the Bible speaks these two words of comfort. First, God is sovereign over all our suffering. Second, Jesus himself is praying for us, even as he prayed for Simon.

We tend to view Peter's final statement with a degree of skepticism, since we all know that he will deny Jesus in a few hours. But I would like to remind you that after he had "turned around," Peter indeed did go to prison and eventually to his death for Jesus—for the One who prayed for him from the very beginning and who prays for you.

Just before they leave, to make their way to the Mount of Olives, Jesus reminds them of their earlier "marching orders." (This passage points to the necessity of keeping track of the flow of the ministry, since Jesus will refer back to something he told the Twelve in Luke 9:3 and the Seventy in Luke 10:4.) He asks them to remember their first mission, when they were told not to take provisions along. Did they lack for anything? No, the disciples answer. Now, however, says Jesus, they should take along a bag for money and another bag to carry extra clothes. They should buy a sword, even if it means selling a robe to get enough money.

It is a puzzling statement, is it not? The Prince of Peace telling his men to buy swords. Next, Jesus says, the prophecy from Isaiah 53:12 "must be fulfilled." This prophecy says that he was "counted among the rebels." Somehow it all fits together.

Although it is Passover and the law forbids them to be armed between the eleven of them they have two swords. Jesus enigmatically responds, "That is enough" (NIV).

Bill Lane once told me that these were some of the most troubling verses in the New Testament for him. From that moment, I made it the goal of my life to "crack" this passage. Just a few weeks before he died, I hazarded a guess at what this business about selling their coats to buy swords was all about.

It has to do with the flow of the ministry. When they were first sent out, the disciples were dependent on Jewish hospitality. This explains why they did not carry provisions. They would have avoided the treacherous Gentile inns. Now they will be sent out beyond Judea. Luke will tell us that story later on in Acts. The disciples will be outside the protective shield of Jewish hospitality. They will need to be able to protect themselves.

When I shared this idea with Bill, he did not respond. Not a single word. A few days later I confessed to him that this had hurt my feelings, since I had spent almost twenty years trying to understand the passage. Finally, after a long pause, he grinned and said, "I think you may have something there."

AN UNSUCCESSFUL ANGEL

³⁹He went out and made His way as usual to the Mount of Olives, and the disciples followed Him. ⁴⁰When He reached the place, He told them, "Pray that you may not enter into temptation." ⁴¹Then He withdrew from them about a stone's throw, knelt down, and began to pray, ⁴²"Father, if You are willing, take this cup away from Me—nevertheless, not My will, but Yours, be done."

[⁴³Then an angel from heaven appeared to Him, strengthening Him. ⁴⁴Being in anguish, He prayed more fervently, and His sweat became like drops of blood falling to the ground.] ⁴⁵When He got up from prayer and came to the disciples, He found them sleeping, exhausted from their grief. ⁴⁶"Why are you sleeping?" He asked them. "Get up and pray, so that you won't enter into temptation."

We can only imagine how the Eleven must feel as they leave the upstairs room and follow Jesus in the darkness, across the Kidron Valley and into the darker shadows of Gethsemane. As they move into the safety of the trees, Jesus tells them to go to prayer. Then he moves deeper still into the darkness of the olive grove. John tells us that he asks the Three to accompany him.

Luke gives us only a brief sketch. But Luke also tells us something none of the other Gospels do: an angel comes to comfort Jesus

This is not the first time angels have come to comfort Jesus. As Jesus suffered temptation in the wilderness, Mark tells us that "angels attended Him" (Mk 1:13 NIV). Perhaps they brought food and water to relieve Jesus after his forty-day fast. Now, as that earthly ministry comes to a close, Luke tells us a single angel has come to give him strength for the final battle that lies ahead. Perhaps the angel is reminding him of all the promises God has made. Perhaps the angel is simply silently present to let Jesus know that, for now anyway, he is not alone.

But, in the end, it is an unsuccessful mission for the nameless angel. In the next verse (v. 44), Luke speaks of the intensification of Jesus' sorrow, of his anguish and bloody sweat. He *is* alone after all, and beyond all comfort, even the comfort of an angel.

In a moment Jesus will be surrounded by a hostile crowd of soldiers and later by the Sanhedrin and the rabble of Jerusalem. He is nevertheless strangely *alone* for the remainder of the Passion story. It is not until after the resurrection that he seems once more to be *together* with those he loves. Their presence will ultimately comfort the still wounded but resurrected One. He will break bread with them and their eyes will be opened. And we are left to wonder if an unseen and unsuccessful angel looked on with a certain satisfaction at seeing his beloved Jesus, smiling and satisfied once more.

THE TRAITOR'S KISS

[47] While He was still speaking, suddenly a mob was there, and one of the Twelve named Judas was leading them. He came near Jesus to kiss Him, [48] but Jesus said to him, "Judas, are you betraying the Son of Man with a kiss?"

⁴⁹When those around Him saw what was going to happen, they asked, "Lord, should we strike with the sword?" ⁵⁰Then one of them struck the high priest's slave and cut off his right ear.

⁵¹But Jesus responded, "No more of this!" And touching his ear, He healed him. ⁵²Then Jesus said to the chief priests, temple police, and the elders who had come for Him, "Have you come out with swords and clubs as if I were a criminal? ⁵³Every day while I was with you in the temple complex, you never laid a hand on Me. But this is your hour—and the dominion of darkness."

*T*he mob comes upon them suddenly. Luke tells us they are armed. John tells us they have torches and lanterns, although according to the Jewish lunar-based calendar, there is a full Passover moon in the sky (Jn 18:3). Judas seems brazen to be leading the mob. He slithers up to Jesus and gives him what is, in all likelihood, their normal greeting: a kiss. The irony is not lost on Jesus. He asks Judas a question for which he does not expect an answer. "Judas, are you betraying the Son of Man with a kiss?"

The response of the disciples in Luke 22:49 makes perfect sense in light of what we have read in the previous passage. Jesus told them a time was coming when they would need a sword. We know they possessed two swords among them, but only one has the courage to draw his, even in the face of such overwhelming odds. Luke does not tell us who it was. Mark, who is recording Peter's account of Jesus' life, does not tell us either; only John does (Jn 18:10). Peter makes a horizontal stroke, aiming for the neck of the slave named Malchus, whose name also only John knows.

Though he believes he has responded courageously and in defiance of Jesus' earlier prediction that he would deny him, Peter is nonetheless rebuked. Jesus touches the slave's right ear lobe, and what would have been a prodigious flow of blood is stanched.

Before he is dragged away, Jesus, who has spoken so much about their hypocrisy, points out what hypocrites they all are for arresting him, like a criminal, when for a week he was teaching in the temple in broad daylight. But it is dark now, and these men, whose dominion is darkness, drag Jesus away.

When I was in college, I read a book that said that those of us who follow Jesus today still betray him with a kiss. It was a disturbing thing to read, and I must confess that for a good while I hated the author for writing those words. It seemed easier to hate him than to hate myself, since what he said was true. I know something now that I didn't know then. Even though each one of us does betray him, time and time again, the point is not to try to fix us. We are unfixable. Judas will try to fix what he had done by returning the money. But it won't be enough. It will never be enough. The point is to follow Peter's lead. The main difference between Peter and Judas is that only Peter weeps in repentance. That is what I know now that I didn't know when I read the book. While we cannot avoid the sin, we can live a life of repentance.

THE GAZE

54 They seized Him, led Him away, and brought Him into the high priest's house. Meanwhile Peter was following at a distance. 55 They lit a fire in the middle of the courtyard and sat down together, and Peter sat among them. 56 When a servant saw him sitting in the firelight, and looked closely at him, she said, "This man was with Him too."

57 But he denied it: "Woman, I don't know Him!"

58 After a little while, someone else saw him and said, "You're one of them too!"

"Man, I am not!" Peter said.

59 About an hour later, another kept insisting, "This man was certainly with Him, since he's also a Galilean."

60 But Peter said, "Man, I don't know what you're talking about!" Immediately, while he was still speaking, a rooster crowed. 61 Then the Lord turned and looked at Peter. So Peter remembered the word of the Lord, how He had said to him, "Before the rooster crows today, you will deny Me three times." 62 And he went outside and wept bitterly.

*J*esus is first taken to the house of Annas, a former high priest and still the most powerful man in Jerusalem. He is held there while the Sanhedrin can be gathered for what, in Jewish law, would have been an illegal midnight meeting (Jn 18:13). By law the council was only sup-posed to gather during the daylight hours. Luke does not mention this meeting. Later, while Jesus is being interrogated, Peter and John are outside huddled beside the fire.

Peter, who has been following at a distance, is allowed into the courtyard because John spoke to the slave girl at the gate and obtained permission for Peter to come in (Jn 18:16). He is quickly recognized by two people as someone who has been with Jesus. He denies it both times. Luke gives us the detail that an hour later a third person, whom John identifies as "a relative of the man whose ear Peter had cut off" (Jn 18:26), confronts Peter. He apparently recognizes Peter by his thick Galilean accent. The third time Peter denies Jesus, he calls down curses on himself to strengthen his denial (Mk 14:71).

In the midst of this heated denial, the rooster crows just as Jesus had said it would. Luke 22:61 explores the real reason for Peter's repentant breakdown, and it is not the sound of the rooster. Only Luke tells us that upon Peter's third denial, Jesus turns and gazes knowingly at him. The Greek word used to describe the way Jesus looked at Peter is *emblepō*. John uses the same word to describe the very first time Jesus laid eyes on Peter (Jn 1:42). "Gaze knowingly" is a good way to render *emblepō*.

Try to imagine what Jesus' gaze communicates to Peter that would make him respond the way he does. It surely is not an angry "I told you so" kind of expression. My best guess is that Jesus looks at him with compassion. After all, Jesus has been praying for him.

The difference between Peter and Judas, who both betray Jesus in their own way, is that one tries to fix it and the other recognizes that things are beyond fixing. So Judas hangs himself (Mt 27:5), while Peter is eventually restored to become the first great leader of the church.

THE EARLY-MORNING HEARING

*⁶³The men who were holding Jesus started mocking and beating Him.
⁶⁴After blindfolding Him, they kept asking, "Prophesy! Who hit You?" ⁶⁵And they were saying many other blasphemous things against Him.*

⁶⁶When daylight came, the elders of the people, both the chief priests and the scribes, convened and brought Him before their Sanhedrin. ⁶⁷They said, "If You are the Messiah, tell us."

But He said to them, "If I do tell you, you will not believe. ⁶⁸And if I ask you, you will not answer. ⁶⁹But from now on, the Son of Man will be seated at the right hand of the Power of God."

⁷⁰They all asked, "Are You, then, the Son of God?"

And He said to them, "You say that I am."

⁷¹"Why do we need any more testimony," they said, "since we've heard it ourselves from His mouth?"

$\mathcal{T}$hat Jesus is still in Jewish hands is revealed by the details of the mocking he receives at the hands of the temple police. They are putting Jesus to a cruel test. There was a tradition concerning the Messiah that was based on Isaiah 11:3, which reads; "He will not judge by what he sees with his eyes, or decide by what he hears with his ears" (NIV). The conclusion of this spurious tradition was that the Messiah would judge by what he smelled. This explains the bizarre behavior of the servants of the high priest who blindfold Jesus and keep demanding that he "prophesy" who hit him.

In verse 66 we come to the early morning. A charge has already been concocted during the illegal midnight meeting. This morning trial is only a kangaroo court, a mock trial. This helps us to understand Jesus' response to their questions. Initially, he protests that even if he admits being the Messiah, they will not believe. Giving way to the desire to testify to the truth, in verse 69 Jesus states that he will soon be seated at the right hand of the "Power of God." They respond, point-blank, "Are you, then, the Son of God?"

Jesus answers pointedly, "You say that I am."

With this verdict, the Jewish trials of Jesus come to an end. In the next chapter we will proceed to the three Roman trials.

LUKE 23

THE INNOCENCE OF JESUS: PILATE

23:1-5 The first Roman hearing.

THE INNOCENCE OF JESUS: HEROD

23:6-12 Jesus sent to Herod.

BARABBAS!

23:13-25 Pilate continues to protest that Jesus is innocent.

THE GOD-FORSAKEN GOD

23:26-43 The crucifixion.

THE DEATH OF JESUS

23:44-49 The darkness of death.

THE WITNESSES

23:50-56 Jesus placed in the tomb.

THE INNOCENCE OF JESUS: PILATE

¹Then their whole assembly rose up and brought Him before Pilate. ²They began to accuse Him, saying, "We found this man subverting our nation, opposing payment of taxes to Caesar, and saying that He Himself is the Messiah, a King."

³So Pilate asked Him, "Are You the King of the Jews?"

He answered him, "You have said it."

⁴Pilate then told the chief priests and the crowds, "I find no grounds for charging this man."

⁵But they kept insisting, "He stirs up the people, teaching throughout all Judea, from Galilee where He started even to here."

$\mathcal{M}$ore than any other Gospel writer, Luke focuses on Jesus' innocence. This unique perspective finds its sharpest focus in chapter 23, with the Roman trial of Jesus. During the previous three Jewish "hearings," Jesus was pronounced guilty on the basis of the conflicting evidence of false witnesses and Jesus' own confession that they were right in saying that he is the Son of God (Lk 22:70). But in the two separate hearings before Pilate that follow, and in a single appearance before Herod, the lips of two of the most irreligious, deceitful and bloodthirsty despots in the New Testament declare the truth that Jesus is, in fact, innocent.

The Jews bring the condemned Jesus to Pontius Pilate early in the morning (Mt 27:1), knowing they must speak to the governor before he begins his highly orchestrated day of leisure, principally at the baths. Their initial religious charge of blasphemy has been reshaped into three separate civil charges: rebellion, tax evasion and usurpation of the throne.

Pilate, who sees the incident as just another annoyance, asks Jesus one simple question: "Are you the king of the Jews?" Jesus responds, "Yes, it is as you say" (Lk 23:3 NIV). Certainly something more is going on than the matter of question and answer. Jesus' response should have resulted in, at most, a verdict of guilty or, at least, cause for further investigation. But apparently wanting to brush aside the whole affair, Pilate here pronounces Jesus innocent for the first time.

THE INNOCENCE OF JESUS: HEROD

⁶When Pilate heard this, he asked if the man was a Galilean. ⁷Finding that He was under Herod's jurisdiction, he sent Him to Herod, who was also in Jerusalem during those days. ⁸Herod was very glad to see Jesus; for a long time he had wanted to see Him, because he had heard about Him and was hoping to see some miracle performed by Him. ⁹So he kept asking Him questions, but Jesus did not answer him. ¹⁰The chief priests and the scribes stood by, vehemently accusing Him. ¹¹Then Herod, with his soldiers, treated Him with contempt, mocked Him, dressed Him in a brilliant robe, and sent Him back to Pilate. ¹²That very day Herod and Pilate became friends. Previously, they had been hostile toward each other.

*A*nother indication that Pilate was simply a busy Roman administrator who wanted to get Jesus off his hands so he could resume his day of organized leisure comes in Luke 23:6-7. As soon as he gets wind that Jesus is from Galilee, he bundles Jesus off to Herod, to whom the Romans have given responsibility over the province.

What was it like for Jesus to appear before the same man who had executed his cousin John? What was the prospect of being judged by a man who had married his own brother's wife? In light of the fact that Pilate had earlier killed a number of Herod's subjects (Lk 13:1), what did it feel like to be used as a pawn between two ruthless rulers?

Only Luke tells us about Jesus being sent to Herod Antipas for what is supposedly further investigation. Apparently only Luke knows about Herod wanting to see Jesus perform a miracle. (Compare with Mk 6:20, where the same Herod is pictured enjoying listening to John, who he later executed.) And although Jesus has responded to the questions of both the Sanhedrin and Pilate, now before Herod he apparently sees that it is useless to respond and so remains silent (see Is 53:7). After Herod and his soldiers tire of ridiculing Jesus, they dress him up in an elegant robe, wrapping him up like a present, and send him back to the ruthless Roman governor. Pilate clearly sees it as yet another indication of Jesus' innocence. Herod has also concluded that Jesus has done nothing to deserve death (Lk 23:15).

Luke, who alone tells us this part of Jesus' trial, seems to have had access to information that the other Gospel writers did not have. Since, by his own acknowledgment, we know that Luke was not an eyewitness to Jesus' life (Lk 1:2-3), we are left to search his Gospel for clues to just where he heard this particular story.

In Luke 8:3, we read that one of the women who followed Jesus and helped support him was the wife of a man named Chuza, who just happened to be the manager of Herod's household. Her name was Joanna. It seems reasonable to suppose that she was one of the "eyewitnesses" Luke interviewed for the writing of his Gospel and that she was the source for this scene of Jesus' story. She would have almost certainly had access to the behind-the-scenes information regarding Herod's confusion about who Jesus really was (Lk 9:7-9), as well as the fact that early on Herod had decided that he wanted to see Jesus (Lk 23:8).

If the pieces of this puzzle form a likely picture, then perhaps Joanna is even there that morning, in the old Hasmonean palace in Jerusalem. Perhaps she hears, through Chuza, that someone is coming to the house, sent by Pilate, for judgment. I imagine her standing beside the outer doorway to the palace. I can see the painful look of recognition dawning on her face when she recognizes the familiar face of Jesus, now covered with spit and blood. Perhaps she has heard that Pilate has pronounced him innocent. Maybe she is there to hear Herod come to the same conclusion. If so, she would be the only one there who knows that it is really true: that Jesus is an innocent man.

BARABBAS!

¹³Pilate called together the chief priests, the leaders, and the people, ¹⁴and said to them, "You have brought me this man as one who subverts the people. But in fact, after examining Him in your presence, I have found no grounds to charge this man with those things you accuse Him of. ¹⁵Neither has Herod, because he sent Him back to us. Clearly, He has done nothing to deserve death. ¹⁶Therefore I will have Him whipped and [then] release Him." [¹⁷For accord-

ing to the festival he had to release someone to them.]

¹⁸*Then they all cried out together, "Take this man away! Release Barabbas to us!"* ¹⁹*(He had been thrown into prison for a rebellion that had taken place in the city, and for murder.)*

²⁰*Pilate, wanting to release Jesus, addressed them again,* ²¹*but they kept shouting, "Crucify! Crucify Him!"*

²²*A third time he said to them, "Why? What has this man done wrong? I have found in Him no grounds for the death penalty. Therefore I will have Him whipped and [then] release Him."*

²³*But they kept up the pressure, demanding with loud voices that He be crucified. And their voices won out.* ²⁴*So Pilate decided to grant their demand* ²⁵*and released the one they were asking for, who had been thrown into prison for rebellion and murder. But he handed Jesus over to their will.*

*H*erod Antipas has Jesus brought back to Pilate, probably still wearing the gaudy robe in which he dressed him as a sick joke. It is not difficult to imagine the urgency in Pilate's voice when he calls the Jewish leadership back in. He has examined Jesus and finds no grounds to charge him with anything. Jesus has been sent to Herod, Pilate tells them, and Herod found nothing with which to charge him. It is approximately at this time that Matthew tells us that Pilate's wife sends word to her husband to have nothing to do with this "innocent man" (Mt 27:19 NIV).

Pilate, almost desperate at this point to be rid of Jesus, throws Roman law out the window and offers to have Jesus flogged in order to appease the leadership. But they do not want a flogging. They want a crucifixion.

When they hear the mention of releasing Jesus, the crowd responds with an orchestrated cry for Barabbas. Barabbas has been found guilty and been thrown into prison for murder. In Luke 23:20 Pilate tries again to speak to the crowd but is apparently shouted down. In verse 22 (Luke counts this as the third time), the Roman governor appeals to the crowd once more, giving them a summary of his findings. Again he proposes having Jesus flogged. But the crowd won't hear of it. Eventually Pilate, a Roman official charged by Tiberius with maintaining the *Pax Romana*, or peace of Rome, hands Jesus over to the will of the mob and releases a convicted murderer.

Of all the men who pronounce Jesus' innocence in Luke 23, no one has less to gain than Pilate. It is impossible to tell if his verdict is based on his own hatred of the Jews or some infinitesimal speck of compassion he might have for Jesus.

THE GOD-FORSAKEN GOD

26 As they led Him away, they seized Simon, a Cyrenian, who was coming in from the country, and laid the cross on him to carry behind Jesus. 27 A great multitude of the people followed Him, including women who were mourning and lamenting Him. 28 But turning to them, Jesus said, "Daughters of Jerusalem, do not weep for Me, but weep for yourselves and your children. 29 Look, the days are coming when they will say, 'Blessed are the barren, the wombs that never bore, and the breasts that never nursed!' 30 Then they will begin to say to the mountains, 'Fall on us!' and to the hills, 'Cover us!' 31 For if they do these things when the wood is green, what will happen when it is dry?"

32 Two others—criminals—were also led away to be executed with Him. 33 When they arrived at the place called The Skull, they crucified Him there, along with the criminals, one on the right and one on the left. [34 Then Jesus said, "Father, forgive them, because they do not know what they are doing."] And they divided His clothes and cast lots.

35 The people stood watching, and even the leaders kept scoffing: "He saved others; let Him save Himself if this is God's Messiah, the Chosen One!" 36 The soldiers also mocked Him. They came offering Him sour wine 37 and said, "If You are the King of the Jews, save Yourself!"

38 An inscription was above Him:

> *THIS IS*
> *THE KING OF THE JEWS*

39 Then one of the criminals hanging there began to yell insults at Him: "Aren't You the Messiah? Save Yourself and us!"

40 But the other answered, rebuking him: "Don't you even fear God, since you are undergoing the same punishment? 41 We are punished justly, because we're getting back what we deserve for the things we did, but this man has *done nothing wrong." *⁴²Then he said, "Jesus, remember me when You come into Your kingdom!"*

⁴³And He said to him, "I assure you: Today you will be with Me in paradise."

*T*he seizure of Simon from Cyrene is an example of Roman "impressment." Roman law provided that a soldier could "impress" anyone to carry a burden the distance of one mile. In Matthew 5:41, Jesus told his disciples that if they were called upon to carry a burden for one mile, they should acquiesce and carry it for two. Interestingly, two of the later followers of Jesus, Alexander and Rufus (Rom 16:13), were the sons of this same Simon of Cyrene (Mk 15:21). Cyrene was a Roman province in North Africa that had a large Jewish population. Simon had come to Jerusalem to celebrate Passover. He never could have imagined how his life would be changed by this moment.

A mixed multitude is following. Some are mocking while others are mourning. Jesus speaks to a group of weeping women in verses 28-31. It is a lengthy prophetic utterance describing the upcoming destruction of Jerusalem. This is the last long utterance we will hear from Jesus. From now on there will only be short gasping phrases.

From this moment in Luke's narrative, an Old Testament passage will be represented by every statement. In fact, the description of Jesus' crucifixion in the Old Testament is far more detailed than it is in the New Testament.

Luke 23:32: Jesus is led between two criminals (Is 53:12).

Luke 23:33: He is crucified (Zech 12:10).

Luke 23:34: They cast lots for his clothing (Ps 22:18).

Luke 23:35: The people standing by mock and sneer (Ps 22:7; 109:25).

Luke 23:36: The soldiers offer him sour wine (Ps 69:21).

Luke refers to the Roman *titulus*, the sign hanging over Jesus' head that bears an inscription describing his crime. Luke records that it reads, "This is the king of the Jews." One of the men being crucified with Jesus shouts out in derision that if he really is the Messiah, he should save all three of them. But the other criminal joins with Pilate and Herod and from his own cross also pronounces Jesus innocent.

Now, at the end of Jesus' earthly ministry, Luke finds another example of the theme he loves so well. As Jesus hangs on the cross, surrounded by howling religious leaders who have condemned him, a convicted criminal sees the truth to which their hatred has blinded them.

The criminal hanging beside Jesus has most likely been flogged, as Jesus has, since flogging before crucifixion was the normal custom. Although for some reason artists through the ages have been unwilling to depict it, he has probably also been nailed hand and foot to the cross just like Jesus. If you and I had been passing by the scene that Friday afternoon, we would not have been able to recognize a single difference between the repentant thief and the Savior of the world—aside from the fact that the charges scribbled in red across a gypsum-covered placard over their heads would have been different. Scholars tell us that it is probably more accurate to say that the two thieves were insurrectionists, since simple robbery was not punishable by crucifixion.

The criminal has absolutely nothing to gain by declaring Jesus innocent. He has nothing to gain, and yet he has everything to gain. As he hangs next to the blood-soaked rabbi from Nazareth, gasping for breath, he pushes up on the nails in his ankles. Like Jesus, he speaks in short gasping phrases. "Remember me," he whimpers. In that luminous moment, he sees two simple truths: his guilt, and Jesus. And that seeing becomes his salvation.

THE DEATH OF JESUS

[44]It was now about noon, and darkness came over the whole land until three, [45]because the sun's light failed. The curtain of the sanctuary was split down the middle. [46]And Jesus called out with a loud voice, "Father, into Your hands I entrust My spirit." Saying this, He breathed His last.

[47]When the centurion saw what happened, he began to glorify God, saying, "This man really was righteous!" [48]All the crowds that had gathered for this spectacle, when they saw what had taken place, went home, striking their chests. [49]But all who knew Him, including the women who had followed Him from Galilee, stood at a distance, watching these things.

*A*mos 8:9-10 prophetically describes a darkness that will cover the earth someday. God says he will make it like a time of mourning for an only son. Inside the temple, strong invisible hands now tear the foot-thick material of the curtain from top to bottom. Now the way into the Holy of Holies would be open, not blocked by a dividing curtain. Holiness is being released, set free on the earth. The image of the suffering servant from Isaiah 53 has been perfectly fulfilled in every detail. All that is left is for Jesus to "dismiss" his spirit. He does so using the words of Psalm 31:5: "Into Your hand I entrust my spirit."

Polybius tells us that centurions were an exceptional class of men.[13] Without exception, when centurions are portrayed in the New Testament, it is in a thoroughly positive light. Now, at the end of his ministry, Jesus amazes the hardened soldier by the way he dies. He does not succumb to exhaustion or loss of blood; instead, he shouts triumphantly. The centurion has never seen anything like it before. The way Jesus dies wins praise for God.

In John 19:35-36, a mysterious voice interrupts the text. We are told it is the voice of someone who actually witnessed the piercing of Jesus' side and saw both blood and water pouring from the wound. The voice tells us that he is testifying so that we, his hearers, might have faith. Clearly it is the voice of one of the members of John's congregation. Perhaps he is even the bearer of the Gospel of John, carrying it along the postal road where the seven churches lie. Over time I have come to believe that it is the same voice that called out at the cross, "This man really was righteous!" The word Luke uses, *dikaios*, means both "righteous" and "innocent."

The crowds that have come together to witness the gruesome sight begin to melt away. Some respond by beating their breasts, a sign of mourning in the Near East that continues today. As the people file past, a group of women, their eyes almost swollen shut from weeping, stand with their eyes fixed on the last image they ever thought they would see. They have followed him all the way from Galilee and have supplied his needs from their own finances. We know some of their names because Luke has named them for us. Since all but a few of the disciples have fled, they must take on the important role of being the authoritative witnesses.

THE WITNESSES

⁵⁰There was a good and righteous man named Joseph, a member of the Sanhedrin, ⁵¹who had not agreed with their plan and action. He was from Arimathea, a Judean town, and was looking forward to the kingdom of God. ⁵²He approached Pilate and asked for Jesus' body. ⁵³Taking it down, he wrapped it in fine linen and placed it in a tomb cut into the rock, where no one had ever been placed. ⁵⁴It was preparation day, and the Sabbath was about to begin. ⁵⁵The women who had come with Him from Galilee followed along and observed the tomb and how His body was placed. ⁵⁶Then they returned and prepared spices and perfumes. And they rested on the Sabbath according to the commandment.

*A*ll four of the Gospels introduce Joseph of Arimathea to us at this point in the narrative. Scholars say he might have been one of the wealthiest men in Jerusalem. He was a member of the aristocratic Sanhedrin, which means he was almost certainly a Sadducee. Luke tells us that he had not agreed with what they had done. He might have been one of the only dissenting voices. John tells us he was already a secret disciple of Jesus (Jn 19:38).

By coming to Pilate and asking for Jesus' body, he is identifying with a known criminal. Mark even goes so far as to say that he came "boldly" (Mk 15:43). He takes the body down, wrapping it in expensive linen. John tells us that this is done with the help of a prominent Pharisee named Nicodemus, who brings a hundred pounds of myrrh and aloes to wrap up with the body. Earlier the Sadducees and Pharisees, normally adversaries, had come together to condemn Jesus. Now these two representatives of their divided parties come together to show Jesus the ultimate act of *hesed*.

Verse 55 tell us that the witnesses, the women who had come from Galilee, were there . . . watching.

LUKE 24

NO EXPECTATIONS

24:1–12 The resurrection.

RECOGNIZED BY THE BROKEN BREAD

24:13–35 The road to Emmaus.

THE PERSISTENCE OF DOUBT

24:36–53 The ascension.

NO EXPECTATIONS

¹On the first day of the week, very early in the morning, they came to the tomb, bringing the spices they had prepared. ²They found the stone rolled away from the tomb. ³They went in but did not find the body of the Lord Jesus. ⁴While they were perplexed about this, suddenly two men stood by them in dazzling clothes. ⁵So the women were terrified and bowed down to the ground.

"Why are you looking for the living among the dead?" asked the men. ⁶"He is not here, but He has been resurrected! Remember how He spoke to you when He was still in Galilee, ⁷saying, 'The Son of Man must be betrayed into the hands of sinful men, be crucified, and rise on the third day'?" ⁸And they remembered His words.

⁹Returning from the tomb, they reported all these things to the Eleven and to all the rest. ¹⁰Mary Magdalene, Joanna, Mary the mother of James, and the other women with them were telling the apostles these things. ¹¹But these words seemed like nonsense to them, and they did not believe the women. ¹²Peter, however, got up and ran to the tomb. When he stooped to look in, he saw only the linen cloths. So he went home, amazed at what had happened.

*I*n order to fully grasp the amazement of Easter morning, there is one precondition: you must realize that *no one* was expecting Jesus to rise from the dead. No one! Here in verse 1 the women—the witnesses—come to the tomb to anoint a dead body. They have zero expectations that he has risen. They are perplexed when they see the body is gone, but no one is shouting, "He is risen!"

The angels appear, terrifying the women, who fall to their knees. Angelic questions usually indicate that the person being addressed has no idea of what is really happening. Angels seem to be aware of another reality. In Acts 1:11 two angels, perhaps the same two, ask the disciples, "Why do you stand looking up into heaven?"

The angels can't seem to understand why the women would come to a tomb to look for Jesus. And then they speak those words that are the spark of the flame of our faith: "He is not here; he has risen!" (Lk 24:6 NIV).

The women run to tell the disciples, who are sadly now referred to as the Eleven. Luke, who has so revered these women, names them for us one more time: Mary Magdalene, Joanna and Mary, the mother of James. But you must remember that the disciples also possess zero expectations. Luke uses a medical term, saying that the women are *delirious*. But Peter gets up and runs to the tomb. John, in his account, will brag that he, being so much younger, outruns Peter (Jn 20:4). When Peter arrives, he sees the empty linens and simply turns and goes home . . . *amazed!*

RECOGNIZED BY THE BROKEN BREAD

13Now that same day two of them were on their way to a village called Emmaus, which was about seven miles from Jerusalem. 14Together they were discussing everything that had taken place. 15And while they were discussing and arguing, Jesus Himself came near and began to walk along with them. 16But they were prevented from recognizing Him. 17Then He asked them, "What is this dispute that you're having with each other as you are walking?" And they stopped [walking and looked] discouraged.

18The one named Cleopas answered Him, "Are You the only visitor in Jerusalem who doesn't know the things that happened there in these days?"

19"What things?" He asked them.

So they said to Him, "The things concerning Jesus the Nazarene, who was a Prophet powerful in action and speech before God and all the people, 20and how our chief priests and leaders handed Him over to be sentenced to death, and they crucified Him. 21But we were hoping that He was the One who was about to redeem Israel. Besides all this, it's the third day since these things happened. 22Moreover, some women from our group astounded us. They arrived early at the tomb, 23and when they didn't find His body, they came and reported that they had seen a vision of angels who said He was alive. 24Some of those who were with us went to the tomb and found it just as the women had said, but they didn't see Him."

25He said to them, "How unwise and slow you are to believe in your hearts all that the prophets have spoken! 26Didn't the Messiah have to suffer these things and enter into His glory?" 27Then beginning with Moses and all the Prophets, He interpreted for them the things concerning Himself in all the Scriptures.

²⁸They came near the village where they were going, and He gave the impression that He was going farther. ²⁹But they urged Him: "Stay with us, because it's almost evening, and now the day is almost over." So He went in to stay with them.

³⁰It was as He reclined at the table with them that He took the bread, blessed and broke it, and gave it to them. ³¹Then their eyes were opened, and they recognized Him, but He disappeared from their sight. ³²So they said to each other, "Weren't our hearts ablaze within us while He was talking with us on the road and explaining the Scriptures to us?" ³³That very hour they got up and returned to Jerusalem. They found the Eleven and those with them gathered together, ³⁴who said, "The Lord has certainly been raised, and has appeared to Simon!" ³⁵Then they began to describe what had happened on the road and how He was made known to them in the breaking of the bread.

*T*he two disciples have given up and are making their way back home to Emmaus. Along the way they are trying to sort out the disappointing reality of what has happened in Jerusalem that week. At this point, being a disciple of Jesus would mean that everything you have given your life to and have given up your home for is over. It is all simply over. Their hope has died with him.

As they mope along, Jesus is suddenly with them. Luke tells us they are "prevented" from recognizing him. At least part of the reason is that they have zero expectations of ever seeing him again.

We can't help but smile as we engage with our imaginations. Jesus asks them what they have been talking about. The question stops them in their tracks.

Cleopas can't imagine how anyone from Jerusalem could possibly *not* know what had just occurred in the city. We smile all the more when Jesus responds simply, "What things?"

Their account says it all. In verse 21, I have underlined their words "but we *were* hoping . . ." They are so confused. They've heard rumors about the delirious women, but after all, they're *only* women. Besides, they checked it out themselves; they went to the tomb but didn't see him. That means that it is over . . . right?

Even as Jesus begins to explain it all, they still have no idea that it is him. Then Luke commits his most grievous error, and I'm not sure I will ever be able to forgive him for it, at least this side of heaven. Luke reports in verse 27 that Jesus explained everything concerning himself in the Old Testament. What was Luke possibly thinking? The greatest Bible lesson of all time, and yet we have not a single word!

The three continue on their walk, and Jesus acts as if he is going to leave them. Their words have always sounded like music to me—almost like words from Shakespeare: "Stay with us, because it's almost evening, and now the day is almost over."

They enter the house and recline around the table. As Jesus breaks the bread, whatever veil has been blocking their understanding is lifted. But as soon as they recognize him, he vanishes!

I have not always been completely convinced of their sincerity in Luke 24:32. Were their hearts really burning? Then how could they have missed "it" . . . missed him? Without waiting around, they run the seven miles back to Jerusalem to find the Eleven. The group is buzzing about an unrecorded appearance Jesus has made to Simon Peter. It is mentioned here in Luke and also in 1 Corinthians 15:4-5. We have only the references, but not a single word of what might have passed between them. The next time Peter sees Jesus, in John 21, there is no hesitation whatsoever. He leaps into the lake and swims to get to Jesus as fast as he can. Whatever it is that they talk about during that unrecorded appearance, apparently the conversation settles the issues of Peter's denials.

What is most significant about this appearance at Emmaus is the fact that Jesus is recognized in the breaking of the bread. It is a truth that is lived out thousands of times every day all over the world, whenever the faithful come with open eyes and recognize in the bread and the cup the presence of Jesus. And in keeping with Luke's perspective of the spiritual life as a journey, Jesus' first resurrection appearance is to two disciples walking together down the road.

THE PERSISTENCE OF DOUBT

³⁶And as they were saying these things, He Himself stood among them. He said to them, "Peace to you!" ³⁷But they were startled and terrified and

thought they were seeing a ghost. [38]*"Why are you troubled?" He asked them. "And why do doubts arise in your hearts?* [39]*Look at My hands and My feet, that it is I Myself! Touch Me and see, because a ghost does not have flesh and bones as you can see I have."* [40]*Having said this, He showed them His hands and feet.* [41]*But while they still could not believe because of [their] joy and were amazed, He asked them, "Do you have anything here to eat?"* [42]*So they gave Him a piece of a broiled fish,* [43]*and He took it and ate in their presence.*

[44]*Then He told them, "These are My words that I spoke to you while I was still with you—that everything written about Me in the Law of Moses, the Prophets, and the Psalms must be fulfilled."* [45]*Then He opened their minds to understand the Scriptures.* [46]*He also said to them, "This is what is written: the Messiah would suffer and rise from the dead the third day,* [47]*and repentance for forgiveness of sins would be proclaimed in His name to all the nations, beginning at Jerusalem.* [48]*You are witnesses of these things.* [49]*And look, I am sending you what My Father promised. As for you, stay in the city until you are empowered from on high."*

[50]*Then He led them out as far as Bethany, and lifting up His hands He blessed them.* [51]*And while He was blessing them, He left them and was carried up into heaven.* [52]*After worshiping Him, they returned to Jerusalem with great joy.* [53]*And they were continually in the temple complex blessing God.*

*H*e has been coming and going, appearing out of the shadows through locked doors for a number of days. They have seen him and spoken to him and witnessed the identifying marks on his hands and feet and side. They have surely seen but still not completely believed.

Perhaps it is his ordinariness that causes them to stumble. It is still just Jesus, the same man they have known from the beginning. He appears, not with echoing pronouncements but with what amounts to an ordinary "Hi": *Shalom.*

Perhaps it is the sheer impossibility of it all. He has been three days dead in that tomb! Dead people simply don't get up again; that is impossible. But there he stands, asking not for a robe or a crown but for a piece of broiled fish.

Even Jesus seems a bit dismayed. "Why do doubts arise in your hearts?" he says with an incredulous smile. Then once more he extends his warm, living hands and feet for them to touch. "It is I," he says, looking them straight in the eye.

Even Luke does not seem to totally understand the persistence of their doubt. Perhaps it is due to their joy, he writes—the indescribable marvel of having him in their midst once more. Maybe it is the sheer weight of their unexpected happiness that keeps their minds from realizing that Jesus has made possible what was impossible, and that he has entered fully into their ordinary world with the intention of transforming it. From now on, nothing will ever be the same, because nothing ever can be the same. It was not too good to be true, as Frederick Buechner has said; it was too good *not* to be true.

We have missed the point of this passage if we fail to realize that our own doubt is just as persistent, just as pernicious. Not often enough is our struggle due to joy, to the heart-pounding hope that it truly *is Jesus.* Some of us beg for signs and proof, for the extraordinary to occur and dispel our doubt.

But then Jesus comes, in the midst of the ordinary. "Hi," he says. "It truly is me," he whispers. "Do you have anything like a piece of fish?"

Luke tells us that the joyful disciples are, even then, unable to believe due to the fact that they are "amazed." That word, so central to the meaning of Luke's Gospel, literally refers to the feeling you get when you are cast into a *maze*—that is, when you follow one path only to find a dead end, then turn around to try to find your way to the end. One by one, beginning with Zechariah, they have experienced this feeling when asked to believe the unbelievable truth that the Messiah has come.

I enjoy reading certain books backwards, beginning with the last chapter and moving toward the front. Not every book can be read this way, but a surprising number of them become clearer when you begin with the writer's conclusion. Also, there is something to be said for listening to an author's final words with the same intensity and freshness usually reserved for hearing their first. When you listen this way, a writer's last words become their first.

We have just read Jesus' final words in Luke's account of his life. The scene opens with a moment for which they have all been waiting, a moment for which many of us have been waiting: the moment that Jesus opens their minds to understand the Scriptures.

Perhaps you remember the first instance when you understood a passage in the Bible with more than your own mind—when the words came to life and became incarnate in your imagination. For me, it was a passage I had heard all my life. I could have quoted it. But in that moment, the words spoke in a way that connected the pieces of my life with Scripture like a puzzle. I was hearing what I thought I knew for the first time. The last words became, in a sense, the first words.

"Thus it is written . . ." (Lk 24:46 ESV): Jesus begins and then he unfolds, in a sentence that can be spoken in a single breath, what it had taken an eternity to accomplish. First suffering, then resurrection, then the message of repentance and forgiveness preached to all the nations. It will all begin where it had just ended, in Jerusalem. And so he sends them back to the city to wait for the coming of the Spirit that will empower them from on high.

Now that their minds are open, he leads them out to Bethany and pronounces one last *berakah*. While it is still ringing in their ears, they notice that Jesus is ascending, being "carried up." He is going away, but he is not going away. With the coming of the Spirit, he will be closer, more present, than any of them could have imagined. He will be as close as their new understanding of the Word. That blessing—those final words—were, in a sense, the first words they had ever truly heard.

APPENDIX

Beyond providing more parables than any other Gospel, Luke also gives us the context, the audience and the impact of the parables more often. This complete list of the parables illustrates those unique to Luke in bold type. Of the thirty-three parables listed, Matthew tells eighteen of them but only provides a context or an outcome for seven. Mark, who tells six, only provides a context or outcome for two. But Luke, who tells fully twenty-one of the parables, provides a context and or an outcome for seventeen. This is where we see most vividly Luke's concern to show us the parables at work.

1. The Wise and Foolish Builders (Mt 7:24-27; Lk 6:47-49): neither context nor outcome

2. **The Debtors** (Lk 7:41-47): context and outcome

3. **The Rich Fool** (Lk 12:16-21): context

4. **The Waiting Servants** (Lk 12:35-40): outcome

5. **The Barren Fig Tree** (Lk 13:6-9): context

6. The Sower (Mt 13:3-9, 18-23; Mk 4:1-9, 14-20; Lk 8:5-8, 11-15): all three Gospels give context and outcome

7. The Tares (Mt 13:24-30, 36-43): outcome only

8. The Secret Seed (Mk 4:26-29): neither context nor outcome

9. The Mustard Seed (Mt 13:31-32; Mk 4:30-32; Lk 13:18-19): only Luke gives context

10. The Leaven (Mt 13:33-34; Lk 13:20-21): neither context nor outcome

11. Hidden Treasure (Mt 13:44): context and outcome from a block of parables

12. Pearl of Great Price (Mt 13:45-46): context and outcome from a block of parables

13. The Net (Mt 13:47-50): context and outcome from a block of parables

14. The Unmerciful Servant (Mt 18:23-35): context

15. **The Good Samaritan** (Lk 10:30-37): context and outcome

16. **The Friend at Midnight** (Lk 11:5-8): context

17. **The Great Supper** (Lk 14:15-24): context

18. The Lost Sheep (Mt 18:12-14; Lk 15:3-7): context only in Luke

19. **The Lost Coin** (Lk 15:8-10): context only in Luke

20. **The Lost Son** (Lk 15:11-32): context only in Luke

21. **The Unjust Steward** (Lk 16:1-9): outcome

22. **The Rich Man and Lazarus** (Lk 16:19-31): neither context nor outcome

23. **The Stubborn Widow** (Lk 18:1-8): context

24. **The Pharisee and the Tax Collector** (Lk 18:9-14): context

25. The Laborers in the Vineyard (Mt 20:1-16): neither context nor outcome

26. **The Minas** (Lk 19:11-27): context

27. The Two Sons (Mt 21:28-32): neither context nor outcome

28. The Tenants (Mt 21:33-44; Mk 12:1-12; Lk 20:9-18): Matthew and Mark give outcome; Luke gives context and outcome

29. The Wedding Feast (Mt 22:1-14): neither context nor outcome

30. The Fig Tree (Mt 24:32-33; Mk 13:28-29; Lk 21:29-31): neither context nor outcome

31. The Long Journey (Mk 13:34-37): neither context nor outcome

32. The Ten Virgins (Mt 25:1-13): neither context nor outcome

33. The Talents (Mt 25:14-30): neither context nor outcome

NOTES

[1]William Westermann, *The Slave Systems of Greek and Roman Antiquity* (Philadelphia: The American Philosophical Society, 1955), pp. 114–15.

[2]James S. Jeffers, *The Greco-Roman World of the New Testament Era* (Downers Grove, Ill: InterVarsity Press, 1999), p. 224. See also J. D. V. D. Balsdon, *Life and Leisure in Ancient Rome* (London: Phoenix Press, 1969), p. 132.

[3]Dietrich Bonhoeffer, *The Cost of Discipleship* (New York: Macmillan, 1963), p. 103.

[4]Clinton E. Arnold, ed., *Zondervan Illustrated Bible Backgrounds Commentary* (Grand Rapids: Zondervan, 2002), 1:339.

[5]T. B. Ketuboth, quoted in William Lane, *The Gospel According to Mark,* The New International Commentary on the New Testament (Grand Rapids: Eerdmans, 1974), p. 52.

[6]Herbert Danby, *The Mishnah* (London: Oxford University Press, 1933), *Yoma* 8:6, p. 172.

[7]*Shaliakh:* "a delegate appointed to a mission or task." From Ernest Klein, *A Comprehensive Etymological Dictionary of the Hebrew Language for Readers of English* (Jerusalem: Carta Jerusalem, 1987), p. 661. "Even Judaism had an office known as apostle" *[shaliakh]:* Walter Bauer, William Arndt and F. Wilbur Gingrich, *A Greek-English Lexicon of the New Testament* (Chicago: University of Chicago Press, 1957), p. 99.

[8]*Tosefta Sotah* 59.

[9]For a discussion of different-sized baskets for the feeding of the four thousand and the five thousand, see Marvin Vincent, *Word Studies of the New Testament* (New York: Scribner and Sons, 1914), 1:85.

[10]See Acts 9:25 when the same word is used to describe a basket that is big enough to hold Paul.

[11]Darrell Bock, *Luke*, Baker Exegetical Commentary of the New Testament (Grand Rapids: Baker, 1996), p. 1464.

[12]Xavier Leon-Dufour, *Dictionary of the New Testament* (San Francisco: Harper, 1980), pp. 173-74.

[13]Polybius, *The Histories,* Loeb Classical Library, vol. 3 (Cambridge, Mass.: Harvard University Press, 1944), p. 24.

RESOURCES

Bock, Darrell L. *Luke*. InterVarsity Press New Testament Commentary. Downers Grove, Ill.: InterVarsity Press, 1994.

Borgman, Paul C. *The Way According to Luke: Hearing the Whole Story of Luke-Acts*. Grand Rapids: Eerdmans, 2006.

Green, Joel B. *The Gospel of Luke*. The New International Commentary on the New Testament. Grand Rapids: Eerdmans, 1997.

Marshall, I. Howard. *The Gospel of Luke: A Commentary on the Greek Text*. Grand Rapids: Eerdmans, 1978.

Morris, Leon. *The Gospel According to Luke: An Introduction and Commentary*. Grand Rapids: Eerdmans, 2002.

ABOUT THE AUTHOR

*F*or over thirty years Michael Card has endeavored to engage with the text of Scripture, whether through the writing of music and books or in the context of the conference or classroom. The fruit of this approach is seen in well-known songs like "El Shaddai," "Immanuel" and more recently "Come Lift Up Your Sorrows." In the course of thirty albums, twenty-two books and numerous concerts he has invited listeners and readers to honestly wrestle with the Bible, seeking to grasp the meaning of the text with all the heart and mind.

A graduate of Western Kentucky University, he received his bachelor's and master's degrees in biblical studies. At Western he first met Dr. William Lane, who mentored him in this imaginative approach to studying the Bible. He has received honorary Ph.D.s in music and Christian education from Whitfield Seminary and Philadelphia Biblical University. He lives in Franklin, Tennessee, where he and a group of close friends pursue racial reconciliation and neighborhood renewal. He and his wife, Susan, have four children.

Michael Card Music, LLC
801 North Atlantic Ave.
Kansas City, MO 64116
info@michaelcard.com
www.michaelcard.com

ALSO AVAILABLE FROM INTERVARSITY PRESS

Luke: *A World Turned Upside Down*
music CD
ISBN: 978-0-8308-3801-1

Scribbling in the Sand:
Christ and Creativity
168 pages, paperback
ISBN: 978-0-8308-3254-5

A Fragile Stone:
The Emotional Life of Simon Peter
192 pages, paperback
ISBN: 978-0-8308-3445-7

A Better Freedom: *Finding*
Life as Slaves of Christ
168 pages, paperback
ISBN: 978-0-8308-3714-4

For more information on the Biblical Imagination Series go to the Facebook page for "Biblical Imagination with Michael Card" or visit www.biblicalimagination.com.

Forthcoming in the Biblical Imagination Series:

Mark: *The Gospel of Passion* (2012)
Matthew: *The Gospel of Fulfillment* (2013)
John: *The Gospel of Wisdom* (2014)